Perl

PROGRAMMER'S REFERENCE

Martin C. Brown

Osborne/**McGraw-Hill**

Berkeley ▪ New York ▪ St. Louis ▪ San Francisco
Auckland ▪ Bogotá ▪ Hamburg ▪ London
Madrid ▪ Mexico City ▪ Milan ▪ Montreal
New Delhi ▪ Panama City ▪ Paris ▪ São Paulo
Singapore ▪ Sydney ▪ Tokyo ▪ Toronto

Osborne/**McGraw-Hill**
2600 Tenth Street
Berkeley, California 94710
U.S.A.

For information on translations or book distributors outside the U.S.A.,
or to arrange bulk purchase discounts for sales promotions, premiums, or
fund-raisers, please contact Osborne/**McGraw-Hill** at the above address.

Perl Programmer's Reference

Publisher   Brandon A. Nordin
Associate Publisher and
Editor-in-Chief   Scott Rogers
Acquisitions Editor   Megg Bonar
Project Editor   Mark Karmendy
Editorial Assistant   Stephane Thomas
Technical Editor   Ann-Marie Mallon
Copy Editor   Sally Engelfried
Proofreader   Brian Galloway
Indexer   Jack Lewis
Computer Designer   E. A. Pauw and Ann Sellers
Series Design   Peter Hancik

1234567890 DOC DOC 90198765432109

ISBN 0-07-212142-4

This book was composed with Corel VENTURA.

CONTENTS

iv Contents

Part 3
Standard Perl Library 125

Part 6

ACKNOWLEDGMENTS

Once again I find myself thanking my wife, who continues to stand by me on this crazy idea of becoming a writer full time. Without her support I'd still be doing a 9-to-5 job somewhere without ever realizing how much of a pleasure writing full time is.

The real thanks go to Megg Bonar, the acquisitions editor at Osborne/McGraw-Hill, for offering me the book, and Wendy Rinaldi who suggested my name in the first place. Both have given me the necessary prods and pokes to keep me going on the *Perl: The Complete Reference* and *Perl Programmer's Reference* titles. Steph Thomas helped keep me on track timewise, and reminded me when I forgot to send edits. I'd also like to thank the rest of the production team, including Mark Karmendy who handled the final round of edits.

For technical input, thanks go to Ann-Marie Mallon for the primary technical edits. Ann-Marie managed to spot more errors than I care to mention and without her help the book would be pretty useless. I also need to thank Rima S. Regas and Mark Strivens who both provided additional input when it was needed.

It's not possible to write a Perl book without thanking Perl's original author and the current maintainers. These include Larry Wall, Tom Christiansen, Randal L. Schwartz, Sriram Srinivasan, Gurusamy Sarathay, and many, many others.

As always, if there's anybody I've forgotten to acknowledge, I apologize unreservedly in advance now. I have done my best to check and verify all sources and contact all parties involved, but it's perfectly possible for me to make a mistake.

INTRODUCTION

Perl is many different things to many different people. The most fundamental aspect of Perl is that it's a high-level programming language written originally by Larry Wall and now supported and developed by a cast of thousands. The Perl language semantics are largely based on the C programming language, inheriting many of the best features of **sed**, **awk**, the Unix **shell**, and at least a dozen other tools and languages.

Although it is a bad idea to pigeonhole any language and attribute it to a specific list of tasks, Perl is particularly strong at process, file, and text manipulation. This makes it especially useful for system utilities, software tools, systems management tasks, database access, graphical programming, networking, and world web programming. These strengths make it particularly attractive to CGI script authors, systems administrators, mathematicians, journalists, and just about anybody who needs to write applications and utilities very quickly.

Perl has its roots firmly planted in the Unix environment, but it has since become a cross-platform development tool. Perl runs on IBM mainframes; AS/400s; Windows NT, 95, and 98; OS/2; Novell Netware; Cray supercomputers; Digital's VMS; Tandem Guardian; HP MPE/ix; MacOS; and all flavors of Unix, including Linux. In addition, Perl has been ported to dozens of smaller operating systems, including BeOS, Acorn's RISCOS, and even machines such as the Amiga.

Perl Programmer's Reference is designed to sit on your desktop and provide you with quick access to information on the core elements of the Perl language. It consists of a number of sections that provide a concise description of the Perl language up to and including v5.005. *Perl Programmer's Reference* is designed as a quick tool, not a complete guide, and as such you will need to know Perl, or have access to another Perl book to make use of the information supplied in this manual.

In this book you'll find the following information:

- **Part 1**, "Perl Fundamentals," includes data structures, references, control structures, built-in operators and variables, regular expressions, and information on the Perl format system.

- **Part 2**, "Function Reference," incorporates details on all the built-in functions that come with Perl.

- **Part 3**, "Standard Perl Library," includes detailed information on all the modules supplied as standard with the Perl 5 distribution.

- **Part 4**, "Sample Scripts," contains scripts that will work right off the page that do everything from processing text to a simple web server, to processing scripts for downloading and uploading entire websites.

- **Part 5**, "Execution Environment," details how to use Perl on the command line, and how its behavior can be controlled from the environment.

- **Part 6**, "Compiler and Debugger," incorporates information on how best to use the Perl compiler for producing stand-alone Perl applications, and the Perl debugger for tracing and resolving errors.

- **Appendix**, "Resource Reference," covers websites, mailing lists, and books that should help you in your Perl development process.

If you want more detailed and in-depth information on Perl, then you might consider the sister publications, *Perl: The Complete Reference* and *Perl Annotated Archives*. The former gets into every corner of Perl and describes it in detail, whilst the latter gives further in-depth and annotated examples of real-world Perl scripts.

Conventions Used in This Book

All Perl keywords are highlighted in **bold**, but functions are listed without parentheses. This is because the C functions on which the Perl versions may be based are shown like **this()**.

```
Examples and code are displayed using a fixed-width font.
```

Function descriptions are formatted using the same fixed-width font.

Note: Notes are formatted like this and include additional information about a particular topic.

Contacting the Author

I always welcome comments and suggestions on my work. I particularly appreciate guides and recommendations on better ways of achieving different goals, especially with a language as varied and capable as Perl. The best way to contact me is via e-mail. You can use either books@mcwords.com (preferred) or mc@whoever.com. Alternatively, visit my website, http://www.mcwords.com, which contains resources and updated information about the scripts and contents of this book.

About the Author

Martin C. Brown is an IT Manager and freelance consultant with 15 years of multi-platform administration and programming experience in Perl, Shellscript, Basic, Pascal, C/C++, Java, JavaScript, VBScript, and Awk. Martin is also the author of two computer books.

Part 1
Perl Fundamentals

A Perl script is made up of a combination of declarations and statements:

- A *declaration* is a statement of fact. It defines the existence of something and probably its value or format. There is no commitment in a declaration of how the entity will be used or indeed if it will be used at all. For example, when you create a variable and assign it a value, it is a declaration.

- A *statement* is a command or instruction to perform a particular operation. The act of adding two numbers together is an example of a statement.

In addition, statements are made up of a combination of operators and functions.

- An *operator* performs an operation on a value and should be thought of as a verb. For example, when you add two numbers together, you use an operator: the plus (+) sign. Individual operators also have expectations on the types of data and arguments they expect, and imply the type of data that is returned.

- A *function* should be thought of as a list of statements and operators combined into a single verb. Perhaps the easiest analogy is a sentence or paragraph.

If you put all of these elements together, you can produce a simple Perl script that adds two numbers together (with the plus operator). The result is assigned to a variable (using the equal sign operator), making a declaration. The result is then printed out (using a function), which forms the statement. You can see the Perl version here:

```
$result = 45 + 25;
print "$result\n";
```

Note: The terms *operator*, *function*, and *subroutine* tend to be used interchangeably. It is best not to get bogged down in the detail of which element is which.

Variables

There are three basic types of variables within Perl: the scalar, the array (of scalars), and the hash (of scalars). You can identify the type by the preceding character:

```
$scalar;
@array;
%hash
```

In the case of arrays and hashes, the use of the @ and % signs indicates that you want to refer to the entire hash or array.

To populate or access the contents of an array, you use the square brackets to specify the numeric index element. Note that index elements start at zero:

```
$days[0] = "Sun";
$days[1] = "Mon";
...$days[6] = "Sat";
```

Alternatively, when populating an array you can use parentheses to indicate a list:

```
@days = ("Sun", "Mon", "Tue", "Wed",
         "Thu", "Fri", "Sat");
```

or use the **qw//** operator, which returns a list when given a list of white space–separated words:

```
@days = qw/Sun Mon Tue Wed Thu Fri Sat/;
```

The scalar value of an entire array is the number of elements it contains, for example:

```
print scalar @days;
```

will print **7**, since there are seven days defined. To find the highest index in the array use **$#array**.

When using a hash, you use braces to specify the string of the individual element you want to access:

```
$monthtonum{'Jan'} = 1;
$monthtonum{'Feb'} = 2;
...$monthtonum{'Dec'} = 12;
```

Alternatively, you can use the same list operation to populate the hash. The list will be parsed in pairs. The first element in the pair will be used as the key, and the second argument will be used as the value.

```
%longday = ("Sun", "Sunday", "Mon", "Monday", "Tue",
            "Tuesday", "Wed", "Wednesday", "Thu",
            "Thursday", "Fri", "Friday","Sat", "Saturday");
```

When creating hashes you can use the **=>** operator to separate key/value pairs. It's synonymous with the normal comma, but it makes more sense when you are examining code.

```
%longday = ("Sun" => "Sunday",
            "Mon" => "Monday",
            "Tue" => "Tuesday",
            "Wed" => "Wednesday",
            "Thu" => "Thursday",
            "Fri" => "Friday",
            "Sat" => "Saturday"
           );
```

Note that when used as the argument to a function or operator using a list, the reverse is also true—the list will consist of the same key/value pairs. To extract the individual key/value pairs, use the **keys**, **values,** or **each** functions. Note that in all cases, a hash has no specific sort order. If you want sorted output, then use **sort**, or, if your system supports it, use **DB_File** to create an in memory hash.

In a scalar context, a hash returns a string that defines the number of allocated blocks (called buckets) and used blocks in the entire hash structure. If you want to obtain the number of elements in the hash, imply scalar context on the **keys** functions. For example, the script

```
%hash = glob('/usr/lib/*');

print scalar %hash,"\n";
print scalar keys %hash,"\n";
```

returns

```
64/128
105
```

On my machine, this indicates that there are 105 key/value pairs, but 64 out of 128 buckets have been used to store the information.

A typeglob is just a pointer to a name within a symbol table. The prefix for a typeglob is the asterisk *. In most cases, you will want to use a reference—the only exception is when you want to pass a filehandle, which cannot be passed directly to a function. For example:

```
open(FILE, ">file.txt");
myprint(*FILE, 'Come grow old along with me');

sub myprint
{
    my $file = shift;
    my $message = shift;
    print $file "Text: $message\n";
}
```

References

A reference is a scalar (or array of scalars or hash of scalars) that references to another scalar, array, hash, or code item. You can use a reference to create complex nested structures or to pass information between functions without having to pass the entire data structure. Some examples of different references are listed next.

Scalar references

```
$scalar = 'Hello';
$ref    = \$scalar    # Creates a reference to $scalar
$$ref   = 'World';    # Updates the value of $scalar using $ref
print $$ref;          # Prints the value of $scalar
```

Array references

```
@array = qw/Hello World/;
$ref   = \@array;
       # Creates a reference to @array
$ref   = [ 'Hello', 'World' ];
       # Creates a reference to an anon array
print join(' ', @$ref);
       # Prints out the entire anon array
print $ref->0;
       # Prints the first element of anon array
```

Note the use of the -> operator, otherwise known as the *infix operator*. It allows you to refer to an individual element of a reference to an array or hash. If you are using nested data structures, the infix operator is implied. See the examples following.

Hash references:

```
%hash = ('Name' => 'Martin',
         'Hair' => 'Brown');
$ref = \%hash;
     # Creates a reference to %hash
$ref = {'Name' => 'Martin',
        'Hair' => 'Brown'};
     # Creates a reference to an anon hash
print (keys %$ref);
     # Prints the keys of the hash
print $ref->{Name};
     # Prints out a single element of anon hash
```

Code references:

```
$ref = \&function;
     # Creates a reference to an existing function
$ref = sub {print 'Boo'};
     # Creates a reference to an anon sub, note ;
&$ref(); # Calls the subroutine
```

In all of the above examples, we used a simple dereference operator. There are occasions, however, when you need to use more complex references, particularly when referring to entire arrays or hashes. In these instances, you must use the block quoting mechanism. To do this, you put braces around the reference and prefix it with required data type. For example, the above dereferences could be rewritten as:

```
print ${$ref};
print join(' ', @{$ref});
print (keys %{$ref});
&{$ref}();
```

Using references, you can create complex structures that are arrays of hashes, hashes of arrays, arrays of arrays, or hashes of hashes. Since an array or hash is made up of scalars, you can create any level of any structure, nested in any way you like.

Consider the following nested hash of arrays of hashes, which emulates a database that supports multiple tables.

```
%db = (
      cont => [
               { 'name' => 'Martin',
                 'email' => 'mc@mcwords.com' },
               { 'name' => 'Bob',
                 'email' => 'bob@bob.com' },
              ],
      app => [
               { 'Date' => '22/3/98',
                 'Time' => '10:30',
                 'Title' => 'Dentist' },
               { 'Date' => '5/5/98',
                 'Time' => '00:00',
                 'Title' => 'Birthday' },
             ]
      );
```

To make the process of building complex structures easier, you can also copy references so that a particular element points to some other part of the structure. For example, you might want to create a new appointment and add a new field—say, an array of contacts who will attend the meeting:

```
%appt = ( 'Date' => '4/5/1999',
          'Time' => '10:30',
          'Title' => 'Production Meeting',
          'Members' => [ $db{'contacts'}[0],
                         $db{'contacts'}[1] ]
          );

push @{$db{'app'}}, \%appt;
```

The new *Members* element of the hash contains an array, which has two references to the two contacts created above. You can access their e-mail addresses directly with:

```
print ${$db{app}[2]{Members}[0]}{email},"\n";
```

But note that because it's a reference, an assignation like this:

```
${$db{app}[2]{Members}[0]}{email} = 'foo@goo.bar';
```

updates the value of the contact's record directly, so that both

```
print ${$db{app}[2]{Members}[0]}{email},"\n";
```

and

```
print $db{contacts}[0]{email},"\n";
```

print out the new *foo@goo.bar* e-mail address.

Objects

Objects are easy in Perl—there is no specific format for creating an object. There are, however, a number of rules:

- An object is a reference that knows to what class it belongs.
- Objects are blessed into a class; a reference is not.
- A class is a package that happens to provide methods for dealing with object references.
- A method is just a function that expects an object reference or a package name as the first argument.
- Inheritance of a method is controlled by the **@ISA** array. If you call a method on an object and the definition is not found within the specified class, then the classes in **@ISA** are searched recursively until all possible avenues have been exhausted.

For example:

```
package Vegetable;
sub new
{
    my $object = {};
    return bless $object;
}
```

The code above creates a new package, **Vegetable**, with a single method, **new**, which is the default name for an object constructor. The **new** method returns a reference to a hash, defined in **$object**, which has been blessed using the **bless** function into an object reference. Although we've used a hash as the base data type here, you can also use arrays and scalars for creating objects.

You can now create a new **Vegetable** object by using this code:

```
$carrot = new Vegetable;
```

Any additional arguments to the **new** method are passed as normal, so you can use this for initializing an object when it is created.

Methods should be defined like this:

```
sub boil
{
    my $self = shift;
    $self->{'State'} = 'Boiled';
}
```

The object reference will always be passed as the first argument to a method. You call methods using one of the following two forms:

```
object->method parameters
method object parameters
```

Note the lack of a comma in the second form.

There are three standard methods:

```
can METHOD
```

returns a reference to the **METHOD** if the object supports it.

```
isa CLASS
```

returns true if the object is blessed into **CLASS** or a subclass of it.

```
VERSION [NEED]
```

returns the version of the class or checks the version against **NEED** if it is supplied.

Standard Variables

Perl supports a number of core variables that can be used both to access information and to control different aspects of the Perl interpretation process. The following table lists the available standard variables.

Perl variable	Description
$-	The number of lines available for printing for the current page. Part of the Perl format system
$!	Returns the error number or error string, according to context
$"	List separator

Perl variable	Description
$#	Default number format when printing numbers
$$	The process ID of the Perl interpreter
$%	Current page number of the current output channel
$&	The string matched by the last successful pattern match
$(	The real group ID of the current process
$)	The effective group ID of the current process
$*	Set to 1 to do multiline pattern matching. Use is deprecated by /s and /m modifiers
$,	Current output field separator
$.	The current input line number of the last file from which you read
$/	The current input record separator, newline by default
$:	The set of characters after which a string may be broken to fill continuation fields
$;	Separator used when emulating multidimensional arrays
$?	The status returned the last external command
$@	The error message returned by the Perl interpreter from an **eval** statement
$[	The index of the first element in an array
$\	Current output record separator
$]	The version+patchlevel/1000 of the Perl interpreter
$^	The name of the current top of page output format for the current channel
$^A	Variable used to hold formatted data before it is printed
$^D	The value of the debugging flags
$^E	Extended OS error information for OSs other than Unix
$^F	The maximum file descriptor number
$^H	The status of syntax checks enabled by the compiler
$^I	The value of the inplace edit extension
$^L	The character used to send a formfeed to the output channel
$^M	The size of the emergency memory pool

Perl variable	Description
$^O	The operating system name
$^P	The internal variable which specifies the current debugging value
$^R	The value of the last evaluation in a block in a regular expression
$^S	The current interpreter state
$^T	The time the script starts running in seconds since the epoch
$^W	The current value of the warning switch
$^X	The name of the Perl binary being executed
$_	Default input/output and pattern matching space
$|	Controls buffering on the currently selected output filehandle
$~	The name of the current report format
$'	The string preceding the information matched by the last pattern match
$'	The string following the information matched by the last pattern match
$+	The last bracket match by the last regular expression search pattern
$<	The real ID of the user currently executing the interpreter
$<digits>	Contains the result of the corresponding parentheses from the last regular expression match
$=	The number of printable lines for the current page
$>	The effective user ID of the current process
$0	The name of the file containing the script currently being executed
$ARGV	The name of the current file when reading from the default filehandle
%ENV	List of environment variables
%INC	List of files included via do or require
%SIG	List of signals and how they are to be handled
@_	List of parameters supplied to a subroutine
@ARGV	The list of command line arguments supplied to the script
@INC	The list of directories to be searched when importing modules

For English versions of the variables in this table, see the **English** module in Part 3, "Standard Perl Library."

Quoting

Perl supports two types of quoting, the customary (preferred) format and the alternative functional generic style. Different quote operators imply different evaluations, and only some interpolate values and variables. These are summarized in the following table.

Customary	Generic	Meaning	Interpolates
"	q//	Literal	No
""	qq//	Literal	Yes
``	qx//	Command	Yes
()	qw//	Word list	No
//	m//	Pattern match	Yes
s///	s///	Substitution	Yes
y///	tr///	Translation	No

Operators

Operators listed in the following table are listed in precedence order.

Order	Operator	Description
Left	List operators	Functions, variables, parentheses
Left	->	Dereferencing operator
NonA	++ --	Increment, decrement
Right	**	Exponential
Right	! ~ + -\	Not, bit negation, reference op, unary +/- (-4)
Left	=~ . !~	Matching operators for regular expressions
Left	* / % x	Multiplication, division, modulus, string multiplication

Order	Operator	Description
Left	+ - .	Addition, subtraction, string concatenation
Left	<< >>	Binary left and right shift
NonA	Named unary operators	Functions that take one argument, file test operators
NonA	< > <= >=	Numeric less than, greater than, less than or equal to, greater than or equal to
NonA	lt gt le ge	String less than, greater than, less than or equal to, greater than or equal to
NonA	== != <=>	Numeric equal to, not equal to, comparison operator
NonA	eq ne cmp	String equal to, not equal to, comparison operator
Left	&	Bitwise and
Left	| ^	Bitwise or and xor
Left	&&	And
Left	||	Or
NonA	, ..	List generator
Right	?:	Conditional
Right	= += -= *= **= &= <<= >>= &&= ||=	Equals, plus equals, etc.
Left	=> ,	List separators
Left	not	Lower precedence !
Left	and	Lower precedence &&
Left	or	Lower precedence ||
Left	xor	Lower precedence ^

For example, the + and – operators have a higher precedence than * and /, thus the statement:

```
print 4+5*4-2/3;
```

prints a value of 23.3333 because it's interpreted as

```
print (4+(5*4))-2/3;
```

Control Statements, Functions, Packages

Listed next are the Perl control statements and the definitions for creating new functions (subroutines) and packages.

```
if (EXPR)
if (EXPR) {BLOCK}
if (EXPR) {BLOCK} else {BLOCK}
if (EXPR) {BLOCK} elsif (EXPR) {BLOCK} ...
if (EXPR) {BLOCK} elsif (EXPR) {BLOCK} ... else
{BLOCK}
```

The **if** statement tests **EXPR**; if it returns true, it executes the first block. If supplied, it also tests additional **elsif** expressions. Once all **if** and **elsif** expressions have been resolved, it executes the **else** block if supplied.

```
while EXPR
LABEL while (EXPR) {BLOCK}
LABEL while (EXPR) {BLOCK} continue {BLOCK}
```

executes **BLOCK** while **EXPR** returns true. It runs the **continue** block at the end of each loop.

```
until (EXPR) {BLOCK}
```

executes **BLOCK** until **EXPR** returns true and evaluates **EXPR** before executing the **BLOCK**.

```
do {BLOCK} until (EXPR)
```

executes **BLOCK** until **EXPR** returns true and executes **BLOCK** once before any evaluation.

```
LABEL for (EXPRA; EXPRB; EXPRC) {BLOCK}
```

initializes the variables with **EXPRA** before loop, tests each iteration with **EXPRB**, and evaluates **EXPRC** at the end of each **BLOCK**.

```
LABEL foreach VAR (LIST) {BLOCK}
LABEL foreach VAR (LIST) {BLOCK} continue {BLOCK}
```

iterates through each element of **LIST**, assigning the value of each element to **VAR** or **$_** if not specified.

```
next LABEL
```

skips execution to next iteration of the current loop or the loop referred to by **LABEL**. It always runs **continue** block.

```
last
```

ends iteration of the current loop, always skipping the rest of the statements in the main block and those that are defined by the **continue** block.

```
redo LABEL
```

reexecutes the iteration of the current block without reevaluating the expression for the loop and redoes the loop **LABEL** if specified.

```
sub NAME {BLOCK}
```

defines the function (subroutine) **NAME** to execute the code contained in **BLOCK** and can be used to define an anonymous function if **NAME** is skipped and result is assigned to a scalar reference.

```
package NAME;
```

defines the current namespace as **NAME**. When used within a script, defines a new package.

Standard Filehandles

The following table shows the standard filehandles available to all Perl scripts.

Filehandle	Description
ARGV	The special filehandle that iterates over command line filenames in **@ARGV**. Usually written as the null filehandle <>
STDERR	The filehandle used for printing error messages

Filehandle	Description
STDIN	The filehandle used for standard input
STDOUT	The filehandle used for standard output
DATA	Refers to the information contained after the **__END__** token in a script. Can also be used to read data after the **__DATA__** token
_	The filehandle used to cache information from the last **stat**, **lstat**, or **file** test operator

To use the **DATA** filehandle, you include a **__DATA__** tag at the end of your script. Perl then uses the text after this tag as the source of the **DATA** filehandle. For example:

```
while(<DATA>)
{
    print $_;
}


__DATA__

Hello!
This is a multiline test message!
```

Note that the **DATA** filehandle is already open, since it's part of the script source. Also, note that it must be the last portion of the file.

Perl Formats

A format is a definition for formatting text for output in a structured form. The format for a format definition is

```
format NAME =
FORMLIST
.
```

The formlist is a specification, character by character, for each line of the report. The period on a single line terminates the format specification. Valid characters are shown in the following table.

Picture Character Description

@	Defines a field picture.
<	Specifies left justification; the number of repetitions specifies the field width.
>	Specifies right justification; the number of repetitions specifies the field width.
|	Specifies centered justification; the number of repetitions specifies the field width.
#	Specifies numbered justification; usually used for floating point fields. See the example in the text.
^	Defines a split field; information will be printed at the specified width but will span multiple lines.
~	Indicates that blank lines in a format should be ignored. This means that if you specify multiple ^ fields but the information does not fill all the lines, blanks won't be printed instead.

Using the information in this table, you can create definitions accordingly. For example,

```
format STDOUT =
@<<<<<<<< @|||||| @####.## @>>>>
$prodid,  $type,   $cost,    $instock
.
```

prints out each line with an eight-character, left-justified product ID; a centered type; a cost, printed as a formatted floating point value; and a right-justified stock level. The repetition of the individual format characters specifies the field width. Therefore, in the example of the cost field, it is printed as four digits, a decimal point, and two more digits.

To specify a format to appear on the header of each page, append **_TOP** to the specified format:

```
format STDOUT_TOP =
Product   Type    Cost      Stock  Description
-------   ------  --------  -----  --------------------
.
```

The format system also uses the variables shown in the following table to format each line page and specify the current format name.

Variable	English	Description
$~	$FORMAT_NAME	Current format name
$^	$FORMAT_TOP_NAME	Current top-of-form format name
$%	$FORMAT_PAGE_NUMBER	Current page number (within current format)
$=	$FORMAT_LINES_PER_PAGE	Number of printable lines on a current page
$-	$FORMAT_LINES_LEFT	Number of printable lines left on the page
$^L	$FORMAT_FORMFEED	String to be output before each top of the page (except the first)

Regular Expressions

A regular expression is used to match or substitute a string against a search or substitution expression.

```
$string =~ m/pattern/x;
     # Returns true if pattern matches
$string
$string !~ m/pattern/x;
     # Returns true pattern does not match
$string
$string =~ s/pattern/replace/x;
     # Replaces pattern with replace in
$string
```

The *pattern* in the above examples is the regular expression, and *replace* is the text with which to replace it. The *x* character is a modifier for the regular expression. (See Table 1-1.)

The **m** and **s** prefixes are not compulsory; they are implied when a regular expression is identified. The // characters can be replaced with alternative characters that naturally match. For example, **s###** and **m()** are valid, but you must specify the prefix character.

Individual regular expressions recognize the metacharacters described in the following table.

Metacharacter(s)	Description
\	Treats the following metacharacter as a real character, ignoring any associations with a Perl regexp metacharacter. Known as the escape character.
^	Matches from the beginning of the string (or the line if **/m** modifier in place).
$	Matches from the end of the string (or the line if **/m** modifier in place).
.	Matches any character except the newline character.
l	Allows you to specify alternate matches within the same regexp. Known as the OR operator.
()	Groups expressions together.
[]	Looks for a set of characters.

Patterns that match expressions grouped with the () operator are available in replacement strings as the variables **$1**, **$2**, and so on, where each group matches each number. Note that they start from one onwards, for example:

```
$date = '03/26/1999';
$date =~ s#((\d+)/(\d+)/(\d+))#Date $1 = $4$2$3#;
print "$date\n";
```

The match operator also returns the group matches as part of the expression, so we can extract the date from a string as follows:

```
$date = '03/26/1999';
($month, $day, $year) = ($date =~ m#(\d+)/(\d+)/
                         (\d+)#);
```

Regular expressions can also use the special characters shown in the following table to identify specific characters or character sequences.

Sequence	Purpose
\w	Matches an alphanumeric character (including _).
\W	Matches a nonalphanumeric character.
\s	Matches a white-space character (spaces, tabs).
\S	Matches a nonwhite-space character.
\d	Matches a digit.
\D	Matches a nondigit character.
\b	Matches a word boundary.

Sequence	Purpose
\B	Matches a nonword boundary.
\A	Matches only the beginning of a string.
\Z	Matches only the end of a string.
\G	Matches where previous m//g operation left off (only works with /g modifier).
\t	Matches tab.
\n	Matches newline.
\r	Matches carriage return.
\f	Matches form feed.
\a	Matches alarm (bell).
\e	Matches escape.
\b	Matches backspace within a [ ] block.
\033	Matches octal character.
\x1B	Matches hex character.
\c[	Matches control character.
\l	Makes next character lowercase.
\u	Makes next character uppercase.
\L	Specifies lowercase till \E.
\U	Specifies uppercase till \E.
\E	Ends case modification.
\Q	Quotes (disables) regexp metacharacters till \E.

You can quantify any regular expression by specifying the number of repetitions to accept in a regular expression. The supported quantifiers are shown in the following table. A maximal quantifier will match as many characters as possible before it attempts the next match. A minimal quantifier will match as few characters as possible before attempting the next match.

Maximal	Minimal	Purpose
*	*?	Matches 0 or more items.
+	+?	Matches 1 or more items.
?	??	Matches 0 or 1 items.
{n}	{n}?	Matches exactly n times.
{n,}	{n,}?	Matches at least n times.
{n,m}	{n,m}?	Matches at least n times but no more than m times.

All regular expressions using the **m//** and **s//** formats support the modifiers shown in Table 1-1 for the specified pattern.

Modifier	Description
g	Matches/replaces globally every occurrence within a string, not just the first.
i	Makes the match case-insensitive.
m	Specifies that if the string has newline or carriage return characters, the ∧ and $ operators match the start and end of the string, rather than individual lines.
o	Evaluates the expression only once.
s	Allows use of . to match a newline character.
x	Allows you to use white space in the expression for clarity.
e	Evaluates replacement string as an expression (substitution only).

Table 1-1.   Modifiers for Substitutions and Matches

In addition to the above regular expressions, metacharacters, and qualifiers, you can also place individual assertions on regular expressions using the patterns in the following table.

Assertion	Meaning
(?#text)	Comment-text within the brackets is ignored.
(?:pattern)	Identical to grouping, but does not populate **$1**, **$2**, and so on, on a match.
(?imsx:pattern)	Identical to grouping, but does not populate **$1**, **$2**, and so on, on a match; embeds pattern match modifiers for the duration of the specified pattern, according to Table 1-1.
(?=pattern)	Matches if the regular expression engine would match **pattern** next without affecting the result of the match. For example, the expression **\w+(?=\t)/** would match a tab following a word without the tab being added to the value of **$&**.

Assertion	Meaning
(?!pattern)	Matches if the regular expression engine would not match **pattern** next. For example, the expression **foo($!bar)**/ would match only if there was an occurrence of *foo* not followed by *bar*.
(?<=pattern)	Matches the next statement only if **pattern** would have matched with the following expression but without placing the result of **pattern** into the **$&** variable. For example, to test for a word following a tab, but without placing the tab into **$&**, you would use /(?<=\t)\w+/.
(?<!pattern)	Matches the next statement only if **pattern** would not have matched with the following expression but without placing the result of **pattern** into the **$&** variable. For example, to match any occurrence of *foo* that isn't following *bar*, you might use /(?<!bar)foo/.
(?{ code })	Experimental—the intended use for this is for **code** to be executed and, if it returns true, the result is considered as a match along the same lines as the **(?:pattern)** assertion. The **code** does not interpolate variables. This assertion only works if you have the **use re 'eval'** pragma in effect.
(?>pattern)	Matches the substring that a stand-alone **pattern** would match if the **pattern** were anchored at the current position. For example, the regexp /^(?>a*)ab/ will never match since the assertion **(?>a*)** will match all characters *a* at the beginning of the string, effectively removing the *a* required to match *ab*.
(?(condition)yes-pattern | no-pattern) (?(condition)yes-pattern)	Conditional expression—the **(condition)** element should either be an integer in parentheses or an assertion.

Assertion	Meaning
(?imsx) **(?-imsx)**	Embedded pattern match modifiers, according to Table 1-1. Useful when you want to embed an expression modifier within a variable, which may then be used in a general regexp that does not specify its own modifiers. Anything following a – switches off the modifier for the duration or until another embedded modifier is in place.

For example:

```
$string = 'The cat sat on the mat';
$string =~ s/cat/dog/;
```

would replace *cat* with *dog* in **$string**.

For a demonstration of the minimal and maximal pattern quantifiers:

```
$string = "There was a food shortage in foodham";
print "Maximal:",($string =~ /(.*)foo/),"\n";
print "Minimal:",($string =~ /(.*?)foo/),"\n";
```

If you run this, the result is

```
Maximal:There was a food shortage in
Minimal:There was a
```

Translation

Translation is similar, but not identical, to the principles of substitution. The idea has been taken from the **sed** translation operation and the Unix command line **tr** utility. The translation operators are

```
tr/SEARCHLIST/REPLACEMENTLIST/cds
y/SEARCHLIST/REPLACEMENTLIST/cds
```

The translation replaces all occurrences of the characters in **SEARCHLIST** with the corresponding characters in **REPLACEMENTLIST**.

In both s/// and tr///, the **SEARCHLIST** and **REPLACEMENTLIST** arguments to the operator do not need to use the same delimiters. As long as the **SEARCHLIST** is naturally paired with delimiters such as parentheses or braces, the **REPLACEMENTLIST** can use its own pair. This can make some expressions easier to read:

```
$string =~ s(cat)/dog/;
```

The same feature can be used to make certain character sequences seem clearer, such as the one below, which converts an 8-bit string into a 7-bit string, albeit with some loss of information:

```
tr [\200-\377]
   [\000-\177]
```

Three modifiers are supported by the **tr** operator, as seen in the following table.

Modifier	Meaning
c	Complement **SEARCHLIST**.
d	Delete found but unreplaced characters.
s	Squash duplicate replaced characters.

Documentation

Perl documentation is written in POD format, a simple text markup system that can be easily converted to other formats.

Supported tags for the main layout are shown in the following table.

Command	Result
=head1 text	Applies first-level heading, using *text* as the description.
=head2 text	Applies second-level heading, using *text* as the description.
=over n	Starts a section for the generation of a list. The value of *n* is used as the indentation value.
=item text	Specifies the title for an item in a list. The value of text will be interpreted differently, according to the translator.

Command	Result
=back	Ends a list/indentation.
=for format	Allows you to specify that the following paragraph be inserted exactly as supplied, according to the specified format. For example: **=for html <font size=+1>Heading</font>** would be inserted into the translated file only by an HTML translator.
=begin format =end format	Acts similarly to =**for**, except that all the paragraphs between =**begin** and =**end** are included by the specified format translator as preformatted text.
=pod	Specifies the start of a POD document. It is best used when the documentation is included as part of a script. The =**pod** command paragraph tells the compiler to ignore the following text.
=cut	Specifies the end of an =**pod** section.

Individual strings can also be formatted within textual elements using the formats shown in the following table.

Sequence	Description
I<text>	Italic text
B<text>	Boldfaced text
S<text>	Text with nonbreaking spaces (spaces within text that will not be used to wrap or split lines)
C<code>	Literal code fragment (for example, the C<printf()> function)
L<name>	A link or cross-reference to another section, identified by name. Links are further subdivided as follows:
L<name>	Manual page
L<name/ident>	Item or section within a manual page
L<name/"sec">	Section in other manual page

Sequence	Description
L<"sec">	Section within the current manual page (quotes are optional, as in L<name>)
L</"sec">	Same as above
L<text | name> L<text | name/ident> L<text | name/"sec"> L<text | "sec"> L<text | /"sec">	Same as above, but destination is identified by *name* but displayed as *text*; the *text* element cannot contain | or >
F<file>	Used for filenames
X<index>	An index entry
Z<>	A zero-width character
E<escape>	A named character (similar to HTML escapes):
E<lt>	A literal <
E<gt>	A literal >
E<n>	Character number (in ASCII)

Part 2
Function Reference

This part contains a complete functional reference for the built-in features of Perl. Additional functions and abilities may be provided by external packages and modules, both within the standard Perl library (see Part 3) and from CPAN and other sources (see the Appendix).

Note that this is intended as a quick reference for the arguments and values returned by each function. For a full discussion on how to use the function in a script, please refer to the corresponding part.

In all cases, unless otherwise noted, the functions return either zero or undef on failure. Most functions will also set the value of **$!** to the corresponding system error number returned.

```
-X FILEHANDLE
-X EXPR
-X
```

File test, where **X** is one or more of the letters listed in the following table. The function takes one operator, either a file name or a **FILEHANDLE**. The function tests the associated file to see if the selected option is true. If **EXPR** and **FILEHANDLE** are omitted, the function tests **$_**, except for **–t**, which tests **STDIN**.

Test	Result
–r	File is readable by effective uid/gid.
–w	File is writable by effective uid/gid.
–x	File is executable by effective uid/gid.
–o	File is owned by effective uid.
–R	File is readable by real uid/gid.
–W	File is writable by real uid/gid.
–X	File is executable by real uid/gid.

Test	Result
–O	File is owned by real uid.
–e	File exists.
–z	File has zero size.
–s	File has nonzero size (returns size in bytes).
–f	File is a plain file.
–d	File is a directory.
–l	File is a symbolic link.
–p	File is a named pipe (**FIFO**), or **FILEHANDLE** is a pipe.
–S	File is a network socket.
–b	File is a block special file.
–c	File is a character special file.
–t	File is opened to a tty (terminal).
–u	File has setuid bit set.
–g	File has setgid bit set.
–k	File has sticky bit set.
–T	File is a text file.
–B	File is a binary file (opposite of –T).
–M	Age of file in days when script started.
–A	Time of last access in days when script started.
–C	Time of last inode change when script started.

Returns

0 if false
1 if true
Special conditions exist for some operators; see the previous table.

Reference:

stat

```
abs EXPR
abs
```

Returns the absolute value of **EXPR**, or **$_** if omitted.

Returns
Absolute value

accept

```
accept NEWSOCKET, GENERICSOCKET
```

Accepts an incoming connection on **GENERICSOCKET**, assigning the new connection information to the **NEWSOCKET** filehandle.

Returns
0 on failure
Packed address of remote host on success

References:

connect, listen

alarm

```
alarm EXPR
alarm
```

Sets the "alarm," causing the current process to receive a **SIGALRM** signal in **EXPR** time. If **EXPR** is omitted, the value of **$_** is used instead. The actual time delay is not precise, since different systems implement the system differently. The actual time may be up to a second more or less than the requested value. You can only set one alarm timer at any one time. If a timer is already running and you make a new call to the alarm function, the alarm timer is reset to the new value. A running timer can be reset without setting a new timer by specifying a value of zero.

Returns
Integer, number of seconds remaining for previous timer

atan2

```
atan2 Y,X
```

Returns the arctangent of Y/X in the range π to $-\pi$.

Returns
Floating point number

bind

```
bind SOCKET, ADDRESS
```

Binds the network address **ADDRESS** to the **SOCKET** filehandle. The **ADDRESS** should be a packed address of the appropriate type for the socket being opened.

Returns
0 on failure
1 on success

References:

connect, accept, socket

binmode

```
binmode FILEHANDLE
```

Sets the format for **FILEHANDLE** to be read from and written to as binary on the operating systems that differentiate between the two. Files that are not in binary have **CR LF** sequences converted to **LF** on input and **LF** to **CR LF** on output. This is vital for operating systems that use two characters to separate lines within text files (MS-DOS), but has no effect on operating systems that use single characters (Unix, MacOS, QNX).

Returns

undef on failure or invalid **FILEHANDLE**
1 on success

bless

```
bless REF, CLASSNAME
bless REF
```

Tells the entity referenced by **REF** that it is now an object in the **CLASSNAME** package, or the current package if **CLASSNAME** is omitted.

Returns

The reference **REF**

caller

```
caller EXPR
caller
```

Returns the context of the current subroutine call; returns the caller's package name in a scalar context. Without an argument, returns the package name, file name, and line within file in a list context, as in:

```
($package, $filename, $line) = caller;
```

If **EXPR** is specified, **caller** returns extended information, relative to the stack trace. That is, if you specify a value of one, the parent subroutine information will be printed; a value of two, the grandparent subroutine; and so forth. The information returned is

```
($package, $filename, $line, $subroutine,
$hasargs, $wantarray, $evaltext, $is_require) = caller($i);
```

The **$evaltext** and **$is_require** values are only returned when the subroutine being examined is actually the result of an **eval()** statement.

Returns

undef on failure
Basic information (list) in a list context with no expression
Extended information (list) in a list context with an expression

chdir

```
chdir EXPR
chdir
```

Changes the current working directory to **EXPR**, or user's home directory if none specified.

Returns

0 on failure
1 on success

chmod

```
chmod MODE, LIST
```

Changes the mode of the files specified in **LIST** to the **MODE** specified. The value of **MODE** should be in octal.

Returns

0 on failure
Integer, number of files successfully changed

References:

–X, stat

chomp

```
chomp EXPR
chomp LIST
chomp
```

Removes the last character if it matches the value of **$/** from **EXPR**, each element of **LIST**, or **$_** if no value is specified. Note that this is a safer version of the **chop** function since it only removes the last character if it matches **$/**. Removes all trailing newlines from the string or strings if in paragraph mode (when **$/** = "").

Returns

Integer, number of bytes removed for all strings

Reference:

chop

chop

```
chop EXPR
chop LIST
chop
```

Removes the last character from **EXPR**, each element of **LIST**, or **$_** if no value is specified.

Returns

The character removed from **EXPR**, or from last element of **LIST**

Reference:

chomp

chown

```
chown USERID, GROUPID, LIST
```

Changes the user and group to the IDs specified by **USERID** and **GROUPID** on the files specified in **LIST**. Note that **USERID** and **GROUPID** must be the numeric IDs, not the names. If you specify a value of **–1** to either argument then the user or group ID is not updated.

Returns

Number of files successfully changed

chr

```
chr EXPR
chr
```

Returns the character represented by the numeric value of **EXPR**, or **$_** if omitted, according to the current character set.

Returns

Character

Reference:

ord

chroot

```
chroot EXPR
chroot
```

Changes the root directory for all pathnames beginning with "/" to the directory specified by **EXPR**, or **$_** if none is specified. For security reasons, this function, which is identical to the system **chroot()** function, is restricted to the superuser and cannot be undone.

Returns

0 on failure
1 on success

close

```
close FILEHANDLE
close
```

Closes **FILEHANDLE**, flushing the buffers, if appropriate, and disassociating the **FILEHANDLE** with the original file, pipe, or socket. Closes the currently selected filehandle if none is specified.

Returns
0 on failure
1 if buffers were flushed and the file was successfully closed

Reference:

open

closedir

```
closedir DIRHANDLE
```

Closes the directory handle **DIRHANDLE**.

Returns
0 on failure
1 on success

Reference:

opendir

connect

```
connect SOCKET, EXPR
```

Connects to the remote socket using the filehandle **SOCKET** and the address specified by **EXPR**. The **EXPR** should be a packed address of the appropriate type for the socket.

Returns
0 on failure
1 on success

continue

```
continue BLOCK
```

Not a function. This is a flow control statement that executes
BLOCK just before the conditional for the loop is evaluated.

Returns
Nothing

cos

```
cos EXPR
cos
```

Returns the cosine of **EXPR**, or **$_** if **EXPR** is omitted. The value
should be expressed in radians.

Returns
Floating point number

crypt

```
crypt EXPR, SALT
```

Encrypts the string **EXPR** using the system **crypt()** function. The
value of **SALT** is used to select an encrypted version from one of a
number of variations.

Returns
Encrypted string

dbmclose

```
dbmclose HASH
```

Closes the binding between a hash and a DBM file.

Note: The use of this function is deprecated in favor of the more efficient facilities provided by the **tie** and **untie** functions in combination with one of the supported **DBM** modules. Use the **Any_DBM** module if you are unsure what is supported on your machine.

Returns
0 on failure
1 on success

References:

dbmopen, tie

---

dbmopen

dbmopen HASH, EXPR, MODE

Binds the database file specified by **EXPR** to the hash **HASH**. If the database does not exist, then it is created using the mode specified by **MODE**. The file **EXPR** should be specified without the **.dir** and **.pag** extensions.

Note: The use of this function is deprecated in favor of the **tie** and **untie** functions in combination with one of the supported **DBM** modules. Use **Any_DBM** if you are unsure what is supported on your machine.

Returns
0 on failure
1 on success

Reference:

dbmclose

defined

```
defined EXPR
defined
```

Returns **TRUE** if **EXPR** has a value other than the **undef** value, or **$_** if **EXPR** is not specified. This can be used with many functions to detect a failure in operation, since they return **undef** if there is a problem. A simple Boolean test does not differentiate between **FALSE**, zero, an empty string, or the string "0", which are all equally false.

If **EXPR** is a function or function reference, then it returns **TRUE** if the function has been defined. When used with entire arrays and hashes, it will not always produce intuitive results. If a hash element is specified, it returns **TRUE** if the corresponding value has been defined, but does not determine whether the specified key exists in the hash.

Returns
0 if **EXPR** has not been defined
1 if **EXPR** has been defined

delete

```
delete LIST
```

Deletes the specified keys and associated values from a hash. Deleting from the **$ENV** hash modifies the current environment, and deleting from a hash tied to a DBM database deletes the entry from the database file.

Returns
undef if the key does not exist
Each value associated with the corresponding key that was deleted

die

```
die LIST
```

Outside an **eval**, prints the value of **LIST** to **STDERR** and calls **exit** with the error value contained in **$!**. If **$!** is zero, then it prints the value of (**$?** >> 8) (for use with backtick commands). If (**$?** >> 8) is zero, then the exit status value returned is 255.

Inside an **eval**, the value of **LIST** is inserted in the **$@** variable, and the **eval** block exits with an undefined value. You should therefore use **die** to raise an exception within a script.

If the value of **LIST** does not end in a newline, then Perl adds the current script and input line number to the message that is printed. If **LIST** is empty and **$@** already contains a value, then the string "\t...propagated" is appended; if **LIST** is empty, the string "Died" is printed instead.

Returns
Nothing

References:

exit, eval, warn

do

```
do EXPR
```

If **EXPR** is a subroutine, executes the subroutine using the supplied arguments; otherwise, uses **EXPR** as a file name and executes the contents of the file as a Perl script.

Note: This is a deprecated form of a subroutine call. Use **sub** and **&function** or **function()** instead.

Returns

undef if file is not accessible; if the file cannot be read it puts the error in $!, and if the file cannot be compiled then it puts the error in $@
0 on failure (not a Perl script)
Value of the last expression evaluated on success

dump

```
dump LABEL
```

Dumps the currently executing Perl interpreter and script into a core dump. Using the **undump** program, you can then reconstitute the dumped core into an executable program. If so, execution in the dumped program starts at **LABEL** or if **LABEL** is omitted then execution restarts from the beginning. The process is usually unsuccessful, since core dumps do not necessarily make good fodder for a new program. If you want to produce an executable version of a Perl script, use the Perl-to-C compiler.

Note: This is a deprecated feature. Use the Perl compiler instead (see Part 6).

Returns

Nothing

each

```
each HASH
```

In a list context, returns a two-element list referring to the key and value for the next element of a hash, allowing you to iterate over it. In a scalar context, returns only the key for the next element in the hash. Information is returned in a random order, and a single iterator is shared among each—keys and values. The iterator can be reset by evaluating the entire hash or by calling the **keys** function in a scalar context.

Returns

In a list context, null array at end of hash
In a scalar context, **undef** at end of hash
In a list context, key and value for the next element of a hash
In a scalar context, key only for the next element of a hash

II

endgrent

endgrent

Tells the system you no longer expect to read entries from the
groups file using **getgrent**.

Returns

Nothing

References:

getgrent, setgrent

endhostent

endhostent

Tells the system you no longer expect to read entries from the
hosts file using **gethostent**.

Returns

Nothing

References:

gethostent, sethostent

endnetent

```
endnetent
```

Tells the system you no longer expect to read entries from the
networks list using **getnetent**.

Returns
Nothing

References:

getnetent, setnetent

endprotoent

```
endprotoent
```

Tells the system you no longer expect to read entries from the
protocols list using **getprotoent**.

Returns
Nothing

References:

getprotoent, setprotoent

endpwent

```
endpwent
```

Tells the system you no longer expect to read entries from the
password file using **getpwent**.

Returns
Nothing

References:

getpwent, setpwent

endservent

```
endservent
```

Tells the system you no longer expect to read entries from the
services file using **getservent**.

Returns
Nothing

References:

getservent, setservent

eof

```
eof FILEHANDLE
eof()
eof
```

Returns true if the next read on the specified **FILEHANDLE** will
return end of file, or if **FILEHANDLE** is not currently associated
with an open file. If **FILEHANDLE** is not specified, it returns the
condition for the last accessed file.

If the **eof()** format is used, it checks the input status of the list of
files supplied on the command line (with the **–p**, **–n** options) and,
hence, allows you to detect the end of the file list instead of the
end of the current file.

Normally, you should never need to use **eof** since all filehandle-
compatible functions return false values when no data remains, or
if there was an error.

Returns
undef if **FILEHANDLE** is not at end of file
1 if **FILEHANDLE** will report end of file on next read

References:

while, open, close

```
eval EXPR
eval BLOCK
```

Evaluates **EXPR** at execution time as if **EXPR** were a separate Perl script. This allows you to use a separate, perhaps user-supplied, piece of Perl script within your program. An **eval EXPR** statement is evaluated separately each time the function is called. If **EXPR** is not specified, then it evaluates **$_**.

The second form evaluates **BLOCK** when the rest of the script is parsed (before execution).

In both cases, the evaluated **EXPR** or **BLOCK** has access to the variables, objects, and functions available within the host script.

You can use **die** and **warn** to raise exceptions within an **eval** block. Calling **die** immediately exits the block and sets the value of the **$@** variable to the string passed to **die**.

Returns
Value of last evaluated statement in **EXPR** or **BLOCK**

```
exec LIST
```

Executes a system command as a direct replacement for the currently executing script. The new command is not run using a shell and never returns to the calling script, except on error. The first element of **LIST** is taken as the program name; subsequent elements are passed as arguments to the command executed.

You should use **system** if you want to run a subcommand as part of a Perl script.

Returns

0 only if the command specified cannot be executed

exists

```
exists EXPR
```

Returns **TRUE** if the specified hash key exists, regardless of the corresponding value.

Returns

0 if hash element does not exist
1 if hash element does exist

exit

```
exit EXPR
exit
```

Evaluates **EXPR**, exits the Perl interpreter, and returns the value as the exit value. Always runs all **END{}** blocks defined in the script (and imported packages) before exiting. If **EXPR** is omitted, then the interpreter exits with a value of zero. Should not be used to exit from a subroutine; instead, use either **eval** and **die** or **return**.

Returns

Nothing

```
exp EXPR
exp
```

Returns e (the natural logarithm base) raised to the power of **EXPR**,
or **$_** if omitted.

Returns
e raised to the power

fcntl

```
fcntl FILEHANDLE, FUNCTION, SCALAR
```

The Perl version of the system **fcntl()** function. Performs the
function specified by **FUNCTION**, using **SCALAR** on **FILEHANDLE**.
SCALAR either contains a value to be used by the function, or is
the location of any returned information. The functions supported
by **fcntl()** are entirely dependent on your system's implementation.
If your system does not support **fcntl()**, then a fatal error will occur.

Returns
undef on failure
0 but true if the return value from the **fcntl()** is 0
Value returned by system

Reference:

ioctl

```
fileno FILEHANDLE
```

Returns the file descriptor number (as used by C and POSIX functions) of the specified **FILEHANDLE**. This is generally useful only for using the **select** function and any low-level tty functions.

Returns

undef if **FILEHANDLE** is not open
File descriptor (numeric) of **FILEHANDLE**

Reference:

select

flock

```
flock FILEHANDLE, OPERATION
```

Supports file locking on the specified **FILEHANDLE** using the system **flock()**, **fcntl()** locking, or **lockf()**. The exact implementation used is dependent on what your system supports. **OPERATION** is one of the static values defined in the following table.

Operation	Result
LOCK_SH	Sets shared lock.
LOCK_EX	Sets exclusive lock.
LOCK_UN	Unlocks specified file.
LONG_NB	Sets lock without blocking.

In nearly all cases, file locking is generally advised, especially if the underlying implementation is through the **flock()** function.

Returns

0 on failure to set/unset lock
1 on success to set/unset lock

Reference:

fcntl

fork

```
fork
```

Forks a new process using the **fork()** system call. Any shared sockets or filehandles are duplicated across processes. You must ensure that you wait on your children to prevent "zombie" processes from forming.

Returns
undef on failure to fork
Child process ID to parent on success
0 to child on success

format

```
format NAME =
picture line
 LIST
...
```

Declares a picture format for use by the **write** function.

Returns
Nothing

Reference:

write

formline

```
formline PICTURE, LIST
```

An internal function used by the **format** function and related operators. It formats **LIST** according to the contents of **PICTURE** into the output accumulator variable **$^A**. The value is written out to a filehandle when a write is done.

Returns
1 (always)

References:

format, write

getc

```
getc FILEHANDLE
getc
```

Reads the next character from **FILEHANDLE** (or **STDIN** if none specified), returning the value.

Returns
undef on error
Null (empty) string on end of file
Value of character read from **FILEHANDLE**

getgrent

```
getgrent
```

Iterates over the entries in the **/etc/group** file. Returns the following in a list context:

```
($name, $passwd, $gid, $members)
```

The **$members** scalar contains a space-separated list of the login names that are members of the group. Returns the group name in a scalar context.

Returns
Group name in a scalar context
Group information in a list context

References:

getgrgid, getgrnam

getgrgid

```
getgrgid EXPR
```

Looks up the group file entry by group ID. Returns the following in a list context:

```
($name, $passwd, $gid, $members)
```

The **$members** scalar contains a space-separated list of the login names that are members of the group. Returns the group name in a scalar context. For a more efficient method of retrieving the entire groups file, see **getgrent**.

Returns
Group name in a scalar context
Group information in a list context

References:

getgrnam, getgrent

getgrnam

```
getgrnam EXPR
```

Looks up the group file entry by group name. Returns the following in a list context:

```
($name, $passwd, $gid, $members)
```

The **$members** scalar contains a space-separated list of the login names that are members of the group. Returns the group ID in a scalar context. For a more efficient method of retrieving the entire groups file, see **getgrent**.

Returns

Group ID in a scalar context
Group information in a list context

References:

getgrent, getgrgid

gethostbyaddr

```
gethostbyaddr ADDR, ADDRTYPE
```

Contacts the system's name-resolving service, returning a list of information for the host **ADDR** of type **ADDRTYPE**, as follows:

```
($name, $aliases, $addrtype, $length, @addrs)
```

The **@addrs** array contains a list of packed binary addresses. In a scalar context, returns the host address.

Returns

undef on error in scalar context
Empty list on error in list context
Host name in scalar context
Host information array in list context

Reference:

gethostbyname

gethostbyname

```
gethostbyname NAME
```

Contacts the system's name-resolving service, returning a list of information for **NAME**, as follows:

```
($name, $aliases, $addrtype, $length, @addrs)
```

The @**addrs** array contains a list of packed binary addresses. In a scalar context, returns the host address.

Returns

undef on error in scalar context
Empty list on error in list context
Host address in scalar context
Host information array in list context

Reference:

gethostbyaddr

gethostent

```
gethostent
```

Returns the next entry from the host's file as a list:

```
($name, $aliases, $addrtype, $length, @addrs)
```

Returns

undef on error in scalar context
Empty list on error in list context
Host name in scalar context
Host entry array in list context

References:

sethostent, endhostent

getlogin

```
getlogin
```

Returns the user's name, as discovered by the system function **getlogin()**.

Returns

undef on failure
User's login name

Reference:

getpwuid

getnetbyaddr

```
getnetbyaddr ADDR, ADDRTYPE
```

In a list context, returns the information for the network specified by **ADDR** and type **ADDRTYPE**:

```
($name, $aliases, $addrtype, $net)
```

In a scalar context, returns only the network name.

Returns

undef on error in scalar context
Empty list on error in list context
Network address in scalar context
Network address information in list context

Reference:

getnetbyname

getnetbyname

```
getnetbyname NAME
```

In a list context, returns the information for the network specified by **NAME**:

```
($name, $aliases, $addrtype, $net)
```

In a scalar context, returns only the network address.

Returns

undef on error in scalar context
Empty list on error in list context
Network address in scalar context
Network address information in list context

Reference:

getnetbyaddr

getnetent

```
getnetent
```

Gets the next entry from the **/etc/networks** file, returning:

```
($name, $aliases, $addrtype, $net)
```

Returns

undef on error in scalar context
Empty list on error in list context
Network name in scalar context
Network entry in list context

References:

setnetent, endnetent

getpeername

```
getpeername SOCKET
```

Returns the packed socket address of the remote host attached
via **SOCKET**.

Returns

undef on error
Packed socket address

References:

accept, bind, socket

getpgrp

```
getpgrp EXPR
getpgrp
```

Returns the process group for the process ID specified by **EXPR**, or the current process group if none specified.

Returns
Process group ID

Reference:

setpgrp

getppid

```
getppid
```

Returns the process ID of the parent process.

Returns
Process ID of the parent process

getpriority

```
getpriority WHICH, WHO
```

Returns the current priority for a process (**PRIO_PROCESS**), process group (**PRIO_PGRP**), or user (**PRIO_USER**). The argument **WHICH** specifies what entity to set the priority for, and **WHO** is the process ID or user ID to set. A value of zero for **WHO** defines the current process, process group, or user. This produces a fatal error on systems that don't support the system **getpriority()** function.

Returns
undef on error
Current priority

Reference:

setpriority

getprotobyname

```
getprotobyname NAME
```

Translates the protocol **NAME** into its corresponding number in a scalar context, and translates its number and associated information in a list context:

```
($name, $aliases, $protocol_number)
```

Returns
undef on error in a scalar context
Empty list in a list context
Protocol number in a scalar context
Protocol information in a list context

Reference:

getprotobynumber

getprotobynumber

```
getprotobynumber NUMBER
```

Translates the protocol **NUMBER** into its corresponding name in a scalar context, and translates its name and associated information in a list context:

```
($name, $aliases, $protocol_number)
```

Returns

undef on error in a scalar context
Empty list in a list context
Protocol name in a scalar context
Protocol information in a list context

Reference:

getprotobyname

getprotoent

```
getprotoent
```

Returns the next entry from the list of valid protocols:

```
($name, $aliases, $protocol_number)
```

Returns

undef on error in scalar context
Empty list on error in list context
Protocol name in scalar context
Protocol entry in list context

References:

setprotoent, endprotoent

getpwent

```
getpwent
```

Returns the next password entry from the **/etc/passwd** file. This is used in combination with the **setpwent** and **endpwent** functions to iterate over the password file. In a list context, returns

```
($name, $passwd, $uid, $gid, $quota,
$comment, $gcos, $dir, $shell) = getpwent;
```

In a scalar context, just returns the user name.

Returns
User name in a scalar context
User information in a list context

References:

getpwnam, getpwent

getpwnam

```
getpwnam EXPR
```

In a list context, returns a list of fields, as extracted from the
/etc/passwd file, based on the user name specified by **EXPR**. It's
generally used like this:

```
($name, $passwd, $uid, $gid, $quota,
$comment, $gcos, $dir, $shell) = getpwnam($user);
```

In a scalar context, returns the numeric user ID. If you are
trying to access the whole **/etc/passwd** file, you should use the
getpwent function. If you want to access the details by user ID,
use **getpwuid**.

Returns
User ID in a scalar context
User information in a list context

References:

getpwent, getpwuid

getpwuid

```
getpwuid EXPR
```

In a list context, returns a list of fields, as extracted from the
/etc/passwd file, based on the user name specified by **EXPR**. It's
generally used like this:

```
($name, $passwd, $uid, $gid, $quota,
$comment, $gcos, $dir, $shell) = getpwuid($uid);
```

In a scalar context, returns the user name. If you are trying to access the whole **/etc/passwd** file, you should use the **getpwent** function. If you want to access the details by user name, use **getpwnam**.

Returns
User name in a scalar context
User information in a list context

References:

getpwent, getpwnam

---

getservbyname

```
getservbyname NAME, PROTO
```

Translates the service **NAME** for the protocol **PROTO**, returning the service number in a scalar context, and the number and associated information in a list context:

```
($name, $aliases, $port_number, $protocol_name)
```

Returns
undef on error in a scalar context
Empty list in a list context
Service number in a scalar context
Service information in a list context

Reference:

getservbyport

---

getservbyport

```
getservbyport PORT, PROTO
```

Translates the service number **PORT** for the protocol **PROTO**, returning the service name in a scalar context and the name and associated information in a list context:

```
($name, $aliases, $port_number, $protocol_name)
```

Returns
undef on error in a scalar context
Empty list in a list context
Service name in a scalar context
Service information in a list context

Reference:

getservbyname

getservent

```
getservent
```

Gets the next entry from the list of service entries, returning:

```
($name, $aliases, $port_number, $protocol_name)
```

Returns
undef on error in scalar context
Empty list on error in list context
Protocol name in scalar context
Protocol entry in list context

References:

setservent, endservent

getsockname

```
getsockname SOCKET
```

Returns a packed address of the local end of the network socket **SOCKET**.

Returns

undef on error
Packed address of local socket

References:

getpeername, socket

getsockopt

```
getsockopt SOCKET, LEVEL, OPTNAME
```

Gets the socket options set on **SOCKET** at the socket implementation level **LEVEL** for the option **OPTNAME**. Some sample values for **OPTNAME** at a socket level are given in the following table. The values are defined in the Socket package.

OPTNAME	Result
SO_DEBUG	Gets status of recording of debugging information.
SO_REUSEADDR	Gets status of local address reuse.
SO_KEEPALIVE	Gets status of keep connections alive.
SO_DONTROUTE	Gets status of routing bypass for outgoing messages.
SO_LINGER	Gets status of linger on close if data is present.
SO_BROADCAST	Gets status of permission to transmit broadcast messages.
SO_OOBINLINE	Gets status of out-of-band data in band.
SO_SNDBUF	Gets buffer size for output.
SO_RCVBUF	Gets buffer size for input.
SO_TYPE	Gets the type of the socket.
SO_ERROR	Gets and clears error on the socket.

Returns

undef on error
Option value

Reference:

setsockopt

glob

```
glob EXPR
glob
```

Returns a list of files matching **EXPR** as they would be expanded by the standard Bourne shell. If the **EXPR** does not specify a path, uses the current directory. If **EXPR** is omitted, the value of **$_** is used.

Returns

Empty list on error
List of expanded file names

Reference:

chdir

gmtime

```
gmtime EXPR
gmtime
```

Returns a list of values corresponding to the date and time as specified by **EXPR,** or date and time returned by the **time** function if **EXPR** is omitted, localized for the standard Greenwich mean time. The values returned are as follows:

```
#   0     1     2     3     4     5      6      7      8
($sec, $min, $hour, $mday, $mon, $year, $wday, $yday, $isdst)
    = gmtime(time);
```

The array elements are numeric, taken from the system **struct tm**. The value of **$mon** has a range of **0..11**, **$wday** has a range of **0..6** (Sunday–Saturday), and **$year** is returned as the number of years from 1900; so 2010 is 110.

Returns

In a scalar context, returns a formatted string
In a list context, returns a list of time values

References:

localtime, time

goto

```
goto LABEL
goto EXPR
goto &NAME
```

The first form causes the current execution point to jump to the point referred to as **LABEL**. A **goto** in this form cannot be used to jump into a loop or external function—you can only jump to a point within the same scope. The second form expects **EXPR** to evaluate to a recognizable **LABEL**. In general, you should be able to use a normal conditional statement or function to control the execution of a program, so its use is deprecated.

The third form substitutes a call to the named subroutine for the currently running subroutine. The new subroutine inherits the argument stack and other features of the original subroutine; it becomes impossible for the new subroutine even to know that it was called by another name.

Returns
Nothing

grep

```
grep BLOCK LIST
grep EXPR, LIST
```

Similar to the standard Unix **grep** command. However, the selection process is more widespread and limited to regular expressions. Evaluates the **BLOCK** or **EXPR** for each element of **LIST**, returning the list of elements that the block or statement returns **TRUE**.

Returns

In a scalar context, number of times the expression returned **TRUE**
In a list context, list of matching elements

Reference:

map

hex

```
hex EXPR
hex
```

Interprets **EXPR** as a hexadecimal string and returns the value, or
converts **$_** if **EXPR** is omitted.

Returns

Numeric value

Reference:

oct

index

```
index STR, SUBSTR, POSITION
index STR, SUBSTR
```

Returns the position of the first occurrence of **SUBSTR** in **STR**,
starting at the beginning, or from **POSITION**, if specified.

Returns

–1 on failure
Position of string

Reference:

substr

int

```
int EXPR
int
```

Returns the integer element of **EXPR**, or **$_** if omitted. The **int** function does not do rounding. If you need to round a value up to an integer, you should use **sprintf**.

Returns
Integer

References:

abs, sprintf

ioctl

```
ioctl FILEHANDLE, FUNCTION, SCALAR
```

Performs the function **FUNCTION** using the system function **ioctl()**, using **SCALAR** to set or receive information when appropriate. The available values for **FUNCTION** are completely system independent. You should refer to your ioctl.h C header file, if you have one available, for suitable values.

Returns
undef on failure
0 but true if the return value from the **ioctl()** is 0
Value returned by system

join

```
join EXPR, LIST
```

Combines the elements of **LIST** into a single string using the value of **EXPR** to separate each element. Effectively the opposite of **split**.

Returns
Joined string

Reference:

split

keys

```
keys HASH
```

Returns all the keys of the **HASH** as a list. The keys are returned in random order but, in fact, share the same order as that used by **values** and **each**. You can therefore use the **keys** function to reset the shared iterator for a specific hash.

Returns
List of keys in list context
Number of keys in hash in scalar context

References:

each, values

kill

```
kill EXPR, LIST
```

Sends a signal of the value **EXPR** to the process IDs specified in **LIST**. If the value of **EXPR** is negative, it kills all processes that are members of the process groups specified. You can also use a signal name if specified in quotes. The precise list of signals supported is entirely dependent on the system implementation, but the following table shows the signals that should be supported by all POSIX-compatible operating systems.

Name	Effect
SIGABRT	Aborts the process.
SIGARLM	Alarm signal.
SIGFPE	Arithmetic exception.
SIGHUP	Hangs up.
SIGILL	Illegal instruction.
SIGINT	Interrupts.
SIGKILL	Termination signal.
SIGPIPE	Writes to a pipe with no readers.
SIGQUIT	Quits signal.
SIGSEGV	Segmentation fault.
SIGTERM	Termination signal.
SIGUSER1	Application-defined signal 1.
SIGUSER2	Application-defined signal 2.

Returns

Nothing

last

```
last LABEL
last
```

Not a function. The **last** keyword is a loop control statement that
immediately causes the current iteration of a loop to become the
last. No further statements are executed, and the loop ends.
If **LABEL** is specified, then it drops out of the loop identified by
LABEL instead of the currently enclosing loop.

Returns

Nothing

References:

next, redo

lc

```
lc EXPR
lc
```

Returns a lowercased version of **EXPR**, or **$_** if omitted.

Returns
String

Reference:

lcfirst

lcfirst

```
lcfirst EXPR
lcfirst
```

Returns the string **EXPR**, or **$_** with the first character lowercased.

Returns
String

Reference:

lc

length

```
length EXPR
length
```

Returns the length, in bytes, of the value of **EXPR**, or **$_** if
not specified.

Returns
Integer

link

```
link OLDFILE, NEWFILE
```

Creates a new file name **NEWFILE** linked to the file **OLDFILE**. This is a hard link; if you want a symbolic link, use the **symlink** function.

Returns
0 on failure
1 on success

Reference:

symlink

listen

```
listen SOCKET, EXPR
```

Configures the network socket **SOCKET** for listening to incoming network connections. Sets the incoming connection queue length to **EXPR**.

Returns
0 on failure
1 on success

References:

accept, connect

local

```
local LIST
```

Sets the variables in **LIST** to be local to the current execution block. If more than one value is specified, you *must* use parentheses to define the list. You may wish to use **my** instead, as it's a more specific form of localization.

Returns
Nothing

Reference:

my

localtime

```
localtime EXPR
```

In a list context, converts the time specified by **EXPR**, returning a nine-element array with the time analyzed for the current local time zone. The elements of the array are

```
#  0    1    2    3    4    5    6    7    8
($sec,$min,$hour,$mday,$mon,$year,$wday,$yday,$isdst)
   = localtime(time);
```

If **EXPR** is omitted, uses the value returned by **time**.

In a scalar context, returns a string representation of the time specified by **EXPR**, roughly equivalent to the value returned by **ctime()**.

Returns
In a scalar context, returns a formatted string
In a list context, returns a list of time values

References:

gmtime, time

log

```
log EXPR
log
```

Returns the natural logarithm of **EXPR**, or **$_** if omitted.

Returns

Floating point number

lstat

```
lstat FILEHANDLE
lstat EXPR
lstat
```

Performs the same tests as the **stat** function on **FILEHANDLE**, or the file referred to by **EXPR**, or **$_**. If the file is a symbolic link, it returns the information for the link, rather than the file it points to. Otherwise, it returns the information for the file.

Returns

0 on failure
1 on success

Reference:

stat

m//

m//

is the match operator. Parentheses after initial **m** can be any character and will be used to delimit the regular expression statement.

Returns

0 on failure to match
1 on success
List of values in a grouped regular expression match

References:

s///, tr///

map

```
map EXPR, LIST
map BLOCK LIST
```

Evaluates **EXPR** or **BLOCK** for each element of **LIST**, locally setting **$_** to each element. Returns the evaluated list.

Returns
List of values

mkdir

```
mkdir EXPR, MODE
```

Makes a directory with the name and path **EXPR**, using the mode specified by **MODE** (specified as an octal number).

Returns
0 on failure
1 on success

msgctl

```
msgctl ID, CMD, ARG
```

Calls the system function **msgctrl()** with the arguments **ID**, **CMD**, and **ARG**. You may need to include the **IPC::SysV** package to obtain the correct constants.

Returns
undef on failure
0 but true if the system function returns 0
1 on success

References:

msgget, msgsnd, msgrcv

msgget

```
msgget KEY, FLAGS
```

Returns the message queue ID, or **undef** on error.

Returns
undef on error
Message queue ID

References:

msgctl, msgsnd, msgrcv

msgrcv

```
msgrcv ID, VAR, SIZE, TYPE, FLAGS
```

Receives a message from the queue **ID**, placing the message into the variable **VAR** up to a maximum size of **SIZE**.

Returns
0 on error
1 on success

msgsnd

```
msgsnd ID, MSG, FLAGS
```

Sends the message **MSG** to the message queue **ID**, using the optional **FLAGS**.

Returns
0 on error
1 on success

References:

msgctl, msgget, msgrcv

my

```
my LIST
```

Declares the variables in **LIST** to be local within the enclosing block. If more than one variable is specified, all variables must be enclosed in parentheses.

Returns
Nothing

Reference:

local

next

```
next LABEL
next
```

Not a function. Causes the current loop iteration to skip to the next value or next evaluation of the control statement. No further statements in the current loop are executed. If **LABEL** is specified, then execution skips to the next iteration of the loop identified by **LABEL**.

Returns
Nothing

References:

last, redo

```
no MODULE LIST
no MODULE
```

If **MODULE** supports it, then **no** calls the **unimport** function defined in **MODULE** to unimport all symbols from the current package, or only the symbols referred to by **LIST**. Has some special meanings when used with pragmas.

Returns

Nothing

oct

```
oct EXPR
oct
```

Returns **EXPR**, or **$_** if omitted, interpreted as an octal string. Most often used as a method for returning mode strings as octal values.

Returns

Octal value

Reference:

hex

```
open FILEHANDLE, EXPR
open FILEHANDLE
```

Opens the file specified by **EXPR**, associating it with **FILEHANDLE**. If **EXPR** is not specified, then the file name specified by the scalar variable of the same name as **FILEHANDLE** is used instead. The format of **EXPR** defines the mode in which the file is opened, as shown in the following table.

Expression	Result
"filename"	Opens the file for reading only.
"<filename"	Opens the file for reading only.
">filename"	Truncates and opens the file for writing.
">>filename"	Opens the file for appending (places pointer at end of file).
"+<filename"	Opens the file for reading and writing.
"+>filename"	Truncates and opens the file for reading and writing.
"│ command"	Runs the command and pipes the output to the filehandle.
"command │"	Pipes the output from filehandle to the input of command.
"-"	Opens **STDIN**.
">-"	Opens **STDOUT**.
"<&**FILEHANDLE**"	Duplicates specified **FILEHANDLE** or file descriptor if numeric for reading.
">&**FILEHANDLE**"	Duplicates specified **FILEHANDLE** or file descriptor if numeric for writing.
"<&=N"	Opens the file descriptor matching N, essentially identical to C's **fdopen()**.
"│-" and "-│"	Opens a pipe to a forked command.

You should not ignore failures to the **open** command, so it is usually used in combination with **warn**, **die**, or a control statement.

If you are looking for the equivalent of the system function **open()**, see **sysopen**.

Returns
undef on failure
nonzero on success
Process ID of subprocess if **open** involves a pipe

References:

print, sysopen, close

opendir

```
opendir DIRHANDLE, EXPR
```

Opens the directory **EXPR**, associating it with **DIRHANDLE** for processing, using the **readdir**, **telldir**, **seekdir**, and **closedir** functions.

Returns
0 on failure
1 on success

References:

readdir, rewinddir, telldir, seekdir, closedir

ord

```
ord EXPR
ord
```

Returns the ASCII numeric value of the character specified by **EXPR**, or **$_** if omitted.

Returns
Integer

Reference:

chr

pack

```
pack EXPR, LIST
```

Evaluates the expressions in **LIST** and packs it into a binary structure specified by **EXPR**. The format is specified using the characters shown in the following table.

Character	Description
@	Null fill to absolute position
a	An ASCII string, null padded
A	An ASCII string, space padded
b	A bitstring (ascending bit order)
B	A bitstring (descending bit order)
c	A signed char value
C	An unsigned char value
d	A double-precision float in the native format
f	A single-precision float in the native format
H	A hex string (high nibble first)
h	A hex string (low nibble first)
i	A signed integer value
I	An unsigned integer value
l	A signed long value
L	An unsigned long value
N	A long in "network" (big endian) order
n	A short in "network" (big endian) order
p	A pointer to a null-terminated string
P	A pointer to a structure (fixed-length string)
q	A signed quod (64-bit) value
Q	An unsigned quod value
s	A signed short value
S	An unsigned short value
u	A uuencoded string
V	A long in "VAX" (little endian) order
v	A short in "VAX" (little endian) order
w	A BER-compressed integer
x	A null byte
X	Backs up a byte

Each character may be optionally followed by a number, which specifies a repeat count. A value of * repeats for as many values as are remaining in **LIST**. Values can be unpacked with the **unpack** function.

Returns
Formatted string

Reference:

unpack

```
package NAME
package
```

Changes the name of the current symbol table to **NAME**. The scope of the package name is until the end of the enclosing block. If **NAME** is omitted, there is no current package, and all function and variables names must be declared with their fully qualified names.

Returns
Nothing

```
pipe READHANDLE, WRITEHANDLE
```

Opens a pair of connected communications pipes: **READHANDLE** for reading and **WRITEHANDLE** for writing.

Returns
0 on failure
1 on success

pop

```
pop ARRAY
pop
```

Returns the last element of **ARRAY**, removing the value from the list. If **ARRAY** is omitted, it pops the last value from **@ARGV** in the main program and the @_ array within a subroutine. The opposite of **push**, which, when used in combination, allows you to implement "stacks."

Returns
undef if list is empty
Last element from the array

References:

push, shift, unshift

pos

```
pos EXPR
pos
```

Returns the position within **EXPR**, or **$_**, where the last **m//g** search left off.

Returns
Integer

print

```
print FILEHANDLE LIST
print LIST
print
```

Prints the values of the expressions in **LIST** to the current default output filehandle, or to the one specified by **FILEHANDLE**. If **LIST** is empty, the value in **$_** is printed instead. Because **print** accepts a list of values, every element of the list will be interpreted as an expression. You should therefore ensure that if you are using print within a larger **LIST** context, you enclose the arguments to **print** in parentheses.

Returns

0 on failure
1 on success

References:

printf, sprintf

printf

```
printf FILEHANDLE FORMAT, LIST
printf FORMAT, LIST
```

Prints the value of **LIST** interpreted via the format specified by **FORMAT** to the current output filehandle, or to the one specified by **FILEHANDLE**. Effectively equivalent to

```
print FILEHANDLE sprintf(FORMAT, LIST)
```

Remember to use **print** in place of **printf** if you do not require a specific output format. The **print** function is more efficient. Table 2-1 shows the list of accepted formatting conversions.

Perl also supports flags that optionally adjust the output format. These are specified between the % and the conversion letter, as shown in Table 2-2.

Returns

0 on failure
1 on success

References:

print, sprintf

prototype

```
prototype EXPR
```

Returns a string containing the prototype of function or reference specified by **EXPR**, or **undef** if the function has no prototype.

Format	Result
%%	A percent sign
%c	A character with the given ASCII code
%s	A string
%d	A signed integer (decimal)
%u	An unsigned integer (decimal)
%o	An unsigned integer (octal)
%x	An unsigned integer (hexadecimal)
%X	An unsigned integer (hexadecimal using uppercase characters)
%e	A floating point number (scientific notation)
%E	A floating point number (scientific notation using "E" in place of "e")
%f	A floating point number (fixed decimal notation)
%g	A floating point number (%e or %f notation according to value size)
%G	A floating point number (as %g, but using "E" in place of "e" when appropriate)
%p	A pointer (prints the memory address of the value in hexadecimal)
%n	Stores the number of characters output so far into the next variable in the parameter list
%I	A synonym for %d
%D	A synonym for C %ld
%U	A synonym for C %lu
%O	A synonym for C %lo
%F	A synonym for C %f

Table 2-1. Conversion Formats for **printf**

Returns
undef if no function prototype
String

push

```
push ARRAY, LIST
```

Flag	Result
space	Prefixes positive number with a space.
+	Prefixes positive number with a plus sign.
-	Left-justifies within field.
0	Uses zeros, not spaces, to right-justify.
#	Prefixes nonzero octal with "0" and nonzero hexadecimal with "0x."
number	Minimum field width.
.number	Specifies precision (number of digits after decimal point) for floating point numbers.
l	Interprets integer as C type "long" or "unsigned long."
h	Interprets integer as C type "short" or "unsigned short."
V	Interprets integer as Perl's standard integer type.

Table 2-2.   Formatting Flags for **printf** Conversion Formats

Pushes the values in **LIST** on to the end of the list **ARRAY.** Used with **pop** to implement stacks.

Returns
Number of elements in new array

References:

pop, shift, unshift

quotemeta

```
quotemeta EXPR
quotemeta
```

Returns the value of **EXPR** or **$_** with all nonalphanumeric characters backslashed.

Returns
String

rand

```
rand EXPR
rand
```

Returns a random fractional number between zero and the positive number **EXPR**, or one if not specified. Automatically calls **srand** to seed the random number generator unless it has already been called.

Returns
Floating point number

Reference:

srand

read

```
read FILEHANDLE, SCALAR, LENGTH, OFFSET
read FILEHANDLE, SCALAR, LENGTH
```

Tries to read **LENGTH** bytes from **FILEHANDLE** into **SCALAR**. If **OFFSET** is specified, then reading starts from that point within the input string, up to **LENGTH** bytes. Uses the equivalent of the C **fread()** function. For the equivalent of the C **read()** function, see **sysread**.

Returns
undef on error
0 at end of file
Number of bytes read

Reference:

sysread

readdir

```
readdir DIRHANDLE
```

In a scalar context, returns the next directory entry from the directory associated with **DIRHANDLE**. In a list context, returns all of the remaining directory entries in **DIRHANDLE**.

Returns
undef on failure in scalar context
Empty list on failure in list context
File name in scalar context
List of file names in list context

References:

opendir, rewinddir

readline

```
readline EXPR
```

Reads a line from the filehandle referred to by **EXPR**, returning the result. If you want to use a **FILEHANDLE** directly, it must be passed as a typeglob. In a scalar context, only one line is returned; in a list context, a list of lines up to end of file is returned. Ignores the setting of the **$/** or **$INPUT_RECORD_SEPARATOR** variable. You should use the <> operator in preference.

Returns
undef, or empty list, on error
One line in scalar context
List of lines in list context

readlink

```
readlink EXPR
readlink
```

Returns the path name of the file pointed to by the link **EXPR**, or **$_**
if **EXPR** is not specified.

Returns
undef on error
String

References:

link, symlink

readpipe

```
readpipe EXPR
```

Executes **EXPR** as a command. The output is then returned as a
multiline string in scalar text, or with line returned as individual
elements in a list context.

Returns
String in scalar context
List in list context

Reference:

system

recv

```
recv SOCKET, SCALAR, LEN, FLAGS
```

Receives a message on **SOCKET** attempting to read **LEN** bytes,
placing the data read into variable **SCALAR**. The **FLAGS** argument
takes the same values as the **recvfrom()** system function, on which
the function is based. When communicating with sockets, this
provides a more reliable method of reading fixed-length data
than the **sysread** function or the line-based operator <>.

Returns
undef on error
Number of bytes read

redo

```
redo LABEL
redo
```

Restarts the current loop without forcing the control statement to
be evaluated. No further statements in the block are executed
(execution restarts at the start of the block). A **continue** block, if
present, will not be executed. If **LABEL** is specified, execution
restarts at the start of the loop identified by **LABEL**.

Returns
Nothing

ref

```
ref EXPR
ref
```

Returns a **TRUE** value if **EXPR**, or **$_**, if a reference. The actual
value returned also defines the type of entity the reference refers
to. The built-in types in:

```
REF
SCALAR
ARRAY
HASH
CODE
GLOB
```

Returns
0 if not a reference
1 if a reference

rename

```
rename OLDNAME, NEWNAME
```

Renames the file with **OLDNAME** to **NEWNAME**. Uses the system function **rename()**, and so it will not rename files across file systems or volumes.

Returns

0 on failure
1 on success

require

```
require EXPR
require
```

If **EXPR** (or **$_**, if **EXPR** is omitted) is numeric, then it demands that the script require the specified version of Perl in order to continue. If **EXPR** or **$_** is not numeric, it assumes that the name is the name of a library file to be included. You cannot include the same file with this function twice. The included file must return a true value as the last statement.

This differs from **use** in that included files effectively become additional text for the current script. Functions, variables, and other objects are not imported into the current name space, so if the specified file includes a package definition, then objects will require fully qualified names.

Returns

Nothing

Reference:

use

reset

```
reset EXPR
reset
```

Resets (clears) all package variables starting with the letter range specified by **EXPR**. Generally only used within a **continue** block or at the end of a loop. If omitted, resets **?PATTERN?** matches.

Returns
1 (always)

return

```
return EXPR
return
```

Returns **EXPR** at the end of a subroutine, block, or **do** function. **EXPR** may be a scalar, array, or hash value; context will be selected at execution time. If no **EXPR** is given, returns an empty list in list context, **undef** in scalar context, or nothing in a void context.

Returns
List, interpreted as scalar, array, or hash, depending on context

reverse

```
reverse LIST
```

In a list context, returns the elements of **LIST** in reverse order. In a scalar context, returns a concatenated string of the values of **LIST**, with all bytes in opposite order.

Returns
String in scalar context
List in list context

rewinddir

```
rewinddir DIRHANDLE
```

Sets the current position within the directory specified by
DIRHANDLE to the beginning of the directory.

Returns
Nothing

rindex

```
rindex STR, SUBSTR, POSITION
rindex STR, SUBSTR
```

Operates similar to **index**, except it returns the position of the last
occurrence of **SUBSTR** in **STR**. If **POSITION** is specified, returns the
last occurrence at or before that position.

Returns
undef on failure
Integer

rmdir

```
rmdir EXPR
rmdir
```

Deletes the directory specified by **EXPR**, or **$_** if omitted. Only
deletes the directory if the directory is empty.

Returns
0 on failure
1 on success

Reference:

mkdir

s///

```
s/PATTERN/REPLACE/
```

This is the regular expression substitution operator. Based on the regular expression specified in **PATTERN**, data is replaced by **REPLACE**. Like **m//**, the delimiters are defined by the first character following **s**.

Returns

0 on failure
Number of substitutions made

scalar

```
scalar EXPR
```

Forces the evaluation of **EXPR** to return a value in a scalar context.

Returns

Scalar

seek

```
seek FILEHANDLE, POSITION, WHENCE
```

Positions the file pointer for the specified **FILEHANDLE**. **seek** is basically the same as the **fseek()** C function. The position within the file is specified by **POSITION**, using the value of **WHENCE** as a reference point, as follows:

- **0** sets the new position absolutely to **POSITION** bytes within the file.

- **1** sets the new position to the current position plus **POSITION** bytes within the file.

- **2** sets the new position to **POSITION** bytes, relative to the end of the file.

If you prefer, you can use the constants **SEEK_SET**, **SEEK_CUR**, and **SEEK_END**, provided you have imported the **IO::Seekable** or **POSIX** modules.

If you are accessing a file using **syswrite** and **sysread**, you should use **sysseek** due to the effects of buffering.

The **seek** function clears the **EOF** condition on a file when called.

Returns
0 on failure
1 on success

References:

tell, **sysseek**

seekdir

```
seekdir DIRHANDLE, POS
```

Sets the current position within **DIRHANDLE** to **POS**. The value of **POS** must be a value returned by **telldir**.

Returns
0 on failure
1 on success

References:

rewinddir, **telldir**

select

```
select FILEHANDLE
select
```

Sets the default filehandle for output to **FILEHANDLE**, setting the filehandle used by functions such as **print** and **write** if no filehandle is specified. If **FILEHANDLE** is not specified, then it returns the name of the current default filehandle.

Returns

Previous default filehandle if **FILEHANDLE** specified
Current default filehandle if **FILEHANDLE** not specified

References:

print, autoflush, write

---

select

```
select RBITS, WBITS, EBITS, TIMEOUT
```

Calls the system function **select()** using the bits specified. The
select function sets the controls for handling nonblocking I/O
requests. Returns the number of filehandles awaiting I/O in scalar
context, or the number of waiting filehandles and the time
remaining in a list context.

TIMEOUT is specified in seconds but accepts a floating point
instead of an integer value. You can use this ability to pause
execution for milliseconds instead of the normal seconds available
with **sleep** and **alarm** by specifying **undef** for the first three
arguments.

Returns

The number of filehandles awaiting I/O in a scalar context
The number of filehandles and time remaining in a list context

---

semctl

```
semctl ID, SEMNUM, CMD, ARG
```

Controls a System V semaphore. You will need to import the
IPC:SysV module to get the correct definitions for **CMD**. The
function calls the system **semctl()** function.

Returns

undef on failure
0 but true if the return value from the **semctl()** is 0
Value returned by system

References:

semget, semop

semget

```
semget KEY, NSEMS, FLAGS
```

Returns the semaphore ID associated with **KEY**, using the system
function **semget()**.

Returns

undef on error
Semaphore ID

References:

semctl, semop

semop

```
semop KEY, OPSTRING
```

Performs the semaphore operations defined by **OPSTRING** on
the semaphore ID associated with **KEY**. **OPSTRING** should be a
packed array of **semop** structures, and each structure can be
generated with

```
$semop = pack("sss", $semnum, $semop, $semflag);
```

Returns

0 on failure
1 on success

References:

semctl, semget

send

```
send SOCKET, MSG, FLAGS, TO
send SOCKET, MSG, FLAGS
```

Sends a message on **SOCKET** (the opposite of **recv**). If the socket is unconnected, you must supply a destination to communicate to with the **TO** parameter. In this case, the **sendto** system function is used in place of the system **send** function.

The **FLAGS** parameter is formed from the bitwise **or** of zero and one or more of the **MSG_OOB** and **MSG_DONTROUTE** options. **MSG_OOB** allows you to send out-of-band data on sockets that support this notion. The underlying protocol must also support out-of-band data. Only **SOCK_STREAM** sockets created in the **AF_INET** address family support out-of-band data. The **MSG_DONTROUTE** option is turned on for the duration of the operation. Only diagnostic or routing programs use it.

Returns
undef on error
Integer, number of bytes sent

Reference:

recv

setgrent

```
setgrent
```

Sets (or resets) the enumeration to the beginning of the set of group entries. This function should be called before the first call to **getgrent**.

Returns

Nothing

References:

getgrent, endgrent

sethostent

```
sethostent STAYOPEN
```

Sets (or resets) the enumeration to the beginning of the set of host entries. This function should be called before the first call to **gethostent**. The **STAYOPEN** argument is optional and unused on most systems.

Returns

Nothing

References:

gethostent, endhostent

setnetent

```
setnetent STAYOPEN
```

Sets (or resets) the enumeration to the beginning of the set of network entries. This function should be called before the first call to **getnetent**. The **STAYOPEN** argument is optional and unused on most systems.

Returns

Nothing

References:

getnetent, endnetent

setpgrp

`setpgrp PID, PGRP`

Sets the current process group for the process **PID**. You can use a value of **0** for **PID** to change the process group of the current process. If both arguments are omitted, defaults to values of zero. Causes a fatal error if the system does not support the function.

Returns
undef on failure
New parent process ID

Reference:

getpgrp

setpriority

`setpriority WHICH, WHO, PRIORITY`

Sets the priority for a process (**PRIO_PROCESS**), process group (**PRIO_PGRP**), or user (**PRIO_USER**). The argument **WHICH** specifies what entity to set the priority for, and **WHO** is the process ID or user ID to set. A value of zero for **WHO** defines the current process, process group, or user. Produces a fatal error on systems that don't support the system **setpriority()** function.

Returns
0 on error
1 on success

Reference:

getpriority

setprotoent

`setprotoent STAYOPEN`

Sets (or resets) the enumeration to the beginning of the set of protocol entries. This function should be called before the first call to **getprotoent**. The **STAYOPEN** argument is optional and unused on most systems.

Returns
Nothing

References:

getprotoent, endprotoent

setpwent

`setpwent`

Sets (or resets) the enumeration to the beginning of the set of password entries. This function should be called before the first call to **getpwent**.

Returns
Nothing

References:

getpwent, endpwent

setservent

`setservent STAYOPEN`

Sets (or resets) the enumeration to the beginning of the set of service entries. This function should be called before the first call to **getservent**. The **STAYOPEN** argument is optional and unused on most systems.

Returns
Nothing

References:

getservent, endservent

setsockopt

```
setsockopt SOCKET, LEVEL, OPTNAME, OPTVAL
```

Sets the socket option **OPTNAME** with a value of **OPTVAL** on **SOCKET** at the specified **LEVEL**. You will need to import the **Socket** module for the valid values for **OPTNAME** shown in the following table.

OPTNAME	Description
SO_DEBUG	Enables/disables recording of debugging information.
SO_REUSEADDR	Enables/disables local address reuse.
SO_KEEPALIVE	Enables/disables keep connections alive.
SO_DONTROUTE	Enables/disables routing bypass for outgoing messages.
SO_LINGER	Lingers on close if data is present.
SO_BROADCAST	Enables/disables permission to transmit broadcast messages.
SO_OOBINLINE	Enables/disables reception of out-of-band data in band.
SO_SNDBUF	Sets buffer size for output.
SO_RCVBUF	Sets buffer size for input.
SO_TYPE	Gets the type of the socket (get only).
SO_ERROR	Gets and clears errors on the socket (get only).

Returns
undef on failure
1 on success

References:

getsockopt, socket

---

shift

```
shift ARRAY
shift
```

Returns the first value in an array, deleting it and shifting the elements of the array list to the left by one. If **ARRAY** is not specified, shifts the @_ array within a subroutine, or **@ARGV** otherwise. **shift** is essentially identical to **pop**, except values are taken from the start of the array instead of the end.

Returns
undef if the array is empty
First element in the array

References:

pop, push, unshift

---

shmctl

```
shmctl ID, CMD, ARG
```

Controls the shared memory segment referred to by **ID**, using **CMD** with **ARG**. You will need to import the **IPC::SysV** module to get the command tokens defined in the following table.

Command	Description
IPC_STAT	Places the current value of each member of the data structure associated with **ID** into the scalar **ARG**.
IPC_SET	Sets the value of the following members of the data structure associated with **ID** to the corresponding values found in the packed scalar **ARG**.

Command	Description
IPC_RMID	Removes the shared memory identifier specified by **ID** from the system and destroys the shared memory segment and data structure associated with it.
SHM_LOCK	Locks the shared memory segment specified by **ID** in memory.
SHM_UNLOCK	Unlocks the shared memory segment specified by **ID**.

Returns

undef on failure
0 but true if the return value from the **shmctl()** is 0
Value returned by system

References:

shmget, shmread

shmget

```
shmget KEY, SIZE, FLAGS
shmget KEY
```

Returns the shared memory segment ID for the segment matching **KEY**. A new shared memory segment is created of at least **SIZE** bytes, provided either that **KEY** does not already have a segment associated with it or that **KEY** is equal to the constant **IPC_PRIVATE**.

Returns

Shared memory ID

References:

shmctl, shmread, shmwrite

shmread

```
shmread ID, VAR, POS, SIZE
```

Reads the shared memory segment **ID** into the scalar **VAR** at position **POS** for up to **SIZE** bytes.

Returns

0 on false
1 on success

References:

shmctl, shmget, shmwrite

---

shmwrite

```
shmwrite ID, STRING, POS, SIZE
```

Writes **STRING** from the position **POS** for **SIZE** bytes into the shared memory segment specified by **ID**. The **SIZE** is greater than the length of **STRING**. **shmwrite** appends null bytes to fill out to **SIZE** bytes.

Returns

0 on false
1 on success

References:

shmctl, shmget, shmread

---

shutdown

```
shutdown SOCKET, HOW
```

Disables a socket connection according to the value of **HOW**. The valid values for **HOW** are identical to the system call of the same name. A value of **0** indicates that you have stopped reading information from the socket. A **1** indicates that you have stopped writing to the socket. A value of **2** indicates that you have stopped using the socket altogether.

Returns
0 on failure
1 on success

sin

```
sin EXPR
sin
```

Returns the sine of **EXPR** expressed in radians, or **$_** if not specified.

Returns
Floating point

sleep

```
sleep EXPR
sleep
```

Pauses the script for **EXPR** seconds, or forever if **EXPR** is not
specified. Returns the number of seconds actually slept. Can
be interrupted by a signal handler, but you should avoid
using **sleep** with **alarm** since many systems use **alarm** for the
sleep implementation.

Returns
Integer, number of seconds actually slept

socket

```
socket SOCKET, DOMAIN, TYPE, PROTOCOL
```

Opens a socket in **DOMAIN**, of **TYPE**, using **PROTOCOL**, and attaches it to the filehandle **SOCKET**. You will need to import the **Socket** module to get the correct definitions. For most systems, **DOMAIN** will be **PF_INET** for a TCP/IP-based socket. **TYPE** will generally be one of **SOCK_STREAM** for streams-based connections (TCP/IP) or **SOCK_DGRAM** for a datagram connection (UDP/IP). Values for **PROTOCOL** are system defined, but valid values include **TCP** for TCP/IP, **UDP** for UDP, and **RDP** for the "reliable" datagram protocol.

Returns
0 on failure
1 on success

socketpair

```
socketpair SOCKET1, SOCKET2, DOMAIN, TYPE, PROTOCOL
```

Creates an unnamed pair of connected sockets in the specified **DOMAIN**, of the specified **TYPE**, using **PROTOCOL**. If the system **socketpair()** function is not implemented, then it causes a fatal error.

Returns
0 on failure
1 on success

References:

pipe, socket

sort

```
sort SUBNAME LIST
sort BLOCK LIST
sort LIST
```

Sorts **LIST** according to the subroutine **SUBNAME** or the anonymous subroutine specified by **BLOCK**. If no **SUBNAME** or **BLOCK** is specified, then sorts according to normal alphabetical sequence. If **BLOCK** or **SUBNAME** is specified, then the subroutine should return an integer less than, greater than, or equal to zero according to how the elements of the array are to be sorted.

II

Returns

List

splice

```
splice ARRAY, OFFSET, LENGTH, LIST
splice ARRAY, OFFSET, LENGTH
splice ARRAY, OFFSET
```

Removes the elements of **ARRAY** from the element **OFFSET** for **LENGTH** elements, replacing the elements removed with **LIST** if specified. If **LENGTH** is omitted, removes everything from **OFFSET** onwards.

Returns

undef if no elements removed in a scalar context
Last element removed in a scalar context
Empty list in a list context
List of elements removed in a list context

split

```
split /PATTERN/, EXPR, LIMIT
split /PATTERN/, EXPR
split /PATTERN/
split
```

Splits a string into an array of strings, returning the resultant list. By default, empty leading fields are preserved, and empty trailing fields are deleted.

In a scalar context, returns the number of fields found and splits the values into the @_ array. In a list context, you can force the split into @_ by using **??** as the pattern delimiter. If **EXPR** is omitted, splits the value of **$_**. If **PATTERN** is also omitted, it splits on white space (multiple spaces, tabs). Anything matching **PATTERN** is taken to be a delimiter separating fields and can be a regular expression of one or more characters.

If **LIMIT** has been specified and is positive, splits into a maximum of that many fields (or fewer). If **LIMIT** is unspecified or zero, splitting continues until there are no more delimited fields. If negative, then **split** acts as if an arbitrarily large value has been specified, preserving trailing null fields.

A **PATTERN** of a null string splits **EXPR** into individual characters.

Returns
Integer, number of elements in scalar context
List of split elements

Reference:

join

sprintf

```
sprintf FORMAT, LIST
```

The **sprintf** function uses **FORMAT** to return a formatted string based on the values in **LIST**. Essentially identical to **printf**, but the formatted string is returned instead of being printed. The **sprintf** function is basically synonymous with the C **sprintf** function, but Perl does its own formatting; the C **sprintf** function is not used (except for basic floating point formatting).

The **sprintf** function accepts the same format conversions as **printf** (see Table 2-1). Perl also supports flags that optionally adjust the output format. These are specified between the % and the conversion letter and are the same as those for **printf** (see Table 2-2).

Returns
undef on error
Preformatted string according to **FORMAT** and **LIST**

References:

print, printf

sqrt

```
sqrt EXPR
sqrt
```

Returns the square root of **EXPR**, or **$_** if omitted.

Returns

Floating point number

srand

```
srand EXPR
srand
```

Sets the seed value for the random number generator to **EXPR**, or to a random value based on the time, process ID, and other values if **EXPR** is omitted.

Returns

Nothing

Reference:

rand

stat

```
stat FILEHANDLE
stat EXPR
stat
```

Returns a 13-element array giving the status info for a file, specified by either **FILEHANDLE**, **EXPR**, or **$_**. The list of values returned is shown in the following table. If used in a scalar context, returns **0** on failure, **1** on success.

Element	Description
0	Device number of file system
1	Inode number
2	File mode (type and permissions)
3	Number of (hard) links to the file
4	Numeric user ID of file's owner
5	Numeric group ID of file's owner
6	The device identifier (special files only)
7	File size, in bytes
8	Last access time since the epoch
9	Last modify time since the epoch
10	Inode change time (*not* creation time!) since the epoch
11	Preferred block size for file system I/O
12	Actual number of blocks allocated

Returns

0 on failure in scalar context
1 on success in scalar context
Empty list on failure in list context
List of status on success values in list context

Reference:

−X

study

```
study EXPR
study
```

Takes extra time to study **EXPR** in order to improve the performance on regular expressions conducted on **EXPR**. If **EXPR** is omitted, uses **$_**. The actual speed gains may be very small, depending on the number of times you expect to search the string. You can only study one expression or scalar at any one time.

Returns
Nothing

sub

```
sub NAME BLOCK
sub NAME
sub BLOCK
```

Not a function. This is a keyword that signifies the start of a new subroutine definition. With **NAME** and **BLOCK**, it is a named function and definition. With only **NAME** (and optional prototypes), it is simply a declaration. With only **BLOCK**, it is an anonymous subroutine.

Returns
Nothing

substr

```
substr EXPR, OFFSET, LEN, REPLACEMENT
substr EXPR, OFFSET, LEN
substr EXPR, OFFSET
```

Returns a substring of **EXPR**, starting at **OFFSET** within the string. If **OFFSET** is negative, starts that many characters from the end of the string. If **LEN** is specified, returns that number of bytes, or if not specified, all bytes up until end of string. If **LEN** is negative, leaves that many characters off the end of the string. If **REPLACEMENT** is specified, replaces the substring with the **REPLACEMENT** string.

If you specify a substring that passes beyond the end of the string, then it returns only the valid element of the original string.

Returns
String

symlink

```
symlink OLDFILE, NEWFILE
```

Creates a symbolic link between **OLDFILE** and **NEWFILE**. On systems that don't support symbolic links, causes a fatal error.

Returns
0 on failure
1 on success

syscall

```
syscall EXPR, LIST
```

Calls the system function **EXPR** with the arguments **LIST**. Produces a fatal error if the specified function does not exist.

Returns
–1 on failure of system call
Value returned by system function

sysopen

```
sysopen FILEHANDLE, FILENAME, MODE, PERMS
sysopen FILEHANDLE, FILENAME, MODE
```

Equivalent to the underlying C and operating system call **open()**. Opens the file specified by **FILENAME**, associating it with **FILEHANDLE**. The **MODE** argument specifies how the file should be opened. The values of **MODE** are system dependent, but some values are historically set. Values of zero, one, and two mean read-only, write-only, and read/write. The supported values are available in the **Fcntl** module. Note that **FILENAME** is strictly a file name; no interpretation of the contents takes place, and the mode of opening is defined by the **MODE** argument.

If the file has to be created and the **O_CREAT** flag has been specified in **MODE**, then the file is created with the permissions of **PERMS**. The value of **PERMS** must be specified in traditional Unix-style hexadecimal. If **PERMS** is not specified, then Perl uses a default mode of 0666.

Returns

0 on failure
1 on success

References:

sysread, syswrite, sysseek

sysread

```
sysread FILEHANDLE, SCALAR, LENGTH, OFFSET
sysread FILEHANDLE, SCALAR, LENGTH
```

Tries to read **LENGTH** bytes from **FILEHANDLE**, placing the result in **SCALAR**. If **OFFSET** is specified, then data is written to **SCALAR** from **OFFSET** bytes, effectively appending the information from a specific point. If **OFFSET** is negative, it starts from the number of bytes specified counted backwards from the end of the string. This is the equivalent of the C/operating system function **read()**. Because it bypasses the buffering system employed by functions like **print**, **read**, and **seek**, it should only be used with the corresponding **syswrite** and **sysseek** functions.

Returns

undef on error
0 at end of file
Integer, number of bytes read

References:

syswrite, sysseek

sysseek

```
sysseek FILEHANDLE, POSITION, WHENCE
```

Sets the position within **FILEHANDLE** according to the values of **POSITION** and **WHENCE**. This function is the equivalent of the C function **lseek()**, so you should avoid using it with buffered forms of **FILEHANDLE**. This includes the <**FILEHANDLE**> notation and **print**, **write**, **seek**, and **tell**. Using it with **sysread** or **syswrite** is OK, since they too ignore buffering.

The position within the file is specified by **POSITION**, using the value of **WHENCE** as a reference point, as follows:

- **0** sets the new position to **POSITION**.
- **1** sets the new position to the current position plus **POSITION**.
- **2** sets the new position to **EOF** plus **POSITION**.

If you prefer, you can use the constants **SEEK_SET**, **SEEK_CUR**, and **SEEK_END**, respectively, provided you have imported the **IO::Seekable** or **POSIX** module.

Returns
undef on failure
A position of zero is returned as the string **0 but true**
Integer, new position (in bytes) on success

References:

tell, seek

system

```
system PROGRAM, LIST
system PROGRAM
```

Executes the command specified by **PROGRAM**, passing **LIST** as arguments to the command. The script waits for execution of the child command to complete before continuing. If **PROGRAM** is the only argument specified, then Perl checks for any shell metacharacters and, if found, passes **PROGRAM** unchanged to the user's default command shell. If there are no metacharacters, then the value is split into words and passed as an entire command with arguments to the system **execvp** function.

The return value is the exit status of the program as returned by the **wait** function. To obtain the actual exit value, divide by 256. If you want to capture the output from a command, use the backticks operator.

Returns
Exit status of program as returned by **wait**

syswrite

```
syswrite FILEHANDLE, SCALAR, LENGTH, OFFSET
syswrite FILEHANDLE, SCALAR, LENGTH
```

Attempts to write **LENGTH** bytes from **SCALAR** to the file associated with **FILEHANDLE**. If **OFFSET** is specified, then information is read from **OFFSET** bytes in the supplied **SCALAR**. This function uses the C/operating system **write()** function, which bypasses the normal buffering. You should therefore avoid using functions such as **print** and **read** in conjunction with this function.

Returns
undef on error
Integer, number of bytes written

References:

sysread, sysseek

tell

```
tell FILEHANDLE
tell
```

Returns the current position (in bytes) within the specified **FILEHANDLE**. If **FILEHANDLE** is omitted, then it returns the position within the last file accessed.

Returns

Integer, current file position (in bytes)

References:

seek, sysseek

```
telldir DIRHANDLE
```

Returns the current position within the directory listing referred to by **DIRHANDLE**.

Returns

Integer

```
tie VARIABLE, CLASSNAME, LIST
```

Ties the **VARIABLE** to the package class **CLASSNAME** that provides implementation for the variable type. Any additional arguments in **LIST** are passed to the constructor for the entire class. Typically used to bind hash variables to DBM databases.

Returns

Reference to tied object

References:

tied, untie

tied

```
tied VARIABLE
```

Returns a reference to the object underlying the tied entity **VARIABLE**.

Returns
undef if **VARIABLE** is not tied to a package

References:

tie, untie

time

```
time
```

Returns the number of seconds since the epoch (00:00:00 UTC, January 1, 1970, for most systems; 00:00:00, January 1, 1904, for MacOS). Suitable for feeding to **gmtime** and **localtime**.

Returns
Integer, seconds since epoch

References:

gmtime, localtime

times

```
times
```

Returns a four-element list giving the user, system, child, and child system times for the current process and its children.

Returns
User, system, child, child system times as integer

tr///

```
tr/SEARCHLIST/REPLACEMENTLIST/
```

Not a function. This is the transliteration operator; it replaces all occurrences of the characters in **SEARCHLIST** with the characters in **REPLACEMENTLIST**.

Returns
Number of characters replaced or deleted

truncate

```
truncate FILEHANDLE, LENGTH
```

Truncates (reduces) the size of the file specified by **FILEHANDLE** to the specified **LENGTH** (in bytes). Produces a fatal error if the function is not implemented on your system.

Returns
undef if the operation failed
1 on success

uc

```
uc EXPR
uc
```

Returns an uppercased version of **EXPR**, or **$_** if not specified.

Returns
String

References:

lc, lcfirst, ucfirst

ucfirst

```
ucfirst EXPR
ucfirst
```

Returns the value of **EXPR** with only the first character uppercased.
If **EXPR** is omitted, then uses **$_**.

Returns
String

References:

lc, lcfirst, uc

umask

```
umask EXPR
umask
```

Sets the umask (default mask applied when creating files and
directories) for the current process. Value of **EXPR** must be an octal
number. If **EXPR** is omitted, simply returns the previous value.

Returns
Previous umask value

References:

open, sysopen, mkdir

undef

```
undef EXPR
undef
```

Undefines the value of **EXPR**. Use on a scalar, list, hash, function, or typeglob. Use on a hash with a statement such as **undef $hash{$key}**; actually sets the value of the specified key to an undefined value. If you want to delete the element from the hash, use the **delete** function. If **EXPR** is not specified, returns the undefined value.

Returns
undef

Reference:

delete

unlink

```
unlink LIST
unlink
```

Deletes the files specified by **LIST**, or the file specified by **$_** otherwise.

Returns
Number of files deleted

unpack

```
unpack FORMAT, EXPR
```

Unpacks the binary string **EXPR** using the format specified in **FORMAT**. Basically reverses the operation of **pack**, returning the list of packed values according to the supplied format.

You can also prefix any format field with a **%<number>** to indicate that you want a 16-bit checksum of the value of **EXPR**, instead of the value.

Returns
List of unpacked values

Reference:

pack

unshift

```
unshift ARRAY, LIST
```

Places the elements from **LIST**, in order, at the beginning
of **ARRAY**.

Returns
Number of new elements in **ARRAY**

untie

```
untie VARIABLE
```

Breaks the binding between a variable and a package, undoing the
association created by the **tie** function.

Returns
0 on failure
1 on success

Reference:

tie

use

```
use MODULE LIST
use MODULE
```

```
use VERSION
use MODULE VERSION [LIST]
```

Imports all the functions exported by **MODULE,** or only those referred to by **LIST,** into the name space of the current package. Effectively equivalent to

```
BEGIN
{
    require "Module.pm";
    Module->import();
}
```

Also used to impose compiler directives (pragmas) on the current script, although essentially these are just modules anyway.

Note that a **use** statement is evaluated at compile time. A **require** statement is evaluated at execution time.

If the **VERSION** formats are used, then specifies either the minimum Perl version required, or the minimum version of the imported module required. Exits with a fatal error if the version condition is not met.

Returns
Nothing

Reference:

require

utime

```
utime ATIME, MTIME, LIST
```

Sets the access and modification times specified by **ATIME** and **MTIME** for each file in **LIST.** The values of **ATIME** and **MTIME** must be numerical. The inode modification time is set to the current time.

Returns
Number of files updated

values

```
values HASH
```

Returns the list of all the values contained in **HASH**. In a scalar context, returns the number of values that would be returned. Uses the same iterator, and therefore order, used by the **each** and **keys** functions.

Returns
Number of values in scalar context
List of values in list context

References:

each, keys

vec

```
vec EXPR, OFFSET, BITS
```

Treats the string in **EXPR** as a vector of unsigned integers and returns the value of the bit field specified by OFFSET. BITS specifies the number of bits reserved for each entry in the bit vector. This must be a power of two from 1 to 32.

Returns
Integer

wait

```
wait
```

Waits for a child process to terminate, returning the process ID of the deceased process. The exit status of the process is contained in **$?**.

Returns

–1 if there are no child processes
Process ID of deceased process

Reference:

waitfor

waitpid

```
waitpid PID, FLAGS
```

Waits for the child process with ID **PID** to terminate, returning the
process ID of the deceased process. If **PID** does not exist, then it
returns –1. The exit status of the process is contained in **$?**.

If you import the **POSIX** module, you can specify flags by name,
although all Perl implementations support a value of zero. The
following table lists the flags supported under Solaris. You will
need to check your implementation for the flags your OS supports.

Flag	Description
WIFEXITED	Waits for processes that have exited.
WIFSIGNALED	Waits for processes that received a signal.
WNOHANG	Nonblocking wait.
WSTOPSIG	Waits for processes that received STOP signal.
WTERMSIG	Waits for processes that received TERM signal.
WUNTRACED	Waits for processes stopped by signals.

Returns

–1 if process does not exist
Process ID of deceased process

wantarray

```
wantarray
```

Returns **TRUE** if the context of the currently executing function is looking for a list value. Returns **FALSE** in a scalar context.

Returns
undef if no context
0 in scalar context
1 in list context

warn LIST

Prints the value of **LIST** to **STDERR**. Basically the same as the **die** function except that no call is made to the exit and no exception is raised within an **eval** statement. This can be useful to raise an error without causing the script to terminate prematurely.

If the variable **$@** contains a value (from a previous **eval** call) and **LIST** is empty, then the value of **$@** is printed with "\t...caught" appended to the end. If both **$@** and **LIST** are empty, then "Warning: Something's wrong" is printed.

Returns
Nothing

Reference:

die

write

write FILEHANDLE
write

Writes a formatted record, as specified by **format**, to **FILEHANDLE**. If **FILEHANDLE** is omitted, then writes the output to the currently selected default output channel. Form processing is handled automatically, adding new pages, headers, footers, and so on, as specified by the format for the filehandle.

Returns

0 on failure
1 on success

Reference:

format

y/SEARCHLIST/REPLACEMENTLIST/

Identical to the **tr///** operator; translates all characters in
SEARCHLIST into the corresponding characters in
REPLACEMENTLIST.

Returns

Number of characters modified

Reference:

tr///

Part 3
Standard Perl Library

The standard Perl library comes with a range of modules that have been deemed useful, if not essential, to developing Perl applications. Some of these modules, such as **AutoLoader**, **AutoSplit**, and much of the **ExtUtils** hierarchy, are an essential part of the development process. Others are utility modules, such as the **Text::Tabs** module that supports the expanding and compressing of tabs to and from spaces.

Please note the following:

- References to the **CORE** module refer to the core functions and operators supported natively by the Perl interpreter.

- The actual location of the files will vary according to platform and version. You may need to search the entire Perl 5 library directory to find a specific module. The titles given here will work inside any standard Perl script.

- The list of modules available on your system may be different from that listed here because of differences between the supported features of different operating systems.

AnyDBM_File

```
use AnyDBM_File;
```

This module imports a suitable **DBM** module to enable you to use a DBM database. Care should be taken when doing this, since you cannot normally mix DBM formats. By default, any program wanting to use a DBM file can use this module, which will try to inherit a DBM-handling class first from **NDBM_File** (which is also compatible with **ODBM_File**). Then the module tries to inherit its classes in turn from **DB_File**, **GDBM_File**, **SDBM_File** (which is part of the Perl distribution), and finally, **ODBM_File**.

To use, specify the DBM type as **AnyDBM_File** within the **tie** statement:

```
use Fcntl;
use AnyDBM_File;
```

125

```
tie %myhash, "AnyDBM_File", "mydbm", O_RDWR, 0644;
```

You can override the default list and sequence by redefining the contents of the **@ISA** array within the **AnyDBM_File** module:

```
@AnyDBM_File::ISA = qw(GDBM_File ODBM_File);
```

You can also specify your own preference by importing your DBM module directly. This is less portable, but if you are relying on the feature set of a DBM implementation, especially with the special abilities of **DB_File** and **GDBM_File** in mind, then you may want to use the module directly. See the following table for details of the differences between each DBM version.

Implementation	DBM/ODBM	NDBM	SDBM	GDBM	Berkeley DB
Module	ODBM_File	NDBM_File	SDBM_File	GDBM_File	DB_File
Bucket Limit	1–2K	1–4K	1K (none)	None	None
Disk Usage	Varies	Varies	Small	Big	Big
Speed	Slow	Slow	Slow	OK	Fast
Data Files Distributable	No	No	Yes	Yes	Yes
Byte-order Independent	No	No	No	No	Yes
User Defined Sort Order	No	No	No	No	Yes
Wildcard Lookups	No	No	No	No	Yes

References:

See **DB_File, GDBM_File, NDBM_File, ODBM_File, SDBM_File**

AutoLoader

This module provides a method for automatically loading Perl subroutines from external files that have been split by the **AutoSplit** module. Each subroutine is stored in an individual file within the

./auto directory with the rest of the Perl library modules. For example, the function **Auto::foo** would be in a file **./auto/Auto/foo.al**.

```
package Auto;
use Exporter;
use AutoLoader;
@ISA = qw/Exporter AutoLoader/;
```

Any module using the **AutoLoader** should have the special marker **__END__** prior to any subroutine declarations. These will be used as the declarations for subroutines to be autoloaded from the corresponding .al files. Any code before the marker will be parsed and imported when the module is first used. Any subroutine declared that is not already in memory will then be loaded from the corresponding file by looking into the ./auto directory tree.

Since the **__END__** ends the current scope, you will need to use package globals rather than lexical variables declared with **my**. Remember to use the **vars** pragma to declare them if you are also using the **strict** pragma.

The easiest way to create a module supporting **AutoLoader** is to use the **AutoSplit** module. You may also want to see the **SelfLoader** module, which provides a similar mechanism for loading subroutines.

Also note that this is related to but does not provide the support for the **AUTOLOAD** special subroutine.

References:

See **AutoSplit**, **SelfLoader**, **strict**, **vars**

AutoSplit

This module provides a method for splitting modules into the individual files required by the **AutoLoader** module. This is generally used by the standard Perl library modules and by the XS and **MakeMaker** systems to split C extensions into individual loadable subroutines. The main function is **autosplit**, and it supports the splitting process in a single hit. The typical use is

```
$ perl -MAutoSplit -e 'autosplit(FILE, DIR, KEEP, CHECK, MODTIME)'
```

where **FILE** is the module to split, and **DIR** is the base directory into which the file should be split. The **KEEP** argument defines whether existing **.al** files should be deleted as the module is split. This is the operation when false; if true, files are kept even if the functions do not appear in the new module.

The **CHECK** argument tells **AutoSplit** to check whether the specified module actually includes the **AutoLoader** module. If false, no checks are made. The **MODTIME** argument, if true, only splits the module if its modification time is later than that of the autosplit.ix index file.

Only those functions specified after the __END__ marker are split; other functions are forced to load when the module is imported.

You will be warned if the functions to be split exceed the permitted length for file names on the desired file system. Because of the use of function names as file names, it presents possible naming conflicts that should be resolved. You will also be warned if the directory that you want to split the module into does not exist, or if it can't create directories or files. Warnings are issued and the file is skipped if **AutoSplit** cannot locate either the __END__ marker or specification of the form package NAME.

This module is normally only used as part of the **MakeMaker** process.

References:

See **AutoLoader, ExtUtils::MakeMaker**

autouse

```
use autouse 'Module' => qw(funca funcb);
```

The **autouse** pragma postpones the loading of the **Module** until one of **funca** or **funcb** is actually used. This is similar in principle but not identical to the **Autoloader** module. Note that you must specify the functions that will trigger the **autouse** process;

otherwise, there is no way for the Perl interpreter to identify the functions that should be imported. The line above is therefore equivalent to the standard method for importing selected functions:

```
use Module qw(funca funcb);
```

You can also supply a function prototype to the **autouse** pragma to trap errors during the compilation rather than execution stage:

```
use Module qw(funca($$) funcb($@));
```

B

This module is part of the Perl compiler. The compiler uses many of the objects and methods defined within the **B** module and its hierarchy in order to provide the script with the necessary hooks into its own internals. The module does this by providing its own suite of classes, which allow a Perl script to examine its own objects and classes in detail.

```
use B;
```

Although this module provides the information required during the compilation process of a Perl script into a stand-alone executable, use of this module is not required to make a stand-alone program.

The bulk of the **B** module is the methods for accessing the fields of the objects that describe the internal structures. Note that all access is read-only: you cannot modify the internals by using this module.

The **B** module exports a variety of functions: some are simple utility functions; others provide a Perl program with a way to get an initial "handle" on an internal object. These are listed in the following table.

Function	Description
main_cv	Returns the (faked) **CV** corresponding to the main part of the Perl program.
main_root	Returns the root opcode of the main part of the Perl program.
main_start	Returns the starting op of the main part of the Perl program.

Function	Description
Comppadlist	Returns the **AV** object of the global comppadlist.
sv_undef	Returns the **SV** object corresponding to the C variable **sv_undef** (the undefined value).
sv_yes	Returns the **SV** object corresponding to the C variable **sv_yes** ("true").
sv_no	Returns the **SV** object corresponding to the C variable **sv_no** ("false").
walkoptree(OP, METHOD)	Does a tree-walk of the syntax tree starting at the opcode referenced by **OP**, calling **METHOD** on each opcode in the tree it visits. Each parent node is visited before its children.
walkoptree_debug(DEBUG)	Returns the current debugging flag for **walkoptree**. If the optional **DEBUG** argument is nonzero, it sets the debugging flag to that value.
walksymtable(SYMREF, METHOD, RECURSE)	Walks the symbol table starting at **SYMREF** and calls **METHOD** on each symbol visited. When the walk reaches package symbols **Foo::**, it invokes **RECURSE** and only recurses into the package if that sub returns true.
svref_2object(SV)	Takes any Perl variable and turns it into an object in the appropriate **B::OP**-derived or **B::SV**-derived class.
ppname(OPNUM)	Returns the **PP** function name (for example, **pp_add**) of opcode number **OPNUM**.
hash(STRING)	Returns a string in the form "0x...", representing the hexadecimal value of the internal hash function used by Perl on string **STR**.
cast_I32(I)	Casts **I** to the internal **I32** type used by the current Perl interpreter.
minus_c	Does the equivalent of the **–c** command line option.
cstring(STR)	Returns a double-quote-surrounded escaped version of **STR**, which can be used as a string in C source code.

Function	Description
class(OBJECT)	Returns the class of an object without the part of the class name preceding the first ::.
threadsv_names	In a Perl interpreter compiled for threads, this returns a list of the special per-thread **threadsv** variables.
byteload_fh(FILEHANDLE)	Loads the contents of **FILEHANDLE** as bytecode.

A more in-depth discussion on the use of the Perl compiler, of which the **B** module is a critical part, can be found in Part 6.

References:

See **O**

B::Asmdata

This module is used internally by the **B::Bytecode** and other modules to generate data about Perl opcodes.

References:

See **B::Bytecode**, **O**

B::Assembler

The module used by the **O** Perl compiler interface to assemble Perl bytecode into executable opcodes.

References:

See **B::Bytecode**, **O**

B::Bblock

The module used by the **O** Perl compiler interface to produce a report of the basic blocks that make up a Perl program.

References:

See **O**

B::Bytecode

This module provides the necessary code for translating Perl scripts into Perl bytecode as used by the **O** module and the Perl compiler. For example, you can convert any Perl script into bytecode using

```
$ perl -MO=Bytecode foobar.pl
```

References:

See **O**

B::C

The basic underlying module used by the Perl compiler that produces raw C code in a nonoptimized format, suitable for compiling into a stand-alone program. For an optimized version, you should use the **B:CC** module. The default operation creates a C file that can be separately compiled:

```
$ perl -MO=C foobar.pl
```

If you want to compile a Perl script directly, then use the **perlcc** command:

```
$ perlcc foobar.pl
```

This will generate a stand-alone application called **foobar**.

References:

See **O**

B::CC

This is the optimized interface for creating C code from Perl scripts for compilation into stand-alone applications. For example:

```
$ perl -MO=CC foobar.pl
```

Relatively simple optimizations are supported for the purposes of improving the performance of Perl code into C code.

References:

See **O**

B::Debug

This module produces a Perl syntax tree, providing debug-level information about the opcodes being used. For example:

```
$ perl -M=Debug
```

For a simpler version, you should try the **B::Terse** compiler interface module.

References:

See **O**

B::Deparse

An interface used by the Perl compiler and the **O** module that regurgitates a Perl script based on the internal structure used by the Perl interpreter. The source output matches the format of the script after being parsed by the interpreter and may not match the original source script. It is normally used with the **O** module.

```
$ perl -MO=Deparse foobar.pl
```

References:

See **O**

B::Disassembler

The backend used by the Perl compiler to translate compiled bytecode into raw source code.

References:

See **B::Bytecode, O**

B::Lint

This module expands on the warnings provided by the **–w** switch with additional warnings for some specific statements and constructs in the Perl code. It is used as a backend to the Perl compiler.

```
$ perl -MO=Lint foobar.pl
```

References:

See **O**

B::Showlex

A Perl compiler backend, used with the **O** module. The module produces a list of lexical values used within functions and files.

References:

See **O**

B::Stackobj

A helper module for the Perl compiler.

References:

See **O**

B::Terse

Used with the Perl compiler to provide the syntax tree for a Perl script. Unlike the **Debug** backend, information about individual opcodes within the tree is kept to a minimum.

```
$ perl -MO=Terse foobar.pl
```

References:

See **O**

B::Xref

A Perl compiler backend that produces a report detailing and cross-referencing the variables, subroutines, and formats used in a Perl script on a line-by-line and file-by-file basis.

References:

See **O**

base

The **base** pragma establishes a relationship with a base class at compile (rather than execution) time. In effect, this is equal to adding the specified classes to the **@ISA** array during the module initialization.

```
package Object;
use base qw(Foo Bar);
```

Benchmark

```
use Benchmark;
```

This module provides a constant and consistent interface to aid in the production of benchmarking figures. You can use the **Benchmark** module to time the execution of any Perl statement, function, or even the entire script.

There are three main functions: **timeit**, **timethis**, and **timethese**:

```
timeit(COUNT, 'CODE');
```

Times the execution of a single piece of **CODE**, for **COUNT** iterations. Note that **CODE** is a string containing the code to benchmark. Use the object method shown below to benchmark an arbitrary piece of code.

For example, the code

```
$t = timeit(1000000,'cos(3.141)');
```

will place the timing information for a million iterations of the calculation into **$t**, which will be a reference to a **Benchmark** object. See below for more information on the object interface.

```
timethis(COUNT, 'CODE')
```

Uses **timeit** to run a piece of code, also printing a header to state that it is timing a piece of code and the resulting timing information.

```
timethese(COUNT, CODEHASH)
```

Runs **timethis** on multiple pieces of code. Each piece of code should be placed into the value of a hash element, and the corresponding key will be used as a label for the reported figures.

Note that in all the above cases, the code is embedded into a **for** loop and then **eval**'d in its entirety. As such, lexical values declared outside the **eval** block will not be available within it.

If you want to time arbitrary requests, you need to use the object interface to the module:

```
$ta = new Benchmark;
&render_object();
$tb = new Benchmark;
print "Calculation time: ",
    timestr(timediff($ta,$tb)), "\n";
```

The **timediff** function returns a new object detailing the time difference between two **Benchmark** objects, and you can then print a string of the time difference information with **timestr**.

In all cases, the times reported use the **times** function, so both CPU and user times are reported. The CPU time is the most important, since it should not be affected by other processes. Because it uses the **times** function, measurements are in milliseconds. You should aim to support enough iterations for a reasonable timing figure. Times of at least five seconds are advised; ten seconds or more may give a more precise figure.

blib

The **blib** pragma forces Perl to look in the local **blib** directory for modules. This directory structure is generated when an extension is being built via a Perl-produced Makefile. The normal way to use it is via the command line,

```
$ perl -Mblib script
```

although you can include it in the script if required. This is the usual method for tests conducted during the installation process.

Carp

This module provides a simplified method for reporting errors within modules. A **die** call from a package will report an error with reference to the pacakge file in which it was called. This can cause problems if you are trying to trace errors in a calling script. The **Carp** module provides three functions: **carp**, **croak**, and **confess**. With each function, the location of the error is specified relative to the package that called the function.

```
carp "Didn't work";
```

Equivalent of **warn**; reports an error to **stderr**.

```
croak "Definitely didn't work";
```

Equivalent of **die**.

```
confess "Failed around about there";
```

This is equivalent to **croak** except that a stack trace is printed.

For example, imagine that you have a package called **T**, used in a script called **tm.pl**. The package defines a single function, **only**, which calls **warn** and **carp**; the result is

```
Warning! at T.pm line 11.
Carp warning! at tm.pl line 3
```

You can see from this that the first message, using **warn**, reports the error with reference to the module. The second, using **carp**, reports an error with reference to the original script in which it was called.

The reference is obtained using **caller**, and it goes up exactly one level, so if another package calls a **carp**-using function, the error will be reported with reference to the calling package.

III

CGI

This module provides a set of functions for drawing HTML pages and for both creating HTML forms and post-processing them using the CGI interface.

```
use CGI;
```

The module's primary use is for producing Web forms and parsing their contents once the information has been filled in and returned by a client. The module defines a simple CGI class that can be used to build the pages, although use of the class methods is not exclusive; they can be used as normal functions as well.

For example, to create a "Hello World!" page using the object method:

```
use CGI;
$page = new CGI;
print $page->header,
      $page->start_html('Hello World!'),
      $page->h1('Hello World!'),
      $page->end_html;
```

You can achieve the same result with the functional interface as follows:

```
use CGI qw/:standard/;
```

```
print header,
      start_html('Hello World!'),
      h1('Hello World!'),
      end_html;
```

The module provides three main elements: the HTTP header, HTML-formatted text, and a parsing engine for accepting input from browsers and forms using the various request methods available. In addition, it supports frames, cascading style sheets, cookies, and server-push technologies.

Import Sets

The module supports the import sets shown in the following table.

Import set	Exported symbols/symbol sets
html2	h1 h2 h3 h4 h5 h6 p br hr ol ul li dl dt dd menu code var strong em tt u i b blockquote pre img a address cite samp dfn html head base body Link nextid title meta kbd start_html end_html input Select option comment
html3	div table caption th td TR Tr sup sub strike applet Param embed basefont style span layer ilayer font frameset frame script small big
netscape	blink fontsize center
form	textfield textarea filefield password_field hidden checkbox checkbox_group submit reset defaults radio_group popup_menu button autoEscape scrolling_list image_button start_form end_form startform endform start_multipart_form isindex tmpFileName uploadInfo URL_ENCODED MULTIPART
cgi	param path_info path_translated url self_url script_name cookie dump raw_cookie request_method query_string accept user_agent remote_host remote_addr referer server_name server_software server_port server_protocol virtual_host remote_ident auth_type http use_named_parameters save_parameters restore_parameters param_fetch remote_user user_name header redirect import_names put Delete Delete_all url_param
ssl	https

Import set	Exported symbols/symbol sets
cgi-lib	ReadParse PrintHeader HtmlTop HtmlBot SplitParam
html	html2 html3 netscape
standard	html2 html3 form cgi
push	multipart_init multipart_start multipart_end
all	html2 html3 netscape form cgi internal

III

CGI::Apache

This module supports the use of the **CGI** module when used within the confines of the Perl-Apache API, as supported by the **mod_perl** CPAN module.

```
require CGI::Apache;

my $query = new Apache::CGI;
$query->print($query->header);
```

The module provides a slightly modified interface in order to allow the **CGI** module to work when executing scripts with the Perl-Apache API environment. This imports, and also overrides, some of the methods defined by the **CGI** module.

References:

See **CGI**, **CGI::Switch**

CGI::Switch

This module attempts to load **CGI** constructors from different modules until it successfully loads one.

```
use CGI::Switch;
```

The default packages it attempts to load, in order, are **Apache::CGI**, **CGI::XA**, and **CGI**. You can define a different order or a different selection of modules by specifying them explicitly:

```
use CGI::Switch qw/CGI CGI::Apache/;
```

A call to the **new** method in **CGI::Switch** will return an object of
the first found type:

```
$query = new CGI::Switch;
```

References:

See **CGI**

Class::Struct

This module supports the construction of **struct**-like data types as
Perl classes.

```
use Class::Struct;
```

It supports only one function, **struct**, which builds a new class based
on the information you supply. The new class can be made up of
multiple elements composed of scalars, arrays, hashes, and further
class definitions. This is primarily used for designing or emulating C
struct structures within Perl. The function has three forms:

```
struct(CLASS_NAME => [ ELEMENT_LIST ]);
struct(CLASS_NAME => { ELEMENT_LIST });
struct(ELEMENT_LIST);
```

The first two forms explicitly define the new class to be created,
and the third form assumes the current package name as the new
class. The first form creates an array-based class, which is fast; the
second and third create a hash-based class, which is slower but
more flexible and practical.

The newly created class must not be a subclass of anything other
than **UNIVERSAL**. This is because it will inherit methods, including
new, from its base class, which will override the methods generated
by **struct**.

The **ELEMENT _LIST** argument has the format of a typical hash
assignation:

```
NAME => TYPE
```

The **NAME** is the name of each element in the new class, and
TYPE is one of '**$**', '**@**', '**%**' to create a new scalar, array, or hash
entry; or it can be the name of another class.

For example, to create a Perl version of the **hostent** structure:

```
struct('hostent' => {
                     'h_name' => '$',
                     'h_aliases' => '@',
                     'h_addrtype' => '$',
                     'h_length' => '$',
                     'h_addr_list' => '@',
                   });
```

The name of the new class is **hostent**, but you need to create a new object in order to make use of it; **struct** merely constructs the class definition. Thus,

```
$host = new hostent;
```

will create a new **hostent** structure.

Using Scalar Elements

The scalar is initialized with **undef**. To access the scalar:

```
$obj->scalar
```

To set the value of the scalar:

```
$obj->scalar(value)
```

When defined, if the element type is stated as '**$**', then the element value is returned. If it is defined as '***$**', then a reference to the scalar element is returned.

Using Array Elements

The array is initialized as an empty list. To access the entire array:

```
$obj->array
```

Note that because there is no leading @ sign, you will need to use block notation to use the array in its entirety with many functions, for example:

```
sort @{$obj->array};
```

To access an element from the array,

```
$obj->array(index)
```

where **index** is the numerical index within the array.

To set a value in the array,

```
$obj->scalar(index, value)
```

where **index** is the numerical index within the array, and **value** is the value to be assigned.

When defined, if the element type is stated as '@', then the element value is returned. If it is defined as '*@', then a reference to the element is returned.

Using Hash Elements

The hash is initialized as an empty list. To access the entire hash:

```
$obj->array
```

Note that because there is no leading @ sign, you will need to use block notation to use the array in its entirety with many functions, for example:

```
sort @{$obj->array};
```

To access an element from the hash,

```
$obj->array(key)
```

where **key** is the string value.

To set a value in the hash,

```
$obj->scalar(key, value)
```

where **key** is the string index within the array, and **value** is the value to be assigned.

When defined, if the element type is stated as '%', then the element value is returned. If it is defined as '*%', then a reference to the element is returned.

Using Class Elements

The elements value must be a reference blessed to the named class or to one of its subclasses. The assigned class can have methods and structures and can be used like any other method, albeit within the confines of the class created by **struct**. The main use for this element is to support nested data structures within a **Class::Struct** created class. If the element type does not start with a '*', the accessor returns the element value (after assignment). If the element type starts with a '*', a reference to the element itself is returned.

Example

The code below builds on the **hostent** structure and populates it with the correct information based on the host given.

```
use Class::Struct;
use Socket;

struct('hostent' => {
    'h_name' => '$',
    'h_aliases' => '@',
    'h_addrtype' => '$',
    'h_length' => '$',
    'h_addr_list' => '@',
});

($name, $aliases, $addrtype, $length, @addresses) =
gethostbyname($hostname);

my $host = new hostent;

$host->h_name($name);

@aliases = split / /, $aliases;
foreach($i=0;$i<@aliases;$i++)
{
    $host->h_aliases($i, $aliases[$i]);
}
$host->h_addrtype($addrtype);
$host->h_length($length);

for($i=0;$i<@addresses;$i++)
{
    $host->h_addr_list($i,inet_ntoa($addresses[$i]));
}
```

III

Config

This module provides an interface to the configuration information determined during the build process.

```
use Config;
```

The module exports a single hash, **%Config**, which can be used to access individual configuration parameters by name, for example:

```
print "Built with: $Config{'cc'}
$Config{'ccflags'}\n";
```

You can also optionally import the **myconfig**, **config_sh**, and **config_vars** functions:

```
myconfig
```

This returns a text summary of the main Perl configuration values. This is the method used by the **–V** command line option.

```
config_sh
```

This returns the entire set of Perl configuration information in the form of the **config.sh** file used during the building process.

```
config_vars(LIST)
```

Sends the configuration values for the names specified in **LIST** to **STDOUT**. The information is printed as you would output the values in a simple loop. Thus the code

```
use Config qw/config_vars/;

config_vars(qw/cc ccflags ldflags/);
```

outputs

```
cc='gcc -B/usr/ccs/bin/';
ccflags='-I/usr/local/include';
ldflags=' -L/usr/local/lib';
```

The information contained in the **Config** module is determined during the build process. Since this module could be modified and/or overwritten or copied, the actual configuration information may not match the binary you are currently using.

References:

See **ExtUtils::MakeMaker**

constant

The **constant** pragma enables you to create nonmodifiable constants. The advantages of a constant are obvious: if you use the same constant value throughout all of your calculations and programs, you can be guaranteed that the values calculated will also remain constant.

```
use constant PI => 3.141592654;
```

The value can be any normal Perl expression, including calculations and functions such that the following also work:

```
use constant PI   => 22/7;
use constant USER => scalar getpwuid($<);
```

CPAN

This module provides a simple and programmable interface for downloading and installing modules from the CPAN archives. The module takes into account the requirements of the module you are downloading, automatically including the required modules during the installation process. The module makes use of the **Net::FTP** or **LWP** modules if they are available, or it uses the **lynx** Web browser and even an external ftp client to download the information and modules it needs.

The **CPAN** module therefore takes out a lot of the manual work required when downloading and installing a **CPAN** module. It is in fact the best way to download **CPAN** modules, as it guarantees that you will get the latest version while also ensuring that any required modules will be downloaded and installed.

It works in one of two ways: either within an interactive shell, which is invoked like this:

```
$ perl -MCPAN -e shell;
```

or via a Perl script:

```
use CPAN;
```

Interactive Shell Interface

The shell interface, also known as interactive mode, puts Perl into a simple shell-style interface using the readline line input system. The first time the shell interface is run, you will go through a configuration process that sets up your environment for using the **CPAN** module. This includes configuration of the internal system used to access raw data from the Internet, your preferred download location, and proxy information.

The shell interface supports the commands listed in the following table. You can use the shell to query the CPAN archives and also to download and install modules.

Command	Argument	Description
a	EXPR	Searches authors. **EXPR** should be a simple string, in which case a search will be made for an exact match with the author's ID. Alternatively, you can supply a regular expression that will search for matching author IDs and name details.
b		Displays a list of bundles.
d	EXPR	Performs a regular expression search for a package/module.
m	EXPR	Displays information about the expression matching **EXPR**.
i	EXPR	Displays information about a module, bundle, or user specified in **EXPR**.
r	EXPR	Displays a list of reinstallation recommendations, comparing the existing module list against installed modules and versions. If **EXPR** is not specified, lists all recommendations.

Command	Argument	Description
u	EXPR	Lists all modules not currently installed but available on CPAN.
make	EXPR	Downloads the module specified in **EXPR**, builds it, and installs it. No check is performed to ensure that you need to install the module; it just does it. Use **install** if you want to update a module based on its version number.
test	EXPR	Runs **make test** on the module specified in **EXPR**.
install	EXPR	Downloads and installs the module specified in **EXPR**. Runs **make install**. If **EXPR** is a module, it checks to see if the currently installed version of the module specified in **EXPR** is lower than that available on CPAN. If it is, it downloads, builds, and installs it. If **EXPR** is a distribution file, then the file is processed without any version checking.
clean	EXPR	Runs a **make clean** on the specified module.
force	make | test | install EXPR	Forces a **make**, **test**, or **install** on a command within the current session. Normally, modules are not rebuilt or installed within the current session.
readme		Displays the README file.
reload	index | cpan	Loads the most recent CPAN index files, or the latest version of the **CPAN** module.
h | ?		Displays the help menu.
o		Gets and sets the various configuration options for the **CPAN** module.
!	EXPR	Evaluates the Perl expression **EXPR**.
q		Quits the interactive shell.

To install a module with the interactive shell, the easiest method is to use the **install** command:

```
$ perl -MCPAN -e shell
cpan> install Nice
```

To install a CPAN bundle:

```
cpan> install Bundle::LWP
Fetching with Net::FTP:
  ftp://ftp.demon.co.uk/pub/mirrors/perl/CPAN/
    authors/id/GAAS/libwww-perl-5.42.tar.gz

  CPAN: MD5 security checks disabled because MD5 not
installed.
  Please consider installing the MD5 module.

x libwww-perl-5.42/, 0 bytes, 0 tape blocks
x libwww-perl-5.42/t/, 0 bytes, 0 tape blocks
x libwww-perl-5.42/t/net/, 0 bytes, 0 tape blocks
x libwww-perl-5.42/t/net/cgi-bin/, 0 bytes, 0 tape
    blocks
x libwww-perl-5.42/t/net/cgi-bin/test, 526 bytes, 2
    tape blocks
...
```

In addition to the commands listed in the previous table, the interactive shell supports two commands that should only be used by experienced users: **autobundle** and **recompile**.

The **autobundle** function writes a bundle file into the **$CPAN::Config->{cpan_home}/Bundle** directory. The new bundle contains all of the modules currently installed in the current Perl environment that are also available from CPAN. You can then use this file as the source for installing the same bundle of modules on a number of machines.

The **recompile** function forces the reinstallation of all the installed modules that make use of the XS extension system. This solves problems where an update to the operating system breaks binary compatibility. The function will redownload the necessary modules and rebuild them under the updated environment.

Programmable Interface

Depending on what you are trying to achieve, you might find the programmable interface to be more useful. All of the commands available in the interactive shell are also available as **CPAN::Shell** methods within any Perl script. The methods take the same arguments as their shell interface equivalents.

The **CPAN** module works with a series of subclasses for handling information about authors, bundles, modules, and distributions. The classes are **CPAN::Author**, **CPAN::Bundle**, **CPAN::Module**, and **CPAN::Distribution**. Individual methods are identical to those outlined in the shell in the previous table.

The core of the system is still the **CPAN::Shell** module. Individual methods are identical to their command equivalents, but instead of outputting a list to **STDOUT**, the methods return a list of suitable IDs for the corresponding entity type. This allows you to combine individual methods into entire statements—something not available in the shell. For example,

```
$ perl -MCPAN -e 'CPAN::Shell->install(CPAN::Shell->r)'
```

will reinstall all of the outdated modules currently installed.

The **CPAN::Shell** module also supports a further function, **expand**:

```
expand(TYPE, LIST)
```

This returns an array of **CPAN::Module** objects expanded according to their correct type. The **LIST** is the list of entries to expand. For example, you can expand and install a number of modules at once, using

```
for $module (qw/Bundle::libnet Bundle::LWP/)
{
    my $object = CPAN::Shell->expand('Module',$module);
    $object->install;
}
```

CPAN::FirstTime

This is a utility for configuring the **CPAN** module:

```
CPAN::FirstTime::init();
```

The **init** function asks some simple questions about the current environment and updates the **CPAN::Config** file that will be used by the **CPAN** module when downloading and building extensions.

References:

See **CPAN**

CPAN::Nox

This module supports the normal **CPAN** functionality but avoids the use of **XS** extensions during execution.

```
$ perl -MCPAN::Nox -e shell
```

This is intended for use when the binary compatibility has been broken between the Perl binary and the extensions. The above command puts you into the familiar **CPAN** interactive state.

References:

See **CPAN**

Cwd

This module provides a platform-independent interface for discovering the current working directory. The module provides three functions:

```
use Cwd;
$dir = cwd();
$dir = getcwd();
$dir = fastcwd();
```

The **cwd** function provides the safest method for discovering the current working directory. The **getcwd** function uses the **getcwd()** or **getwd()** C functions, if they are available on your platform.

The **fastcwd** function is a much faster version and can be used in situations where speed may be of great importance. However, it is not a reliable method and may mistakenly indicate that you can **chdir** out of a directory that you cannot change back into. As such, it shouldn't be relied on.

The **Cwd** module also optionally provides a replacement for the CORE **chdir** function that updates the value of the **PWD** environment variable:

```
use Cwd qw/chdir/;
chdir('/usr/local');
print $ENV{PWD};
```

III

References:

See **File::Spec**

Data::Dumper

This module provides methods for resolving a data structure (including objects) into a string format that can be used both to dump the data for printing and for evaluation so that a dumped structure can be reconstituted with **eval** into a valid internal structure.

```
use Data::Dumper;
```

The primary function is **Dumper**

```
Dumper(LIST)
```

This function accepts a list of scalar references to data structures or objects. The return value is a string representation of the structure, produced in normal string syntax format.

For example:

```
use Data::Dumper;

my $ref = { "Name" => "Martin",
            "Size" => "Medium",
            "Dates" => { "Monday" => "170599",
                         "Tuesday" => "180599"
                       }
          };

print Dumper($ref);
```

generates the following:

```
$VAR1 = {
        'Dates' => {
                        'Monday' => 170599,
                        'Tuesday' => 180599
                    },
        'Name' => 'Martin',
        'Size' => 'Medium'
        };
```

Note that references to anonymous variables are labeled with **$VARn**, where **n** is a sequential number relating to the references as they were supplied.

DB_File

This module provides access to the Berkeley DB system—probably the most flexible implementation of the DBM database system. Beyond the basic abilities of supporting a hash-style database, **DB_File** also provides the necessary functions and methods for accessing the database structures and for creating and managing B-Tree structures. The Berkeley DB system also supports a system based on fixed- and variable-length record numbers, which is supported within Perl as a hash using numerical rather than string references.

```
use DB_File ;

[$X =] tie %hash,  'DB_File', [FILENAME, FLAGS, MODE, $DB_HASH] ;
[$X =] tie %hash,  'DB_File', FILENAME, FLAGS, MODE, $DB_BTREE ;
[$X =] tie @array, 'DB_File', FILENAME, FLAGS, MODE, $DB_RECNO ;

# Methods for Hash databases
$status = $X->del(KEY [, FLAGS]);
$status = $X->put(KEY, VALUE [, FLAGS]);
$status = $X->get(KEY, VALUE [, FLAGS]);
$status = $X->seq(KEY, VALUE, FLAGS) ;
$status = $X->sync([FLAGS]);
$status = $X->fd;

# Methods for BTree databases
$count = $X->get_dup(KEY);
@list  = $X->get_dup(KEY);
%list  = $X->get_dup(KEY, 1);
```

```
# Methods for Record Number databases
$a = $X->length;
$a = $X->pop;
$X->push(LIST);
$a = $X->shift;
$X->unshift(LIST);

untie %hash;
untie @array;
```

The different database types are defined in the last argument to the **tie** function, using **DB_HASH** for hashes, **DB_BTREE** for binary trees, and **DB_RECNO** for the record number database.

A **DB_HASH** is identical in most respects to Perl's internal hash structure except that the key/data pairs are stored in data files, not memory. The functionality provided is basically identical to that provided by the other DBM-style database engines. **DB_File** uses its own hashing algorithm for storing and retrieving the key/data pairs, but you can supply your own system if you prefer.

The **DB_BTREE** format follows the same key/data pair structure, but the pairs are stored in a sorted, balanced binary tree. By default, the keys are sorted in lexical order, although you can supply your own comparison routine for use by the binary sorting subsystem.

DB_RECNO supports the storage of fixed- and variable-length records in a flat text using the same key/value hash interface. This may be more suitable to your requirements than using the DBI toolkit, covered later in this part. In order to make the record numbers more compatible with the array system employed by Perl, the offset starts at zero rather than one (as in the Berkeley DB).

You can also create an in-memory database (which is held entirely within memory, just like a standard hash) by specifying a NULL file name (use **undef**). You can use any of the database types for the in-memory database.

References:

See **AnyDBM_File, GDBM_File, NDBM_File, ODBM_File, SDBM_File**

Devel::SelfStubber

This module generates subroutine stubs for use with modules that employ the **SelfLoader** module.

```
use Devel::SelfStubber;

Devel::SelfStubber->stub(MODULE, LIBDIR);
```

It analyzes the module specified in **MODULE** (which should be specified as if it were being imported). The **LIBDIR** argument specifies the directory to search for the module. If left as a blank string, the current directory is used.

The generated output displays the list of subroutine stubs you need to put before the **__DATA__** token in order to support autoloading via the **SelfLoader** module. The stub also ensures that if a method is called, it will get loaded according to the classes and normal inheritance rules, taking into account the effects of autoloading in the inherited modules and classes.

The basic method only produces a list of the correct stubs. To output a complete version of the whole module with the stubs inserted correctly, you need to set the value of the **$Devel::SelfStubber::JUST_STUBS** to zero. For example:

```
use Devel::SelfStubber;

$Devel::SelfStubber::JUST_STUBS = 0;
Devel::SelfStubber->stub(MODULE, LIBDIR);
```

The module uses the **SelfLoader** module to generate its list of stub subroutines and so can be useful if you want to verify what the **SelfLoader** thinks the list of stubs should be.

References:

See **SelfLoader**

diagnostics

The **diagnostics** pragma prints out not only the terse one-line warnings but also the additional descriptive text that you find in the **perldiag** man page. It does not provide you with further information on the error or the reason it has occurred, but it may help to serve as a reminder when a particular warning is produced.

The same module is also used to support the **splain** command, which takes ordinary warnings (from scripts without the **diagnostics** pragma) and regurgitates the errors produced with their full descriptions.

DirHandle

This module supplies an object/method-based interface for directory handles.

```
use DirHandle;
```

It provides an object interface to the directory handle functions **opendir**, **readdir**, **closedir**, and **rewinddir**:

```
$dir = new DirHandle '.';
```

The only argument to the **new** method is the directory to be read, as specified in the **opendir** function. The supported methods then work in a manner identical to their functional equivalents, except that they are known as **open**, **read**, **close**, and **rewind**.

DynaLoader

This module supports the dynamic loading of C libraries into Perl code.

```
package MyPackage;
require DynaLoader;
@ISA = qw/DynaLoader/;

bootstrap MyPackage;
```

It provides a generic interface to the various dynamic linking mechanisms available on the different platforms. This is primarily used with the XS extension system to load external C libraries and functions into the consciousness of the Perl interpreter. The **DynaLoader** module is designed to be easy to use from the user's point of view, in that using a module should be easy, even though the module itself may involve more complex processes to load the module.

To make use of the system within your own module, you only need to supply the information shown above, which will work whether your module is statically or dynamically linked. The Perl and C functions that need to be called to load the dynamic modules are automatically produced for you during the compilation of an XS interface.

The internal interface for communicating with the lower-level dynamic loading systems supported under SunOS/Solaris, HP-UX, Linux, VMS, Windows, and others is high level and generic enough to cover the requirements of nearly all platforms. However, the **DynaLoader** does not produce its own glue code between Perl and C—you must use the XS, SWIG, or other systems for that purpose.

Please refer to the **DynaLoader** man page for details on how to use the internal interface.

References:

See **AutoLoader, SelfLoader**

English

This module produces a set of aliases, as shown in the following table, that provide full text versions of the standard variables. These match those available in **awk** and may also make more sense than the standard variables to most users.

Perl	English
@_	@ARG
$_	$ARG
$&	$MATCH
$'	$PREMATCH
$'	$POSTMATCH
$+	$LAST_PAREN_MATCH
$.	$INPUT_LINE_NUMBER
	$NR
$/	$INPUT_RECORD_SEPARATOR
	$RS
$I	$OUTPUT_AUTOFLUSH
$,	$OUTPUT_FIELD_SEPARATOR
	$OFS
$\	$OUTPUT_RECORD_SEPARATOR
	$ORS
$"	$LIST_SEPARATOR
$;	$SUBSCRIPT_SEPARATOR
	$SUBSEP
$%	$FORMAT_PAGE_NUMBER
$=	$FORMAT_LINES_PER_PAGE
$-	$FORMAT_LINES_LEFT
$~	$FORMAT_NAME
$^	$FORMAT_TOP_NAME
$:	$FORMAT_LINE_BREAK_CHARACTERS
$^L	$FORMAT_LINEFEED
$?	$CHILD_ERROR

III

Perl	English
$!	$OS_ERROR
	$ERRNO
$@	$EVAL_ERROR
$$	$PROCESS_ID
	$PID
$<	$REAL_USER_ID
	$UID
$>	$EFFECTIVE_USER_ID
	$EUID
$(	$REAL_GROUP_ID
	$GID
$)	$EFFECTIVE_GROUP_ID
	$EGID
$0	$PROGRAM_NAME
$]	$PERL_VERSION
$^A	$ACCUMULATOR
$^D	$DEBUGGING
$^F	$SYSTEM_FD_MAX
$^I	$INPLACE_EDIT
$^P	$PERLDB
$^T	$BASETIME
$^W	$WARNING
$^X	$EXECUTABLE_NAME
$^O	$OSNAME

Env

This module imports environment variables into the current package as real scalars, rather than forcing you to use the **%ENV** hash. To import all the variables defined within the **%ENV** hash, just import the whole module:

```
use Env;
```

To import specific environment variables, specify them during the import:

```
use Env qw/PATH/;
```

You can now use and update **$PATH** as if it were **$ENV{PATH}**.

The internal method for supporting this is actually to tie scalar values to the **%ENV** hash. The tie remains in place until the script exits or until you remove a tied variable with **undef**:

```
undef $PATH;
```

Errno

This module defines and exports the constants defined in **errno.h** for error numbers on your system.

```
use Errno;
```

Importing this module has the added effect of exporting **%!**. This allows you to access **$!{}** as a hash element, retaining the look and feel of the special **$!** variable. Each key of the hash is one of the exported error numbers. When an error occurs, the corresponding error(s) that occurred have a nonzero value. Thus you can do more complex error trapping and management by identifying and handling individual error types.

Exporter

This module implements the default import method for modules.

```
package MyModule;
use Exporter;
@ISA = qw/Exporter/;
```

It implements a default **import** method that is called during the **use** statement. Although it is possible for any module to define its own **import** method, this module supplies a sample **import** method that can be inherited by your module to enable you to export symbols to the calling script.

The **Exporter** module and the supplied **import** method use the **@EXPORT**, **@EXPORT_OK**, and **%EXPORT_TAGS** variables to select which symbols to import. The symbols in **@EXPORT** are exported by default, and the symbols in **@EXPORT_OK** only when specifically requested. The **%EXPORT_TAGS** hash defines a number of import sets that can be used to import a named set of symbols at one time.

For example, if the module defines the following variables,

```
@EXPORT      = qw/A B C D E F/;
@EXPORT_OK   = qw/G H I J K L/;
%EXPORT_TAGS = (FIRST => [qw/D E F/],
                SECOND => [qw/J K L/]
               );
```

then you can use the following constructs in a calling script:

```
use MyModule;               # Imports all of @EXPORT
use MyModule qw/G H/        # Only symbols G and H
use MyModule qw/:DEFAULT/;  # All the symbols in @EXPORT
use MyModule qw/:FIRST A B C/;  # The symbols in group FIRST
                               and A B C
use MyModule qw(/^[ACGH]/);    # Only the symbols matching
                               the regex
use MyModule qw/!:FIRST/;      # Only A B C
```

A leading colon indicates that you want to load the symbols defined in the specified group, as defined by **%EXPORT_TAGS**. Note that the symbols exported here must appear either in **@EXPORT** or **@EXPORT_OK**.

A leading exclamation mark indicates that you want to delete the specified symbols from the import list. If such a definition is the first in the import list, then it assumes you want to import the **:DEFAULT** set.

A // regular expression imports the symbols defined in **@EXPORT** and **@EXPORT_OK** according to the regular expression.

You can display the list of symbols to be imported as they are determined by setting the value of **$Exporter::Verbose** to true. You'll need to do this in a **BEGIN** block:

```
BEGIN { $Exporter::Verbose = 1 }
```

Unknown Symbols

You can prevent certain symbols from being exported. You should place the names of symbols that should not be listed into the **@EXPORT_FAIL** array. Any attempt to import any of these symbols will call the **export_fail** method (in the host module) with a list of failed symbols.

If **export_fail** returns an empty list, no error is recorded and the requested symbols are exported. If the list is not empty, an error is generated for each return symbol and the export fails. The default **export_fail** method supported by **Exporter** just returns the list of symbols supplied to it.

III

Tag Handling Functions

You can modify the contents of the @**EXPORT_OK** and @**EXPORT** arrays using the tag sets defined by the %**EXPORT_TAGS** hash and the **Exporter::export_tags** and **Exporter::export_ok_tags** methods.

For example, consider our original example, in which you could have built the contents of @**EXPORT** and @**EXPORT_OK** using

```
@EXPORT       = qw/A B C/;
@EXPORT_OK    = qw/G H I/;
%EXPORT_TAGS  = (FIRST => [qw/D E F/],
                 SECOND => [qw/J K L/]
                 );
Exporter::export_tags('FIRST');
Exporter::export_ok_tags('SECOND');
```

This would populate the arrays with your original values, without requiring you to specify the symbols explicitly. Any names not matching a tag defined in %**EXPORT_TAGS** will raise a warning when the **–w** command line switch is enabled.

Version Checking

The **require_version** method validates that the module being loaded is of a value equal to or greater than the supplied value. The **Exporter** module supplies this method for you, or you can define your own. In the case of the **Exporter** version, it uses the value of the **$VERSION** variable in the exporting module.

Note that the comparison made is numeric, so the version 1.10 will be treated as a lower version than 1.9. You should therefore use an explicit two-digit (or more) format for the version number, for example, 1.09.

ExtUtils::Command

This function is used under Win32 implementations to provide suitable replacements for core Unix commands used by the extension development process. You should not need to use this module directly, but it defines the following functions/commands:

```
cat
eqtime src dst
rm_f files....
touch files ...
mv source... destination
cp source... destination
chmod mode files...
mkpath directory...
test_f file
```

ExtUtils::Embed

This module provides the necessary command line options and other information for use when you are embedding a Perl interpreter into an application. It supports the following functions.

```
xsinit
```

Generates code for the XS initializer function.

```
ldopts
```

Generates command line options for linking Perl to an application.

```
ccopts
```

Generates command line options for compiling embedded Perl programs.

```
perl_inc
```

Generates the command line options for including Perl headers.

```
ccflags
```

Outputs the contents of the **$Config{ccflags}** hash element.

```
ccdlflags
```

Outputs the contents of the **$Config{ccdlflags}** hash element.

```
xsi_header
```

Outputs the string defining the **EXTERN_C** macro used by perlmain.c and includes statements to include perl.h and EXTERN.h.

```
xsi_protos(LIST)
```

Outputs the corresponding **boot_MODULE** prototypes for the modules specified in **LIST**.

```
xsi_body(LIST)
```

Returns a list of the calls to **newXS** that glue each module **bootstrap** function to the **boot_MODULE** function for each module specified in **LIST**.

References:

See **Config, ExtUtils::MakeMaker**

ExtUtils::Install

This module defines two functions: **install** and **uninstall**. These are used during the installation process by the **MakeMaker** system to install files into the destination directory.

ExtUtils::Installed

This module defines a suite of functions that can be used to query the contents of the .packlist files generated during module installation. If you call the **new** function, it constructs the internal lists by examining the .packlist files. The **modules** function returns a list of all the modules currently installed. The **files** and

directories both accept a single argument—the name of a module. The result is a list of all the files installed by the package. The **directory_tree** function reports information for all the related directories. In all cases, you can specify **Perl** to get information pertaining to the core Perl installation.

The **validate** function checks that the files listed in .packlist actually exist. The **packlist** function returns an object as defined by **ExtUtils::Packlist** for the specified module. Finally, **version** returns the version number of the specified module.

ExtUtils::Liblist

This module defines the libraries to be used when building extension libraries and other Perl-based binaries. The information provided here broaches much of the complexity involved in getting an extension to work across many platforms; the bulk of the code relates to the information required for individual platforms.

ExtUtils::MakeMaker

The **MakeMaker** package provides a Perl-based system for producing standard **make** files suitable for installing Perl applications and, more specifically, Perl extensions.

ExtUtils::Manifest

This module provides the functions that produce, test, and update the MANIFEST file. Five of the functions are the most useful, beginning with **mkmanifest**, which creates a file based on the current directory contents. The **maincheck** function verifies the current directory contents against the MANIFEST file, while **filecheck** looks for files in the current directory that are not specified in the MANIFEST. Both **maincheck** and **filecheck** are executed by the **fullcheck** function, and **skipcheck** lists the files in the MAINFEST.SKIP file.

ExtUtils::Miniperl

This module provides the list of base libraries and extensions that should be included when building the **miniperl** binary.

ExtUtils::Mkbootstrap

This module makes a bootstrap file suitable for the **DynaLoader** module.

ExtUtils::Mksymlists

This module produces the list of options for creating a dynamically linked library.

ExtUtils::MM_OS2

MakeMaker specifics for the OS/2 operating system are produced by this module.

ExtUtils::MM_Unix

MakeMaker specifics for the Unix platform are produced by this module. It also includes many of the core functions used by the main **MakeMaker** module irrespective of the host platform.

ExtUtils::MM_VMS

This module produces **MakeMaker** specifics for VMS.

ExtUtils::MM_Win32

This module produces **MakeMaker** specifics for Windows 95/98/NT.

ExtUtils::Packlist

This module supplies the **Packlist** object used by the
ExtUtils::Installed module.

References:

See **ExtUtils::Installed**

Fatal

This module provides a system for overriding functions that normally
provide a true or false return value so that they instead fail (using
die) when they would normally return false. For example,

```
use Fatal qw/open/;
```

overrides **open** so that a failure will call **die** and raise an exception
that can be caught with a suitable **$SIG{__DIE__}** handler. This allows
you to bypass the normal checking that you would conduct on each
call to **open** and instead install a global handler for all **open** calls.

To trap your own calls:

```
sub mightfail {};
import Fatal 'mightfail';
```

Note that you cannot override the **exec** and **system** calls.

Fcntl

This module supplies the constants that are available as standard within the fcntl.h file within C. This supplies all the constants directly as functions—the same as other modules. This information is gleaned during the installation and build process of Perl and should be correct for your operating system, supporting a compatible set of constants.

The module exports the following constants by default. The exact list will vary from system to system; this list comes from MacPerl 5.2.0r4:

```
F_DUPFD F_GETFD F_GETLK F_SETFD F_GETFL F_SETFL
F_SETLK F_SETLKW
FD_CLOEXEC F_RDLCK F_UNLCK F_WRLCK
O_CREAT O_EXCL O_NOCTTY O_TRUNC
O_APPEND O_NONBLOCK
O_NDELAY O_DEFER
O_RDONLY O_RDWR O_WRONLY
O_EXLOCK O_SHLOCK O_ASYNC O_DSYNC O_RSYNC O_SYNC
F_SETOWN F_GETOWN
O_ALIAS O_RSRC
```

The following symbols are available, either individually or via the **flock** group:

```
LOCK_SH LOCK_EX LOCK_NB LOCK_UN
```

To import this group:

```
use Fcntl qw/:flock/;
```

fields

The **fields** pragma affects the compile time error checking of objects. Using the **fields** pragma enables you to predefine class fields, such that a call to a specific class method will fail at compile time if the field has not been specified. This is achieved by populating a hash called **%FIELDS**. When you access a hash with a typed variable holding an object reference, the type is looked up in the **%FIELDS** hash, and, if the variable type exists, the entire operation is turned into an array access during the compilation stage. For example:

```
{
    package Foo;
    use fields qw(foo bar _private);
}
...
my Foo $var = new Foo;
$var->{foo} = 42;
```

If the specified field does not exist, then a compile time error is produced.

For this to work, the **%FIELDS** hash is consulted at compile time, and it's the **fields** and **base** pragmas that facilitate this. The **base** pragma copies fields from the base class definitions, and the **fields** pragma adds new fields to the existing definitions. Field names that start with an underscore character are private to a class; they are not even accessible to subclasses.

The result is that objects can be created with named fields that are as convenient and quick to access as a corresponding hash. You must access the objects through correctly typed variables, or you can use untyped variables, provided that a reference to the **%FIELDS** hash is assigned to the 0th element of the array object. You can achieve this initialization with

```
sub new
{
    my $class = shift;
    no strict 'refs';
    my $self = bless [\%{"$class\::FIELDS"}], $class;
    $self;
}
```

FileCache

This module enables you to keep more files open than the system permits.

```
use FileCache;
```

It remembers a list of valid pathnames that you know you will want to write to and opens and closes the files as necessary to stay within the maximum number of open files supported on your machine. To add a path to the list, you call the **cacheout** function:

```
cacheout $path;
```

FileHandle

This module supports an object-based interface for using filehandles.

```
use FileHandle;
```

The **new** method creates a new **FileHandle** object, returning it to the caller. Any supplied arguments are passed on directly to the **open** method. If the **open** fails, the object is destroyed and **undef** is returned. The newly created object is a reference to a newly created symbol as supported by the **Symbol** module.

```
$fh = new FileHandle;
```

Alternatively, you can use the **new_from_fd** method to create a new **FileHandle** object. It requires two parameters that are passed to **FileHandle::fdopen**.

The **open** method attaches a file to the new filehandle:

```
$fh->method(FILE [, MODE [, PERMS]])
```

The **open** method supports the options as the built-in **open** function. The first parameter is the filename. If supplied on its own, you can use the normal **open** formats such as > or >>, and then it uses the normal **open** function.

If you supply a **MODE** in the format of the **POSIX fopen()**
function—for example, "w" or "w+"—then the built-in **open**
function is also used. If given a numeric **MODE**, then the built-in
sysopen function is used instead. The module automatically
imports the **O_*** constants from **Fcntl** if they are available.

The **fdopen** method is like **open** except that its first argument
should be a filehandle name, **FileHandle** object, or a file descriptor
number.

If supported on your system, the **fgetpos()** and **fsetpos()** functions
are available as the **getpos** and **setpos** methods, respectively. The
getpos works like **tell** and returns the current location. You can
then revisit the location within the file using **setpos**.

The **setvbuf** method is available to you if your system supports the
setvbuf() function, and it sets the buffering policy for the filehandle:

```
$fh->setvbuf(VAR, TYPE, SIZE)
```

The **VAR** parameter should be a suitable scalar variable to hold the
buffer data, and **SIZE** defines the maximum size of the buffer. The
TYPE is specified using a constant, and these are exported by default
by the module. The constants are described in the following table.

Constant	Description
_IOFBF	Causes the input and output to be fully buffered.
_IOLBF	Causes the output to be line buffered. The buffer will be flushed when a newline character is written to the filehandle, when the buffer is full, or when input is requested on the handle.
_IONBF	Causes the input and output to be completely unbuffered.

Warning: You should not modify the contents of the scalar
variable you use for the buffer while it is in use.

The **FileHandle** module also supports the following methods,
which are simply aliases for the corresponding functions:

clearerr	**close**	**eof**	**fileno**	**getc**
gets	**print**	**printf**	**seek**	**tell**

The module also supports methods for setting the individual variables that affect the use of the filehandle directly:

autoflush	**format_formfeed**
format_line_break_characters	**format_lines_left**
format_lines_per_page	**format_name**
format_page_number	**format_top_name**
input_line_number	**input_record_separator**
output_field_separator	**output_record_separator**

Finally, the module also supports two further methods for reading lines from the file:

```
$fh->getline
$fh->getlines
```

The **getline** method returns a single line from the filehandle, just like the **<$fh>** operator when used in a scalar context. The **getlines** method returns a list of lines in a manner identical to the **<$fh>** operator in a list context. The **getlines** method will **croak** if called in a scalar context.

References:

See **Symbol**, **POSIX**

File::Basename

This module supports the **basename** and **dirname** functions for extracting file and directory names for complete paths. It also supports more complex file path parsing functions.

```
use File::Basename;
```

The **File::Basename** module supplies functions for parsing pathnames and extracting the directory, the filename, and, optionally, the extension. The extraction can be made to account for different operating systems and can therefore be used as a cross-platform tool for parsing paths.

The main function is **fileparse**:

```
fileparse PATH, EXTENSION
```

The **fileparse** function separates **PATH** into its components: a directory name, a filename, and a suffix. The directory name should contain everything up to and including the last directory separator in **PATH**. The remainder is then separated into the file name and suffix based on the **EXTENSION** definitions you supply.

This argument should be a reference to an array, where each element is a regular expression used to match against the end of the filename. If the match succeeds, the file is split into its filename and extension. If it does not match, the whole filename is returned and the suffix remains empty.

For example:

```
($name, $path, $suffix) = fileparse('/usr/
    local/bin/script.pl', '\.pl');
```

This will return "script," "/usr/local/bin/," and ".pl," in that order. Note that this is not the same as the order you might expect. The function guarantees that if you combine the three elements returned, you will end up with the original file path.

The syntax used to separate the path depends on the setting of the module. You can change the specification syntax using the **fileparse_set_fstype** function:

```
fileparse_set_fstype EXPR
```

The supplied expression defines the operating system syntax to be used. If **EXPR** contains one of the substrings "VMS," "MSDOS," or "MacOS," then the corresponding syntax is used in all future calls to the **fileparse** function. If **EXPR** does not contain one of these strings, the Unix syntax is used instead. Note that the default operation depends on the value of **$Config{osname}** as determined during the build process.

Two functions, **basename** and **dirname**, are supplied for Unix compatibility:

```
basename EXPR
```

The **basename** function returns the filename of a path. The function uses **fileparse** for its result.

```
dirname EXPR
```

The **dirname** function returns the directory portion of a file path. The result depends on the current syntax being used to extract the information. When using VMS or MacOS, the result is the same as the second argument returned by **fileparse**. If Unix or MS-DOS syntax is used, the value matches what would be returned by the **dirname** Unix command. The function uses **fileparse** for its result.

III

File::CheckTree

This module provides a mechanism for validating a series of files using the standard built-in tests for files. The method is to call the **validate** function with a textual list of files and tests, for example:

```
use File::CheckTree;
$errors += validate(q{
   /test/test.c -e  || die "Can't find test.c"
   /test/test.o -e  || warn "Object file not found"
   /test/test   -ex || warn
});
```

The above tests that the **test.c** file exists; a failure will cause a call to **die**. Warnings are produced if the object and executable do not exist, and also if the executable is not actually executable. The default method is to produce a warning (effectively, | | **warn**) if a file is not specified. Note that the files must be specified exactly. See the **File::Find** module for another alternative.

You can also use a method of **cd**, which indicates the following entries are within the specified directory. Thus, the above example could be rewritten as

```
use File::CheckTree;
$errors += validate(q{
```

```
/test cd
   test.c -e  || die "Can't find test.c"
   test.o -e  || warn "Object file not found"
   test   -ex || warn
});
```

In all cases, provided a fatal error has not occurred, the return
value is the number of files that failed the test.

References:

See **File::Find**

File::Compare

This module compares files or filehandles.

```
use File::Compare;
```

To compare files, you use the **compare** function:

```
print "Equal\n" if (compare('f1','f2') == 0);
```

Either argument to the function can be a filename or filehandle.
The function returns zero if the files are equal, 1 otherwise, or –1 if
an error was encountered.

File::Copy

This module copies or moves files or filehandles.

```
use File::Copy;
```

It supports two functions: **copy** and **move**. The **copy** function
accepts two arguments and copies from the first to the second file.

Either argument can be a filename or filehandle. The following examples are valid:

```
copy('f1', 'f2');
copy(\*STDIN, 'console');
copy('f1', \*STDOUT);
```

The **move** function will move a file from one location to another:

```
move('f1', 'f2');
```

If possible, it will rename the file; but if this does not work, the contents will be copied to the new file, and the old file will be deleted when the copy is complete.

Both functions are platform independent and return 1 on success, zero on failure.

References:

See **Shell**

File::DosGlob

This module provides a DOS-like globbing functionality, with the addition that wildcards are supported in directory and file names.

```
require 5.004;
use File::DosGlob qw/glob/;
```

Note that this function overrides the **CORE** function within the scope of the current package. To override the function in all packages:

```
use File::DosGlob qw/GLOBAL_glob/;
```

You can use spaces to separate individual patterns within the file specification given, for example:

```
$executables = glob('*.exe *.com');
```

Note that in all cases you may have to double the backslashes in file specifications to override the normal parsing that Perl does on quoted strings. Alternatively, use the **q//** operator.

File::Find

This module supports the traversal of a directory tree.

```
use File::Find;
```

It supports two functions: **find** and **finddepth**. The **find** function accepts at least two arguments:

```
find(\&wanted, '/foo', '/bar');
```

The first argument is a reference to a subroutine called each time a file is found. This is called the "wanted" function and is used to process each file as it is found. Further arguments specify the individual directories to traverse.

Because the wanted function is called each time a file is found, the function can perform whatever functions or verifications on each file it needs to. The **$File::Find::dir** variable contains the name of the current directory. Note that the function calls **chdir** to change into each found directory. The special **$_** variable contains the current file name. You can also access **$File::Find::name** to get the full pathname of the current file. Setting the value of **$File::Find::prune** prunes the directory tree.

For example, the script below would print files and directories in the /usr/local tree that are executable by the real and effective uid/gid:

```
use File::Find;

find(\&wanted, '/usr/local');

sub wanted
{
    next unless (-x $_ and -X _);
    print "$File::Find::name\n";
}
```

If you are creating complex wanted functions and know how to use the Unix **find** command, you can use the **find2perl** script, which generates the necessary stand-alone code for you. For example,

```
$ find2perl /usr/local -name "*.html" -mtime -7
```

produces the following stand-alone script:

```
#!/usr/local/bin/perl
    eval 'exec /usr/local/bin/perl -S $0 ${1+"$@"}'
        if $running_under_some_shell;

require "find.pl";

# Traverse desired filesystems


&find('/usr/local');

exit;
sub wanted {
    /^.*\.html$/ &&
    (($dev,$ino,$mode,$nlink,$uid,$gid) = lstat($_)) &&
    (int(-M _) < 7);
}
```

The **finddepth** function is identical to **find** except that it does a depth first search, rather than working from the lowest to the highest depth.

File::Path

This module creates or removes a directory tree.

```
use File::Path;
```

It supplies two functions, **mkpath** and **rmtree**, which make and remove directory trees.

```
mkpath(ARRAYREF, PRINT, MODE)
```

The **ARRAYREF** should either be the name of the directory to create or a reference to a list of directories to be created. All intermediate directories in the specification will also be created as required. If **PRINT** is true (default is false), the name of each directory created will be printed to **STDOUT**. The **MODE** is octal mode to be used for the newly created directories. The function returns a list of all the directories created. For example, to create a typical /usr/local structure:

```
mkpath(['/usr/local/bin',
        '/usr/local/etc',
        '/usr/local/lib'], 0, 0777);
```

The **rmtree** function deletes a directory subtree. All of the directories specified will be deleted, in addition to the subdirectories and files contained within them.

```
rmtime(ARRAYREF, PRINT, SKIP)
```

The **ARRAYREF** should either be the name of a directory to delete or a reference to an array of directories to be deleted. The directory specified and all its subdirectories and files will be deleted.

The **PRINT** argument, if set to true, prints each file or directory and the method used to remove the file or directory. The default value is false. The **SKIP** argument, if set to true, causes the function to skip files and directories that it is unable to remove due to access privileges. The default value for **SKIP** is false.

The function returns the number of files successfully deleted.

Note that you will need to use a **$SIG{__WARN__}** handler to identify files or directories that could not be deleted.

File::Spec

This module is a cross-platform-compatible library for performing operations on filenames and paths.

```
use File::Spec;
```

The module is supported by a number of platform-specific modules that are imported as required, depending on the platform on which the script is running. You shouldn't need to import the support modules individually; use the **File::Spec** module and let it decide which module is required. See the **File::Spec::Unix** module for a list of the supported methods. Other modules override the necessary methods that are specific to that platform.

Since the interface is object oriented, you must call the functions as class methods:

```
$path = File::Spec->('usr','local');
```

References:

See **File::Spec::Mac**, **File::Spec::OS2**, **File::Spec::Unix**, **File::Spec::VMS**, **File::Spec::Win32**

III

File::Spec::Mac

This module supports the MacOS-specific methods for manipulating file specifications.

```
use File::Spec::Mac;
```

It overrides the default methods supported by **File::Spec**. Note that you should not normally need to use this module directory. The methods overridden by this module are given here.

```
canonpath
```

Returns the path it's given; no process is required under MacOS.

```
catdir
```

Concatenates directory names to form a complete path ending with a directory. Under MacOS, the following rules are followed:

Each argument has any trailing : removed.

- Each argument except the first has any leading : character removed.
- All arguments are then joined by a single : character.

To create a relative rather than absolute path, precede the first argument with a : character, or use a blank argument.

```
catfile
```

Concatenates directory names and a file into a path that defines an individual file. Uses **catdir** for the directory names. Any leading or trailing colons are removed from the filename.

`curdir`

Returns a string defining the current directory.

`rootdir`

Returns a string defining the root directory. Under MacPerl this returns the name of this startup volume; under any other Perl, returns an empty string.

`updir`

Returns the string representing the parent directory.

`file_name_is_absolute`

Returns true if the supplied path is absolute.

`path`

Returns the null list under MacPerl, since there is no execution path under MacOS. When used within the MPW environment, returns the contents of **$ENV{Commands}** as a list.

References:

See **File::Spec**

File::Spec::OS2

This module supports methods for manipulating file specifications under the OS/2 platform.

`use File::Spec::OS2;`

It overrides the default methods supported by **File::Spec**. Note that you should not normally need to use this module directory. The supported methods are detailed in the **File::Spec:Unix** module.

References:

See **File::Spec**

File::Spec::Unix

This module supports Unix-specific methods for file specifications.

```
use File::Spec::Unix;
```

It imports and overrides the methods supported by **File::Spec**. It is normally imported by **File::Spec** as needed, although you can import it directly if required. The following methods are supplied.

`canonpath`

Cleans up a given path, removing successive slashes and /.. Note that the physical existence of the file or directory is not verified.

`catdir`

Concatenates one or more directories into a valid path. This strips the trailing slash off the path for all but the root directory.

`catfile`

Concatenates one or more directories and a file name into a valid path to a file.

`curdir`

Returns a string representing the current directory (.).

`rootdir`

Returns a string representing the root directory (/).

`updir`

Returns a string representing the parent directory (..).

`no_upwards`

Removes references to parent directories from a given list of file paths.

`file_name_if_absolute`

Returns true if the given path is absolute.

`path`

Returns the **$ENV{PATH}** variable as a list.

```
join
```

Identical to **catfile**.

References:

See **File::Spec**

File::Spec::VMS

This module supports VMS-specific methods for file specifications.

```
use File::Spec::VMS;
```

It is imported and overrides the methods supplied by **File::Spec** under the VMS platform. The following methods are supported.

```
catdir LIST
```

Concatenates a list of specifications and returns a VMS syntax directory specification.

```
    catfile LIST
```

Concatenates a list of specifications and returns a VMS syntax file specification.

```
curdir
```

Returns the current directory as a string.

```
rootdir
```

Returns the root directory as a string.

```
updir
```

Returns the parent directory as a string.

```
path
```

Translates the logical VMS path defined in **DCL$PATH** rather than splitting the value of **$ENV{PATH}**.

```
file_name_is_absolute
```

Checks that a VMS directory specification is valid. Note that this does not check the physical existence of a file or directory, only that the specification is correct.

References:

See **File::Spec**

File::Spec::Win32

This module provides Win32-specific methods for file specifications.

```
use File::Spec::Win32;
```

This is the module imported internally by **File::Spec** under Win32 platforms. The package overrides the following methods supported by the **File::Spec** module.

```
Catfile LIST
```

Concatenates one or more directory names and a file name to form a complete path to a file.

```
canonpath EXPR
```

Cleans up a supplied pathname for use on Win32 platforms.

References:

See **File::Spec**

FindBin

This module exports variables that define the directory of the original Perl script.

```
use FindBin;
```

It locates the full path to the script's parent directory, as well as the name of the script. This can be useful if you want to install a script in its own directory hierarchy but do not want to hard code the directory location into the script.

The variables available are shown in the following table. The variables are not exported by default; you must explicitly request them or use the fully qualified values.

Variable	Description
$Bin	Path to the directory where the script was located
$Script	The name of the script that was invoked
$RealBin	The value of **$Bin** with all the links resolved
$RealScript	The value of **$Script** with all the links resolved

Note that if the script was invoked from **STDIN** or via the **–e** command line option, the value of **$Bin** is set to the current directory.

GDBM_File

This module provides an interface to the GDBM database system. The main benefit of GDBM over other systems (except Berkeley DB) is that it provides rudimentary database locking and does not have a restricted bucket size, allowing you to store any size object within a GDBM database.

```
use GDBM_File;
tie %db, 'GDBM_File', 'db', &GDBM_WRCREAT, 0640;
untie %db;
```

Instead of using the modes for opening the database that are ordinarily supplied by the **Fcntl** module, the **GDBM_File** module provides its own constants, listed in the following table.

Constant	Description
GDBM_READER	Open for read only.
GDBM_WRITER	Open for read/write.
GDBM_WRCREAT	Open for read/write, creating a new database if it does not already exist, using the mode specified.
GDBM_NEWDB	Open for read/write, creating a new database even if one already exists, using the mode specified.

References:

See **AnyDBM_File, DB_File, NDBM_File, ODBM_File, SDBM_File**

Getopt::Long

This module is suitable for simple scripts and argument passing. However, it falls over if you try to do more complex processing or want to place the extracted information into specific variables and structures. The **Getopt::Long** module implements a more advanced system. It is **POSIX** compliant and therefore suitable for use in scripts that require **POSIX** compliance.

POSIX compliance allows not only the standard single-character matching supported by the **Getopt::Std** module but also string arguments. For example:

```
$ script.pl --inputfile=source.txt
```

The command line option in this case is **--inputfile**. Note that long names as arguments are supported by both the single and double hyphen, although the double hyphen is the **POSIX** default.

Note: The + sign is also supported, but the use of this is deprecated and not part of the **POSIX** specification.

The selection of additional arguments to command line options is supported by appending a specific character sequence to the end of the option name. The list of available modifiers is defined in the following table.

Option specified	Description
!	The option does not accept an optional piece of information and may be negated by prefixing **no**. For example, **opt!**, will set the value of an option **--opt** to one, and **--noopt** to zero.
+	The option does not accept an additional piece of information. Each appearance in the command line options will increment the corresponding value by one, such that **--opt --opt --opt** will set a value of three, provided it doesn't already have a value.
=s	The option requires an additional string argument. The value of the string will be placed into the corresponding variable.
:s	The option accepts an optional string argument. The value of the string will be placed into the corresponding variable.
=i	The option requires an integer argument. The value will be placed into the corresponding variable.
:i	The option accepts an optional integer argument. The value will be placed into the corresponding variable.
=f	The option requires a real number argument. The value will be placed into the corresponding variable.
:f	The option accepts an optional real number argument. The value will be placed into the corresponding variable.

Any elements in the argument list not identified as options remain in the **@ARGV** array.

Linkage

When using a hash reference as the first argument to the **GetOptions** function, additional facilities are available to you for processing more complex command lines. By default, the operation is identical to the

getopts function. You can also use a trailing @ or % sign to signify that an array or hash reference should be returned. In the case of an array reference, this allows you to supply multiple values for a single named option.

For a hash, it supports "–option name=value" command line constructs, where **name** and **value** are the key and value of the returned hash.

If you do not specify a hash reference as the first argument, the function will instead create a new variable of the corresponding type, using the argument name prefixed by **opt_**. So a function call

```
GetOptions("file=s","files=s@","users=s%");
```

may result in a similar assignment to the following:

```
$opt_file = "source.txt";
@opt_files = ('source.txt', 'sauce.txt');
%opt_users = ( 'Bob'  => 'Manager',
               'Fred' => 'Salesman' );
```

You can also use the hash argument feature to update your own variables directly:

```
GetOptions("file=s"   => \$file,
           "files=s@" => \@files,
           "users=s%" => \%users);
```

This last specification method also supports a function that will handle the specified option. The function will receive two arguments— the true option name (see below) and the value supplied.

Aliases

You can support alternative argument names by using | characters to separate individual names. For example:

```
GetOptions("file|input|source=s");
```

The "true" name would be "file" in this instance, placing the value into **$opt_file**. This true name is also passed to a function if specified (see above).

Callback Function

If **GetOptions** cannot identify an individual element of the **@ARGV** array as a true argument, you can specify a function that will handle the option. You do this by using a value of <> as the argument name, as in

```
GetOptions("<>" => \&nonoption);
```

Remember that the **GetOptions** function removes identifiable arguments from **@ARGV** and leaves the remainder of the elements intact if you don't use this facility. You can then process the arguments as you wish after **GetOptions** has completed successfully.

Return Values

The **GetOptions** function returns true (1) if the command line arguments could be identified correctly. If an error occurs (because the user has supplied a command line argument the function wasn't expecting), the function returns false and uses **warn** to report the bad options. If the definitions supplied to the function are invalid, the function calls **die**, reporting the error.

Customizing *GetOptions*

You can control the operation of the **GetOptions** function by passing arguments to **Getopt::Long::Configure**. The list of options is shown in the following table. The values shown in the table *set* the option; to unset, prefix the option with **no_**.

Option	Description
default	Sets all configuration options to their default values.
auto_abbrev	Supports abbreviated option names, provided the arguments supplied can be identified uniquely. This is the default operation, unless the **POSIXLY_CORRECT** environment variable is set.
getopt_compat	Supports the use of + as the prefix to arguments. This is the default operation, unless the **POSIXLY_CORRECT** environment variable is set.

Option	Description
require_order	This specifies that your options must be supplied first on the command line. This is the default operation, unless the **POSIXLY_CORRECT** environment variable is set. This is the opposite of **permute**. If **require_order** is set, processing terminates on the first nonorder item found in the argument list.
permute	Specifies that nonoptions are allowed to be mixed with real options. This is the default operation, unless the **POSIXLY_CORRECT** environment variable is set. This is the opposite of **require_order**.
bundling	Setting this allows single-character options to be bundled into single strings. For example, if set, the string "–vax" will be equivalent to "–v –a –x." This option also allows for integer values to be inserted into the bundled options, such that "–d256aq" is equivalent to "–d 256 –a –q."
bundling_override	If set, the **bundling** option is implied. However, if an option has been defined with the same full name as a bundle, it will be interpreted as the name, not the individual options. For example, if "vax" was specified, then "–vax" would be interpreted as "–vax", but "–avx" would be interpreted as "–a –v –x."
ignore_case	Default; string command line options are interpreted ignoring case.
ignore_case_always	When **bundling** is set, case is also ignored on single-character options.
pass_through	Unrecognized options remain in the @**ARGV** array, instead of producing and being flagged as errors.
prefix	Takes the next argument to the function as a string defining the list of strings that identify an option. The default value is (-- | - | \+), or (-- | -) if the **POSIXLY_CORRECT** environment variable is set.
debug	Enables debugging output.

III

For example, to set auto abbreviation and allow differentiation between upper- and lowercase arguments:

```
Getopt::Long::Configure('auto_abbrev','no_ignore_case');
```

Variables

You can monitor the version number of the **Getopt::Long** module with the **$Getopt::Long::VERSION** variable. You can also identify the major and minor versions using the **$Getopt::Long::major_version** and **$Getopt::Long::minor_version** variables. If you want to identify the version number during import, use the usual

```
use Getopt::Long 3.00;
```

When using the callback function (with <>), you may want to report an error back to the main **GetOptions** function. You can do this by incrementing the **$Getopt::Long::error** variable.

Getopt::Std

This module provides two functions: **getopt** and **getopts**.

```
use Getopt::Std;

getopt('ol');
getopts('ol:');
```

Both functions require a single argument that specifies the list of single-letter arguments you would like to identify on the command line.

In the case of the **getopt** function, it assumes that all arguments expect an additional piece of information. With the **getopts** function, each character is taken to be a Boolean value. If you want to accept arguments with additional information, append a colon.

Variables are created by the function with a prefix of **$opt_**. The value of each variable is one in the case of a Boolean value, or the supplied additional argument. If the command argument is not found, the variable is still created, but the value is **undef**.

In addition, for either function, you can supply a second argument that should be a reference to a hash:

```
getopts('i:',\%opts);
```

Each supplied argument will be used as the key of the hash, and any additional information supplied will be placed into the corresponding values. Thus, a script with the above line when called,

```
$ getopts -i Hello
```

will place the string "Hello" into the **$opts{'i'}** hash element.

If you have the **use strict 'vars'** pragma in effect you will need to predefine the **$opt_** and hash variables before they are called. Either use a **my** definition before calling the function, or, better still, predeclare them with **use vars**.

I18N::Collate

The functionality of the **I18N::Collate** module has been integrated into Perl from version 5.003_06. See the **perllocale** man page for details.

integer

The integer **pragma** forces all calculation within a script, or within a specified block, to be conducted using **integer**, rather than floating point math. Once enabled, the **integer** pragma can be switch off with the **no** keyword:

```
use integer;
print 67/3,"\n";
no integer;
print 67/3,"\n";
```

You can also use **no** within an enclosed block to temporarily turn off integer math.

IO

This module automatically imports a number of base IO modules.

```
use IO;
```

It doesn't provide any modules or functionality on its own, but it does attempt to import the following modules for you:

```
IO::File
IO::Handle
IO::Pipe
IO::Seekable
IO::Socket
```

References:

See **IO::File**, **IO::Handle**, **IO::Pipe**, **IO::Seekable**, **IO::Socket**

IO::File

This module supports the methods for accessing and using filehandles.

```
use IO::File;
```

The **new** method creates a new filehandle, and any arguments are passed to the **open** method. If the **open** fails, the object is destroyed; otherwise, it is returned to the caller.

```
new_tmpfile
```

Creates a new filehandle opened for read/write on the newly created temporary file.

Once created, the object supports the following methods:

```
open(FILENAME [, MODE [, PERMS]])
```

The **open** method supports the options as the built-in **open** function. The first parameter is the filename. If supplied on its own, you can use the normal **open** formats, such as > or >>, and then it uses the normal **open** function.

If you supply a **MODE** in the format of the **POSIX fopen()** function—for example, "w" or "w+"—the built-in **open** function is also used. If given a numeric **MODE**, the built-in **sysopen** function is used instead. The module automatically imports the **O_*** constants from **Fcntl** if they are available.

The **fdopen** method is like **open** except that its first argument should be a filehandle name, **FileHandle** object, or a file descriptor number.

Additional methods are inherited from **IO::Handle** and **IO::Seekable**.

References:

See **IO**, **IO::Handle**, **IO::Seekable**

IO::Handle

This module supports the object methods available for use with other IO handles.

```
use IO::Handle;
```

It provides the base class from which all other IO handle classes inherit.

```
new
```

The **new** method creates a new **IO::Handle** object.

```
new_from_fd(FD, MODE)
```

Creates a new **IO::Handle** object. The **FD** and **MODE** are passed on to the **fdopen** method.

Additional methods match the functionality supported by the following functions.

close	**fileno**	**getc**	**eof**	**read**
truncate	**stat**	**print**	**printf**	**sysread**
syswrite				

The following methods are handle-specific versions of the corresponding Perl variables.

autoflush	**format_formfeed**
format_line_break_characters	**format_lines_left**
format_lines_per_page	**format_name**
format_page_number	**format_top_name**
format_write	**input_line_number**
input_record_separator	**output_field_separator**
output_record_separator	

Additional module-specific methods are described here.

```
$fh->fdopen(FD, MODE)
```

This opens the file like the built-in **open**. The **FD** parameter takes a filehandle name, **IO::Handle** object, or a file descriptor number. The **MODE** is a valid **Fcntl** mode, and the module attempts to import the **O_*** series of constants from **Fcntl** but doesn't **croak** if the modules cannot be imported.

```
$fh->opened
```

Returns true if the object is currently a valid file descriptor.

```
$fh->getline
$fh->getlines
```

The **getline** method returns a single line from the filehandle, just like the **<$fh>** operator when used in a scalar context. The **getlines** method returns a list of lines in a manner identical to the **<$fh>** operator in a list context. The **getlines** method will **croak** if called in a scalar context.

```
$fh->ungetc(ORD)
```

Pushes the character that is the ordinal value **ORD** onto the input stream.

```
$fh->write(BUF, LEN [, OFFSET ] )
```

Writes **BUF** of size **LEN** to the filehandle. This is the implementation of the **write()** C function. If given, then **OFFSET** specifies the location within the file to write the data without requiring you to move to that spot and without modifying the current file pointer. Note that this is identical to the **pwrite()** C function.

```
$fh->flush
```

Flushes the filehandle's buffer.

```
$fh->error
```

Returns true if the filehandle has experienced any errors.

```
$fh->clearerr
```

Clears the error indicator.

```
$fh->untaint
```

Marks the data received on the handle as taint safe.

The **setvbuf** method is available if your system supports the **setvbuf()** function, and it sets the buffering policy for the filehandle:

```
$fh->setvbuf(VAR, TYPE, SIZE)
```

The **VAR** parameter should be a suitable scalar variable to hold the buffer data, and **SIZE** defines the maximum size of the buffer. The **TYPE** is specified using a constant, and these are exported by default by the module. The constants are described in the following table.

Constant	Description
_IOFBF	Causes the input and output to be fully buffered.
_IOLBF	Causes the output to be line buffered. The buffer will be flushed when a newline character is written to the filehandle, when the buffer is full, or when input is requested on the handle.
_IONBF	Causes the input and output to be completely unbuffered.

Warning: You should not modify the contents of the scalar variable you use for the buffer while it is in use.

References:

See **IO**, **IO::File**, **Symbol**

IO::Pipe

This module supports methods for pipes.

```
use IO::Pipe;
```

It provides an object interface for creating pipes between processes.

```
new([READER, WRITER])
```

This creates a new object (as supplied by the **Symbol** package). It takes two optional arguments, which should be **IO::Handle** objects, or an object that is a subclass of **IO::Handle**. These arguments will be used during the **pipe()** system call. If no arguments are supplied, the **handles** method is called.

Supported methods are described here.

```
reader([ARGS])
```

The object is reblessed into a subclass of **IO::Handle** and is the handle at the reading end of the pipe. Any supplied **ARGS** are used when calling **exec** after a **fork**.

```
writer([ARGS])
```

The object is reblessed into a subclass of **IO::Handle** and is the handle at the writing end of the pipe. Any supplied **ARGS** are used when calling **exec** after a **fork**.

```
handles
```

This method returns two objects blessed into **IO::Pipe::End** or a subclass thereof.

References:

See **IO**, **IO::Handle**, **Symbol**

IO::Seekable

This module supplies base seek methods for IO objects.

```
use IO::Seekable;
package IO::Package;
@ISA = qw/IO::Seekable/;
```

It provides base methods for other **IO::*** modules to implement the positional functionality normally handled by the **seek** and **tell** built-in functions. Note that the module does not support any constructor methods of its own. The methods support the seek and location within file descriptors using the **fgetpos()** and **fsetpos()** C functions. The methods are supported within **IO::File** as **IO::File::getpos** and **IO::File::setpos** methods, respectively.

References:

See **IO**, **IO::File**

IO::Select

This module supports an object-oriented interface to the **select()** system call.

```
use IO::Select;
```

The module allows you to monitor which **IO::Handle** objects are ready for reading or writing or have an error pending, just like the **select** built-in function.

You can create a new **IO::Select** object with the **new** method:

```
new([HANDLES])
```

The optional **HANDLES** argument is a list of **IO::Handle** objects to initialize into the **IO::Select** object.

Once created, the new object supports the following, more pragmatic, interface to the **select** function.

```
add(HANDLES)
```

Adds the list of **IO::Handle** objects, integer file descriptor, or array reference, where the first element is an **IO::Handle** object or integer. It is these objects that will be returned when an event occurs. This works by the file descriptor number (as returned by **fileno**), so duplicated handles are not added.

```
remove(HANDLES)
```

Removes the given handles from the object.

```
exists(HANDLE)
```

Returns true if **HANDLE** is a part of the set.

```
handles
```

Returns an array of all the handles within the set.

```
can_read([TIMEOUT])
```

Returns an array of handles that are ready for reading. The method blocks for a maximum of **TIMEOUT** seconds. If **TIMEOUT** is not specified, the call blocks indefinitely.

```
can_write([TIMEOUT])
```

Returns an array of handles that are ready for writing. The method blocks for a maximum of **TIMEOUT** seconds. If **TIMEOUT** is not specified, the call blocks indefinitely.

```
has_error([TIMEOUT])
```

Returns an array of handles that have a pending error condition. The method blocks for a maximum of **TIMEOUT** seconds. If **TIMEOUT** is not specified, the call blocks indefinitely.

```
count
```

Returns the number of handles that will be returned when a **can_*** method is called.

```
bits
```

Returns a bitstring suitable for passing to the built-in **select** function.

```
IO::Select::select(READ, WRITE, ERROR, [, TIMEOUT])
```

The **select** method is a static method that must be called with the package name, as shown above. The function returns an array of three elements. Each is a reference to an array holding the reference to the handles that are ready for reading, writing, and have error conditions waiting, respectively.

The **READ**, **WRITE**, and **ERROR** arguments are **IO::Select** objects, or **undef**. The optional **TIMEOUT** value is the number of seconds to wait for a handle to become ready.

References:

See **IO**, **IO::File**, **IO::Handle**

IO::Socket

This module supports an object interface for socket communications.

```
use IO::Socket;
```

This class supports socket-based communication. It exports the functions and constants supported by **Socket** and also inherits methods from **IO::Handle** in addition to defining a number of common methods suitable for all sockets. The **IO::Socket::INET** and **IO::Socket::UNIX** classes define additional methods for specific socket types.

The **new** method creates a new **IO::Socket** object using a symbol generated by the **Symbol** package.

```
$socket = IO::Socket->new(Domain => 'UNIX');
```

The constructor only identifies one option, **Domain**, which specifies the domain in which to create the socket. Any other options are supplied to the **IO::Socket::INET** or **IO::Socket::UNIX** constructor accordingly.

Note: The newly created handle will be in autoflush mode. This is the default operation from versions above 1.1603 (Perl 5.004_04). You will need to specify this explicitly if you want to remain compatible with earlier versions.

The class supports the following methods:

`accept([PKG])`

This accepts a new socket connection like the built-in **accept** function, returning a new **IO::Socket** handle of the appropriate type. If you specify **PKG**, the new object will be of the specified class, rather than that of the parent handle. In a scalar context, only the new object is returned; in a list context, both the object and the peer address are returned. The method will return **undef** or an empty list on failure.

`timeout([VALUE])`

If supplied without any arguments, the current time-out setting is returned. If called with an argument, it sets the time-out value. The time-out value is used by various other methods.

`sockopt(OPT [, VALUE])`

Gets/sets the socket option **OPT**. If the method is only supplied **OPT**, it gets the current value of the option. To set a value, use the two-argument form.

`sockdomain`

Returns the numerical value of the socket domain type.

`socktype`

Returns the numerical value of the socket type.

`protocol`

Returns the numerical value of the protocol being used on the socket. If the protocol is unknown, zero is returned.

`peername`

This is identical to the built-in **getpeername** function.

`sockname`

This is identical to the built-in **getsockname** function.

The class also supplies frontend methods for the following built-in functions:

```
socket
socketpair
bind
listen
send
recv
```

IO::Socket::INET

The **IO::Socket::INET** class provides a constructor to create a socket within the **AF_INET** family/domain. The constructor accepts a hash that takes the options shown in the following table.

Option	Format	Description
PeerAddr	hostname[:port]	Remote host address (and port). The **address** can be specified as a name (which will be resolved) or as an IP address. The **port** (if specified) should be a valid service name and/or port number as defined in **PeerPort**.
PeerPort	service(port) | port	The service port name and number, or number only.
LocalAddr	hostname[:port]	Local host address to bind to.
LocalPort	service(no) | no	The local service port name and number, or number only.
Proto	"tcp" | "udp" | ...	The protocol name or number. If this is not specified and you give a service name in the **PeerPort** option, then the constructor will attempt to derive **Proto** from the given service name. If it cannot be resolved, then "tcp" is used.
Type	SOCK_STREAM | SOCK_DGRAM | ...	The socket type, specified using a constant as exported by **Socket**. This will be deduced from **Proto** if not otherwise specified.
Listen		The queue size for listening to requests.
Reuse		If true, then it sets the **SO_REUSEADDR** option before binding to the local socket.

If passed a single argument, the constructor assumes that it's a **PeerAddr** specification. For example, to create a connection to a Web server on port 80:

```
$socket = IO::Socket::INET->new(PeerAddr =>
'www.mcwords.com:http(80)');
```

Or to create a local socket for listening:

```
$socket = IO::Socket::INET->new(LocalAddr => 'localhost',
                                LocalPort => '7000',
                                Listen    => '5',
                                Proto     => 'tcp');
```

Note that by specifying **LocalAddr** and **Listen**, the constructor builds a local socket suitable for acting as a server-side socket. You can use the **accept** method (inherited from **IO::Socket**), which works just like the built-in function.

Beyond the methods inherited from **IO::Socket** and **IO::Handle**, the **IO::Socket::INET** class also supports the following methods:

```
sockaddr
```

Returns the 4-byte packed address of the local socket.

```
sockport
```

Returns the port number used for the local socket.

```
sockhost
```

Returns the IP address in the form xxx.xxx.xxx.xxx for the local socket.

```
peeraddr
```

Returns the 4-byte packed address of the remote socket.

```
peerport
```

Returns the port number used for the remote socket.

```
peerhost
```

Returns the IP address in the form xxx.xxx.xxx.xxx for the remote socket.

IO::Socket::UNIX

The **IO::Socket::UNIX** class provides a constructor to create a socket within the **AF_UNIX** family/domain. The constructor accepts a hash that takes the options shown in the following table.

Option	Description
Type	The socket type, **SOCK_STREAM**, **SOCK_DGRAM**, or one of the other constants supported in **Socket**.
Local	Path to the local FIFO file.
Peer	Path to the peer FIFO file.
Listen	If set to true, it creates a socket that can be used to accept new client connections.

Like the **IO::Socket::INET** class, this class supports the methods inherited from **IO::Socket** and **IO::Handle**, in addition to the following methods:

```
hostpath
```

Returns the pathname to the FIFO file at the local end.

```
peerpath
```

Returns the pathname to the FIFO file at the peer end.

References:

See **IO::Handle, IO::Socket, Socket**

IPC::Msg

This module is an object-oriented interface to the System V message system.

```
use IPC::Msg;
```

It provides an alternative interface to the **msg*** range of IPC message queue functions. The **new** method creates a new message queue.

```
new KEY, FLAGS
```

Creates a new message queue associated with **KEY** using **FLAGS** as the permissions for accessing the queue. You will need to import suitable constants from **IPC::SysV**. A new object is created only when all the following conditions are met:

- **KEY** is equal to **IPC_PRIVATE**.
- **KEY** does not already have a message queue associated with it.
- **FLAGS** contains the **IPC_CREAT** constant.

Once created, the following methods are supported:

```
id
```

Returns the system message queue identifier.

```
rcv BUF, LEN [, TYPE [, FLAGS]])
```

Receives a message from the queue into the variable **BUF**, up to a maximum length **LEN**.

```
remove
```

Removes (destroys) the message queue from the system.

```
set STAT
set(NAME => VALUE [, NAME => VALUE...])
```

Sets the values using either an **IPC::Msg::stat** object or the specified hash. Supported elements are **uid**, **gid**, **mode**, and **qbytes**.

```
snd
```

Sends a message to the queue of **TYPE**.

```
stat
```

Returns an **IPC::Msg::stat** object that is a subclass of the **Class::Struct** class. The object consists of the following fields:

uid	gid	cuid	cgid	mode	qnum	qbytes
lspid	lrpid	stime	rtime	ctime		

References:

See **Class::Struct, IPC::SysV**

IPC::Open2

This module allows you to open a piped process for both reading and writing.

```
use IPC::Open2;

$pid = open2(READER, WRITER, LIST);
```

The **open2** function supports the functionality not provided in the built-in **open** function to allow you to open a command for both reading and writing. The **READER** and **WRITER** arguments should be references to existing filehandles to be used for reading from and writing to the piped command. The function does not create the filehandles for you. The **LIST** is one or more arguments defining the command to be run. For example:

```
$pid = open2(\*READ, \*WRITE, '|bc|');
```

The returned value is the process ID of the child process executed. Errors are raised by an exception matching /^**open2:**/. You should probably use this within an **eval** block.

If **READER** is a string and it begins with ">&", then the child will send output directly to that filehandle. If **WRITER** is a string that begins with "<&", then **WRITER** will be closed in the parent, and the child process will read from the filehandle directly. In both cases, the filehandle is duplicated with **dup()** instead of **pipe()**.

Note: The function assumes you know how to read from and write to the child process while preventing deadlocking. Commands that use a fixed input or output length (specified in a number of characters or lines) should prevent the problem.

References:

See **IPC::Open3**

IPC::Open3

This module is similar to **IPC::Open2**, but it opens a command for reading, writing, and error handling.

```
use IPC::Open3;
```

```
$pid = open3(WRITER, READER, ERROR, LIST);
```

The **WRITER**, **READER**, and **ERROR** should be references to existing filehandles to be used for standard input, standard output, and standard error from the command and arguments supplied in **LIST**. Note that the order of the **READER** and **WRITER** arguments is different from that in **open2**. If '' is given as the argument for **ERROR**, then **ERROR** and **READER** use the same filehandle.

All other details are identical to the **open2** call, including the warning on deadlocking.

References:

See **IPC::Open2**

IPC::Semaphore

This module is an object class definition for System V semaphore–based IPC.

```
use IPC::Semaphore;
```

It provides an object interface to the System V semaphore system used for interprocess communication. The **new** method creates a new **IPC::Semaphore** object:

```
$sem = new IPC::Semaphore(KEY, NSEMS, FLAGS);
```

Creates a new semaphore set associated with **KEY**, with **NSEMS** semaphores in the set. The value of **FLAGS** is a list of permissions for the new semaphore set. You will need to import suitable constants from the **IPC::SysV** module.

A new semaphore is created only when all the following conditions are met:

- **KEY** is equal to **IPC_PRIVATE**.
- **KEY** does not already have a semaphore identifier associated with it.
- **FLAGS** contains the **IPC_CREAT** constant.

Once created, the new object supports the following methods:

`getall`

Returns the values contained in the semaphore set as a list.

`getnccnt SEM`

Returns the number of processes waiting for **SEM** to become greater than the current value.

`getpid SEM`

Returns the process ID of the last process that used **SEM**.

`getval SEM`

Returns the current value of **SEM**.

`getzcnt SEM`

Returns the number of processes waiting for **SEM** to become zero.

`id`

Returns the system identifier for the semaphore set.

`op OPLIST`

Performs a specific operation on the semaphore set. **OPLIST** is a multiple of a three-value list that defines the operation to perform. The first argument is the semaphore number, the second is the operator, and the last is the **FLAGS** value.

`remove`

Removes (destroys) the semaphore set.

`set STAT`
`set(NAME => VALUE [, NAME => VALUE...])`

Sets the **uid**, **gid**, and **mode** of the semaphore set. Accepts either an **IPC::Semaphore::stat** object, as returned by the **stat** method (see below), or a hash.

```
setall LIST
```

Sets all the values in the set to those given in **LIST**. The **LIST** must be of the correct length.

```
setval N, VALUE
```

Sets the value of the semaphore at index **N** to **VALUE**.

```
stat
```

Returns an **IP::Semaphore::stat** object that is a subclass of the **Class::Struct** class. The object consists of the following fields:

uid   **gid**   **cuid**   **cgid**   **mode**   **ctime**   **otime**   **nsems**

References:

See **Class::Struct**, **IPC::SysV**

IPC::SysV

This module supplies the System V IPC constants used by the built-in IPC calls.

```
use SysV::IPC;
```

Note that the module does not import any symbols implicitly. You need to specify the symbols you want to use. The list of available symbols is shown here:

GETALL	**GETNCNT**	**GETPID**	**GETVAL**
GETZCNT			
IPC_ALLOC	**IPC_CREAT**	**IPC_EXCL**	**IPC_GETACL**
IPC_LOCKED	**IPC_M**	**IPC_NOERROR**	**IPC_NOWAIT**
IPC_PRIVATE	**IPC_R**	**IPC_RMID**	**IPC_SET**
IPC_SETACL	**IPC_SETLABEL**	**IPC_STAT**	**IPC_W**

III

IPC_WANTED			
MSG_FWAIT	MSG_LOCKED	MSG_MWAIT	MSG_NOERROR
MSG_QWAIT			
MSG_R	MSG_RWAIT	MSG_STAT	MSG_W
MSG_WWAIT			
SEM_A	SEM_ALLOC	SEM_DEST	SEM_ERR
SEM_ORDER	SEM_R	SEM_UNDO	
SETALL	SETVAL		
SHMLBA			
SHM_A	SHM_CLEAR	SHM_COPY	SHM_DCACHE
SHM_DEST	SHM_ECACHE	SHM_FMAP	SHM_ICACHE
SHM_INIT	SHM_LOCK	SHM_LOCKED	SHM_MAP
SHM_NOSWAP	SHM_R	SHM_RDONLY	SHM_REMOVED
SHM_RND	SHM_SHARE_MMU	SHM_SHATTR	SHM_SIZE
SHM_UNLOCK	SHM_W		
S_IRUSR	S_IWUSR	S_IRWXU	
S_IRGRP	S_IWGRP	S_IRWXG	
S_IROTH	S_IWOTH	S_IRWXO	

You can also optionally import the **ftok** function:

```
ftok(PATH, ID)
```

This creates a unique key suitable for use with the **msgget**,
semget, and **shmget** functions.

References:

See **IPC::Msg**, **IPC::Semaphore**

less

```
use less;
```

The intention is to allow you to specify reductions for certain
resources such as memory or processor space.

lib

The **lib** pragma specifies additional libraries to be added to the search path for modules imported by **use** and **require**, adding them to the @**INC** array. This is a neater solution for solving the problem of updating the list of library directories that need to be populated at compilation rather than runtime.

```
use lib LIST;
```

Note that the directories are added before (using **unshift**) the standard directories to ensure that you use the local modules in preference to the standard ones. For all directories added in this way, the **lib** module also checks that a $dir/$archname/auto exists, where $archname is the name of the architecture of the current platform. If it does exist, then it is assumed to be an architecture-specific directory and is actually added to @**INC** before the original directory specification.

locale

The **locale** pragma specifies that the current locale should be used for internal operations such as regular expression, string comparisons, and sorts. To use the current locale:

```
use locale;
```

The default operation for Perl is to ignore locales, meaning that most operations are actually in a quasi-C locale, which sorts and does comparisons based on the ASCII table. If you have switched locales on, you can switch them off with

```
no locale;
```

Math::BigFloat

This module supports the use of floating point numbers of arbitrary length.

```
use Math::BigFloat;
$bigfloat = Math::BigFloat->new($string);
```

The **new** method creates a new floating point object based on the supplied string.

Most operators are overloaded to support the new floating point objects, provided you create the number with

```
$bigfloat
    = new Math::BigFloat '1.23456789012345678901 2345';
```

In addition, you can use the following methods.

```
fadd(STRING)
```

Adds the number **STRING** to the object, returning a number string.

```
fsub(STRING)
```

Subtracts the number **STRING** from the object, returning a number string.

```
fmul(STRING)
```

Multiplies the object by the number **STRING**, returning a number string.

```
fdiv(STRING [,SCALE])
```

Divides the object by the number **STRING**, to the specified **SCALE** places.

```
fneg()
```

Negates the number.

```
fabs()
```

Returns the absolute number.

```
fcmp(STRING)
```

Compares the object to the number **STRING**, returning a value less than, equal to, or greater than zero according to whether the number is less than, equal to, or greater than the given number.

```
fround(SCALE)
```

Rounds the number object to **SCALE** digits, returning the number strings.

```
ffround(SCALE)
```

Rounds the number at the **SCALE**th place within the number.

```
fnorm()
```

Normalizes the floating point, returning a number string.

```
fsqrt([SCALE])
```

Returns the square root of the number object, rounded to the specified **SCALE** if supplied.

References:

See **Math::BigInt**

Math::BigInt

Supports math with integer values of arbitrary sizes.

```
use Math::BigInt;
$int = Math::BigInt->new($string);
```

Basic operators are overloaded, provided you create the new integer with

```
$int = new Math::BigInt '12345678901234567890123456';
```

The following methods are supported by the new object.

```
bneg return BINT                negation
```

Negates the integer and returns an integer string.

```
babs
```

Returns the absolute value as an integer string.

```
bcmp(STRING)
```

Compares the object with the supplied integer **STRING**, returning a value smaller than, equal to, or greater than zero depending on the relationship between the object and the supplied **STRING**.

```
badd(STRING)
```

Adds **STRING** to the object.

```
bsub(STRING)
```

Subtracts **STRING** from the object.

```
bmul(STRING)
```

Multiplies the object by **STRING**.

```
bdiv(STRING)
```

Divides the object by **STRING**, returning the quotient and remainder as strings.

```
bmod(STRING)
```

Returns the modulus of the object and **STRING**.

```
bgcd(STRING)
```

Returns the largest common divisor.

```
bnorm
```

Normalizes the object.

References:

See **Math::BigFloat**

Math::Complex

This module supports the use of complex numbers in mathematical computations.

```
use Math::Complex;
```

You create a new complex number with the **make** method,

```
$z = Math::Complex->make(1,2);
```

the **cplx** function,

```
$z = cplx(1, 2);
```

or directly, using complex notation:

```
$z = 3 + 4*i;
```

In addition, you can specify them in the polar form:

```
$z = Math::Complex->emake(5, pi/3);
$x = cplxe(5, pi/3);
```

The first argument is the modulus, and the second is the angle in radians.

The module also overloads the following operations to allow complex math directly within Perl, where **z** is an imaginary variable.

```
z1 + z2 = (a + c) + i(b + d)
z1 - z2 = (a - c) + i(b - d)
z1 * z2 = (r1 * r2) * exp(i * (t1 + t2))
z1 / z2 = (r1 / r2) * exp(i * (t1 - t2))
z1 ** z2 = exp(z2 * log z1)
~z = a - bi
abs(z) = r1 = sqrt(a*a + b*b)
sqrt(z) = sqrt(r1) * exp(i * t/2)
exp(z) = exp(a) * exp(i * b)
log(z) = log(r1) + i*t
sin(z) = 1/2i (exp(i * z1) - exp(-i * z))
cos(z) = 1/2 (exp(i * z1) + exp(-i * z))
atan2(z1, z2) = atan(z1/z2)
```

You can also use the following methods:

Im(z)	**Re(z)**	**abs(z)**	**acos(z)**
acosh(z)	**acot(z)**	**acoth(z)**	**acsc(z)**
acsch(z)	**arg(z)**	**asec(z)**	**asech(z)**
asin(z)	**asinh(z)**	**atan(z)**	**atanh(z)**
cbrt(z)	**cosh(z)**	**cot(z)**	**coth(z)**
csc(z)	**csch(z)**	**log10(z)**	**logn(z,n)**
sec(z)	**sech(z)**	**sinh(z)**	**tan(z)**
tanh(z)			

Math::Trig

This module defines the full set of trigonometric functions.

```
use Math::Trig;
```

The supplied functions are as follows.

```
tan
```

Returns the tangent.

```
csc, cosec, sec, cot, cotan
```

The cofunctions of sine, cosine, and tangent. The **csc** and **cosec** are aliases for each other, as are **cot** and **cotan**.

```
asin, acos, atan
```

The arcus (inverse) of sin, cos, and tan.

```
atan2(y, x)
```

The principal value of the arctangent of **y/x**.

```
acsc, acosec, asec, acot, acotan
```

The arcus cofunctions.

```
sinh, cosh, tanh
```

The hyperbolic functions.

```
csch, cosech, sech, coth, cotanh
```

The cofunctions of the hyperbolics.

```
asinh, acosh, atanh
```

The arcus of the hyperbolics.

```
acsch, acosech, asech, acoth, acotanh
```

The arcus cofunctions of the hyperbolics.

The module also defines the constant **pi**.

Net::Ping

This module supports a simplified interface to the process of determining a remote host's accessibility.

```
use Net::Ping;
```

The module uses an object-oriented interface and makes use of the **alarm** function and associated signal to test for a suitable time-out value. To create a new **Ping** object:

```
Net::Ping->new([PROTO [, TIMEOUT [, BYTES]]]);
```

Creates a new **Ping** object. The **PROTO**, if specified, should be one of "tcp," "udp," or "icmp." You should use "udp" or "icmp" in preference to "tcp" due to network bandwidth. The default is "udp."

The default **TIMEOUT** should be specified in seconds and be greater than zero. The default value is five seconds. The **BYTES** parameter specifies the number of bytes to be sent to the remote host. The minimum value should be 1 if the protocol is "udp," zero otherwise. The maximum size is 1024 bytes.

The following methods are supported by the new object.

```
ping(HOST [, TIMEOUT]);
```

Pings the remote **HOST** and waits for a response. The method waits the number of seconds defined when the object was created, or **TIMEOUT** seconds if specified. The method returns 1 if the lookup was successful, zero otherwise. The **undef** value is returned if the host cannot be resolved.

```
close();
```

Closes the network connection. The connection is automatically closed if the object goes out of scope.

The module also supports a single function, **pingecho**, for backward compatibility:

```
pingecho(HOST [, TIMEOUT])
```

This pings **HOST** using the **tcp** protocol, returning 1 if the host can be reached, zero otherwise. If the **HOST** cannot be resolved, the function returns **undef**.

NDBM_File

```
use NDBM_File;
use Fcntl;

tie(%db, 'NDBM_File', 'db', O_RDWR|O_CREAT, 0640);
untie %db;
```

This module is an interface supporting, via **tie**, the new (standard) DBM data storage format.

References:

See **AnyDBM_File, DB_File, GDBM_File, ODBM_File, SDBM_File**

This module supports the generic interface to the Perl compiler backends.

```
perl -MO=Backend[OPTIONS] foo.pl
```

Most backends support the following **OPTIONS**. These should be supplied a comma-separated list of words without white space.

V	Puts the backend into verbose mode.
oFILE	Specifies the name of the output **FILE**.
D	Switches on backend debugging flags.

References:

See **B, B::Asmdata, B::Bblock, B::Bytecode, B::C, B::CC, B::Debug, B::Deparse, B::Disassembler, B::Lint, B::Showlex, B::Stackobj, B::Terse, B::Xref**

ODBM_File

```
use ODBM_File;
use Fcntl;
tie(%db, 'ODBM_File', 'db', O_RDWR|O_CREAT, 0640);
untie %db;
```

This is an interface supporting, via **tie**, the old DBM data storage format.

References:

See **AnyDBM_File**, **DB_File**, **GDBM_File**, **NDBM_File**, **SDBM_File**

Opcode

This module is used by the **Safe** module and **ops** pragma to disable named opcodes when compiling Perl scripts.

```
use Opcode;
```

An opcode is the smallest executable element of a Perl program, and it is the internal format of a Perl script once it has been compiled. You shouldn't normally need to use this module; the **Safe** and **ops** interfaces are more practical. However, the information provided here is useful background and reference for both modules.

The module works by creating an opcode mask using the supported functions and defined opcode names and sets. Once the opcode mask has been created, you can execute your program. The execution will croak if an attempt is made to use an opcode defined in the current mask. Note that the created opcode mask only affects the *next* compilation, that is, one executed by **eval**. It does not affect the current script.

Functions

Most functions accept a number of arguments, and these are defined as **OPNAME**, which is the individual name of an opcode, **OPTAG**, for a group of opcodes, or an **OPSET**, which is a binary string that holds a set or zero or more operators. Functions are provided for building **OPSET** strings. Both **OPNAME** and **OPTAG** can be negated by prefixing the name or set with an exclamation mark. **OPTAG** names start with a colon.

```
opcodes
```

In a scalar context, returns the number of opcodes in the current Perl binary. In a list context, returns a list of all the opcodes. This is not yet implemented, so use

```
@names = opset_to_opts(full_opset);
```

to get the full list.

```
opset(OPNAME, ...)
```

Returns an **OPSET** containing the listed operators.

```
opset_to_ops(OPSET)
```

Returns a list of operator names corresponding to those operators in the **OPSET**.

```
opset_to_hex(OPSET)
```

Returns a string representation of an **OPSET**.

```
full_opset
```

Returns an **OPSET** that includes all operators.

```
empty_opset
```

Returns an **OPSET** that contains no operators.

```
invert_opset(OPSET)
```

Returns an **OPSET** that is the inverse set of the one supplied.

```
verify_opset(OPSET, ...)
```

Returns true if **OPSET** is valid; returns false otherwise. If you supply a second argument and it is true, the function calls **croak** if the **OPSET** is invalid.

```
define_optag(OPTAG, OPSET)
```

Creates **OPTAG** as a symbolic name for **OPSET**.

```
opmask_add(OPSET)
```

Adds **OPSET** to the current opcode mask. You cannot unmask opcodes once added.

```
opmask
```

Returns the **OPSET** corresponding to the current opcode mask.

```
opdesc(OPNAME, ...)
```

Returns a list of descriptions for the supplied **OPNAME**s.

```
opdump(PAT)
```

Prints to **STDOUT** a list of opcode names and corresponding descriptions. If **PAT** is supplied, only lines that match the pattern will be listed.

Opcode Sets

A number of predefined **OPSET** values are supplied as standard. They are logically divided into both function and security-conscious sets.

:base_core

aassign	abs	add	aelem
aelemfast	and	andassign	anoncode
aslice	av2arylen	bit_and	bit_or
bit_xor	chomp	chop	chr
complement	cond_expr	const	defined
delete	die	divide	each
enter	entersub	eq	exists
flip	flop	ge	gt
helem	hex	hslice	i_add

i_divide	i_eq	i_ge	i_gt
i_le	i_lt	i_modulo	i_multiply
i_ncmp	i_ne	i_negate	i_postdec
i_postinc	i_predec	i_preinc	i_subtract
index	int	keys	lc
lcfirst	le	leave	leaveeval
leavesub	left_shift	length	lineseq
list	lslice	lt	match
method	modulo	multiply	ncmp
ne	negate	nextstate	not
null	oct	or	orassign
ord	pop	pos	postdec
postinc	pow	predec	preinc
prototype	push	pushmark	qr
quotemeta	return	reverse	right_shift
rindex	rv2av	rv2cv	rv2hv
rv2sv	sassign	scalar	schomp
schop	scmp	scope	seq
sge	sgt	shift	sle
slt	sne	splice	split
stringify	stub	study	substr
subtract	trans	uc	ucfirst
undef	unshift	unstack	values
vec	wantarray	warn	xor

:base_mem

concat	repeat	join	range
anonlist	anonhash		

:base_loop

enteriter	enterloop	goto	grepstart
grepwhile	iter	last	leaveloop
mapstart	mapwhile	next	redo

:base_io

enterwrite	eof	formline	getc
leavewrite	print	rcatline	read
readdir	readline	recv	rewinddir
seek	seekdir	send	sysread
sysseek	syswrite	tell	telldir

:base_orig

bless	crypt	dbmclose	dbmopen
entertry	gelem	getpgrp	getppid
getpriority	gmtime	gv	gvsv
leavetry	localtime	padany	padav
padhv	padsv	pipe_op	prtf
pushre	ref	refgen	regcmaybe
regcomp	regcreset	rv2gv	select
setpgrp	setpriority	sockpair	sprintf
srefgen	sselect	subst	substcont
tie	untie		

:base_math

atan2	cos	exp	log
rand	sin	sqrt	srand

:base_thread

lock	threadsv

:default

This set is made up of the following other sets.

:base_core	:base_mem	:base_loop	:base_io
:base_orig	:base_thread		

:filesys_read

fileno	ftatime	ftbinary	ftblk
ftchr	ftctime	ftdir	fteexec
fteowned	fteread	ftewrite	ftfile
ftis	ftlink	ftmtime	ftpipe
ftrexec	ftrowned	ftrread	ftrwrite
ftsgid	ftsize	ftsock	ftsuid
ftsvtx	fttext	fttty	ftzero
lstat	readlink	stat	

:sys_db

egrent	ehostent	enetent	eprotoent
epwent	eservent	getlogin	ggrent
ggrgid	ggrnam	ghbyaddr	ghbyname
ghostent	gnbyaddr	gnbyname	gnetent
gpbyname	gpbynumber	gprotoent	gpwent
gpwnam	gpwuid	gsbyname	gsbyport
gservent	sgrent	shostent	snetent
sprotoent	spwent	sservent	

:browser

This collection of opcodes is more practical than the :**default** set.

:default	:filesys_read	:sys_db

:filesys_open

binmode	close	closedir	open
open_dir	sysopen	umask	

:filesys_write

chmod	chown	fcntl	link
mkdir	rename	rmdir	symlink
truncate	unlink	utime	

:subprocess

backtick	**fork**	**glob**	**system**
wait	**waitpid**		

:ownprocess

exec	**exit**	**kill**	**time**	**tms**

:others

This set holds a list of other opcodes that are not otherwise handled and don't deserve their own tags.

msgctl	**msgget**	**msgrcv**	**msgsnd**
semctl	**semget**	**semop**	**shmctl**
shmget	**shmread**	**shmwrite**	

:still_to_be_decided

accept	**alarm**	**bind**	**caller**
chdir	**connect**	**dbstate**	**dofile**
entereval	**flock**	**getpeername**	**getsockname**
gsockopt	**ioctl**	**listen**	**pack**
require	**reset**	**shutdown**	**sleep**
socket	**sort**	**ssockopt**	**tied**
unpack			

:dangerous

These are possibly dangerous tags not mentioned elsewhere.

syscall	**dump**	**chroot**

ops

The **ops** pragma switches off specific opcodes during the compilation process. The synopsis is as follows:

```
perl -Mops=:default
```

which enables only reasonably safe operations. Or, you can specify opcodes to be removed from those available using

```
perl -M-ops=system
```

Note that the best way to use this option is via the command line incorporation; otherwise you open yourself up to abuse before the compilation process starts through the use of **BEGIN {}** statements. This pragma makes use of the **Opcode** module.

References:

See **Opcode**

overload

The **overload** pragma enables you to install alternative functions for the core operators defined in Perl. The main syntax is

```
use overload
     '+' => \&myadd,
     '-' => \&mysubtract;
```

The arguments are specified here as a hash, and each key/value pair assigns the operator defined in the key to use the function in the value, instead of using one of the built-in opcodes. The module operates on objects and classes, so the **myadd** function will be called to execute the statement **$a + $b** operator if **$a** is a reference to an object blessed into the current package, or if **$b** is a reference to an object in the current package.

You can overload the following operators and functions:

```
+ += - -= * *= / /= % %= ** **= << <<= >> >>= x x= .
.=
<  <= >  >= == != <=>
lt le gt ge eq ne cmp
& ^ | neg ! ~
++ --
atan2 cos sin exp abs log sqrt
bool "" 0+
```

The pragma also supports three special operators: **nomethod**, **fallback**, and **=**.

Pod::Functions

Used by the internal **Pod** libraries. You shouldn't need to use this function on its own, unless you are developing your own Pod interface.

References:

See **Pod::Html**, **Pod::Text**

Pod::Html

Supports a single function, **pod2html**, for translating POD formatted documents into HTML documents.

```
use Pod::Html;
pod2html("pod2html",
            "--podpath=lib",
            "--podroot=/usr/local/lib/perl5/5.00502/",
            "--htmlroot=/usr/local/http/docs",
            "--recurse",
            "--infile=foo.pod",
            "--outfile=/perl/foo.html");
```

For a full list of supported options see the following table.

Option	Description
--flush	Flushes the contents of the item and directory caches created during the parsing of a POD document.
--help	Prints a help message.
--htmlroot	The base directory from which you reference documents relatively. This is required if you expect to install the generated HTML files onto a Web server. The default is /.

Option	Description
--**index**	Generates an index of =**head1** elements at the top of the HTML file that is generated (default).
--**infile**	The filename to convert. You don't have to use this element; the first nonhyphenated argument is taken as a filename. If you don't specify a file by either method, it will accept input from standard input.
--**libpods**	A colon-separated list of pages searched when referencing =**item** entries. These are not the filenames, just the page names as they would appear in **L<>** link elements.
--**netscape**	Uses Netscape-specific browser directives when necessary.
--**nonetscape**	Prevents the use of Netscape-specific browser directives (default).
--**outfile**	The destination filename for the generated HTML. Uses standard output if none is specified.
--**podpath**	A colon-separated list of directories containing pod files and libraries.
--**podroot**	The base directory prepended to each entry in the **podpath** command line argument. The default is ".", the current directory.
--**noindex**	Don't generate an index at the top of the HTML file that is generated.
--**norecurse**	Don't recurse into the subdirectories specified in the **podpath** option.
--**recurse**	Recurse into the subdirectories specified in the **podpath** option (this is the default behavior).
--**title**	The contents of the <**TITLE**> tag in the created HTML document.
--**verbose**	Produces status and progress messages during production.

References:

See **Pod::Text**

Pod::Text

Supports the **pod2text** script for translating documents from POD format to normal text.

```
use Pod::Text;
pod2text(LIST);
```

If **LIST** is only one argument, it is taken as the name of a file to translate. The translated output is automatically sent to **STDOUT**. If a second argument is specified, it is taken as a reference to a filehandle to which the output should be sent.

You can optionally insert two arguments before the input file. The **–a** option instructs the function to use an alternative format that does not make assumptions about the abilities of the destination output stream. Without this option, termcap may be used to format the document (you can force this by setting **$Pod::Text::termcap** to a value of one), or, if termcap is not available, backspaces will be used to simulate boldfaced and underlined text.

The **–width** argument should be the width of the output device, where **width** is the number of characters to use (the default value is 72 characters) or the value of your terminal, if this can be determined with termcap.

References:

See **Pod::Html**

POSIX

```
use POSIX;
```

The **POSIX** module provides an interface to the POSIX standard—a set of standards designed to provide a common set of features across operating systems, primarily Unix. The **POSIX** module also supports many of the constants and static definitions required when using **fcntl**, **ioctl**, and other I/O-related functions.

The full range of the POSIX functions has been the subject of many books. The best of these is *The POSIX Programmers Guide* by Donald Lewine (O'Reilly & Associates, Sebastopol, CA, 1991).

Where possible, the interface to the underlying POSIX library is made as Perl-compatible as possible. This means that some of the interface is handled by functions and some is handled by objects and classes. As a general rule, when a structure would normally be returned by a function, the Perl equivalent returns a list.

The list of functions supported by the module is shown in the following table. Note that some functions are C-specific and therefore not supported within the interface.

Constant	Description
_exit	Exits the current process.
abort	Aborts the current script, sending the **ABRT** signal to the Perl interpreter.
abs	Identical to the Perl function; returns the absolute value.
access	Returns true if the file can be accessed to the specified level.
acos	Returns the arc cosine of a number.
alarm	Identical to the Perl **alarm** function.
asctime	Converts a time structure to its string equivalent.
asin	Returns the arcsine of a number.
assert	Currently unimplemented. Aborts the current program if the assertion fails.
atan	Returns the arctan of a number.
atan2	Identical to the Perl function.
atexit	Not supported. Use an **END{}** block instead.
atof	C-specific.
atoi	C-specific.
atol	C-specific.
bsearch	Not supported. The functionality can normally be supported by using a hash.
calloc	C-specific.
ceil	Identical to the C function; returns the smallest integer value greater than or equal to the supplied value.

Constant	Description
cfgetispeed	Method for obtaining the input baud rate. See the section on the **POSIX::Termios** import set.
cfgetospeed	Method for obtaining the output baud rate. See the section on the **POSIX::Termios** import set.
cfsetispeed	Method for setting the input baud rate. See the section on the **POSIX::Termios** import set.
cfsetospeed	Method for setting the output baud rate. See the section on the **POSIX::Termios** import set.
chdir	Identical to the Perl function.
chmod	Identical to the Perl function.
chown	Identical to the Perl function.
clearerr	Not supported. Use the **FileHandle::clearerr** function.
clock	Returns an approximation of the amount of CPU time used by the program.
close	Closes the file descriptor created by the **POSIX::open** function.
closedir	Identical to the Perl function.
cos	Returns the cosine of a value.
cosh	Returns the hyperbolic cosine of a value.
creat	Creates a new file, returning the file descriptor.
ctermid	Returns the pathname to the device for controlling terminal for the current program.
ctime	Returns a formatted string for the supplied time. Similar to the scalar value returned by **localtime**.
cuserid	Returns the current user name.
difftime	Returns the difference between two times.
div	C-specific.
dup	Duplicates an open file descriptor.
dup2	Duplicates an open file descriptor.
errno	Returns the value of **errno**.
execl	C-specific. Use the built-in **exec** function instead.
execle	C-specific. Use the built-in **exec** function instead.
execlp	C-specific. Use the built-in **exec** function instead.
execv	C-specific. Use the built-in **exec** function instead.
execve	C-specific. Use the built-in **exec** function instead.

Constant	Description
execvp	C-specific. Use the built-in **exec** function instead.
exit	Identical to the Perl function.
exp	Identical to the Perl function.
fabs	Identical to the built-in **abs** function.
fclose	Use the **FileHandle::close** method instead.
fcntl	Identical to the Perl function.
fdopen	Use the **FileHandle::new_from_fd** method instead.
feof	Use the **FileHandle::eof** method instead.
ferror	Use the **FileHandle::error** method instead.
fflush	Use the **FileHandle::flush** method instead.
fgetc	Use the **FileHandle::getc** method instead.
fgetpos	Use the **FileHandle::getpos** method instead.
fgets	Use the **FileHandle::gets** method instead.
fileno	Use the **FileHandle::fileno** method instead.
floor	Returns the largest integer not greater than the number supplied.
fmod	Returns the floating point remainder after dividing two numbers using integer math.
fopen	Use the **FileHandle::open** method instead.
fork	Identical to the Perl function.
fpathconf	Returns the configural limit for a file or directory using the specified file descriptor.
fprintf	C-specific. Use the built-in **printf** function instead.
fputc	C-specific. Use the built-in **print** function instead.
fputs	C-specific. Use the built-in **print** function instead.
fread	C-specific. Use the built-in **read** function instead.
free	C-specific.
freopen	C-specific. Use the built-in **open** function instead.
frexp	Returns the mantissa and exponent of a floating point number.
fscanf	C-specific. Use <> and regular expression instead.
fseek	Use the **FileHandle::seek** method instead.
fsetpos	Use the **FileHandle::setpos** method instead.
fstat	Gets the file status information for a given file descriptor.
ftell	Use **FileHandle::tell** method instead.

Constant	Description
fwrite	C-specific. Use the built-in **print** function instead.
getc	Identical to the Perl function.
getchar	Returns one character read from **STDIN**.
getcwd	Returns the path to the current working directory.
getegid	Returns the effect group ID for the current process. Use **$)**.
getenv	Returns the value of the specified environment variable. Use **%ENV**.
geteuid	Identical to the Perl function.
getgid	Returns the current process's real group ID. Use **$(**.
getgrgid	Identical to the Perl function.
getgrnam	Identical to the Perl function.
getgroups	Identical to the Perl function.
getlogin	Identical to the Perl function.
getpgrp	Identical to the Perl function.
getpid	Gets the current process ID. Use the **$$** value.
getppid	Identical to the Perl function.
getpwnam	Identical to the Perl function.
getpwuid	Identical to the Perl function.
gets	Returns a line from **STDIN**.
getuid	Gets the current user ID. Use the value of **$<**.
gmtime	Identical to the Perl function.
isalnum	Returns true if the string is composed only of letters (irrespective of case) or numbers.
isalpha	Returns true if the string is composed only of letters (irrespective of case).
isatty	Returns true if the specified filehandle is connected to a TTY device.
iscntrl	Returns true if the string is composed only of control characters.
isdigit	Returns true if the string is composed only of digits.
isgraph	Returns true if the string is composed only of printable characters, except space.
islower	Returns true if the string is composed only of lowercase characters.

Constant	Description
isprint	Returns true if the string is composed only of printable characters, including space.
ispunct	Returns true if the string is composed only of punctuation characters.
isspace	Returns true if the string is composed only of white space characters. Within the default C and POSIX locales are space, form feed, newline, carriage return, horizontal tab, and vertical tab.
isupper	Returns true if the string is composed only of uppercase characters.
isxdigit	Returns true if the string is composed only of hexadecimal characters, "a–z", "A–Z", "0–9".
kill	Identical to the Perl function.
labs	C-specific. Use the built-in **abs** function.
ldexp	Multiplies a floating point number by a power of 2 (**ldexp(num,pow)**).
ldiv	C-specific. Use **int($a/$b)** instead.
localeconv	Gets numeric formatting information. See the **locale_h** import set below.
localtime	Identical to the Perl function.
log	Identical to the Perl function.
log10	Computes the logarithmic value in base 10.
longjmp	C-specific. Use **die** instead.
lseek	Moves the read/write pointer within an open file descriptor.
malloc	C-specific.
mblen	Returns the length of a multibyte string.
mbstowcs	Converts a multibyte string to a wide character string.
mbtowc	Converts a multibyte character to a wide character.
memchr	C-specific. Use the built-in **index** function.
memcmp	C-specific. Use **eq** instead.
memcpy	C-specific. Use = instead.
memmove	C-specific. Use = instead.

Constant	Description
memset	C-specific. Use **x** instead.
mkdir	Identical to the Perl function.
mkfifo	Creates a fifo (named pipe).
mktime	Converts date and time information to a calendar time.
modf	Returns the integral and fractional parts of a floating point number.
nice	Changes the execution priority of a process.
offsetof	C-specific.
open	Opens a file, returning a file descriptor. Accepts three arguments: the file name, mode, and permissions (in octal).
opendir	Identical to the Perl function.
pathconf	Gets configuration values for a specified file or directory.
pause	Suspends the execution of a process until it receives a signal with an associated handler.
perror	Prints the error message associated with the error in **errno**.
pipe	Creates an interprocess communication channel returning file descriptors for use with **open** and related functions.
pow	Raises a number to the specified power (**pow(num,power)**).
printf	Identical to the Perl function.
putc	C-specific. Use the built-in **print** instead.
putchar	C-specific. Use the built-in **print** instead.
puts	C-specific. Use the built-in **print** instead.
qsort	C-specific. Use the built-in **sort** instead.
raise	Sends the specified signal to the current process.
rand	Not supported. Use the built-in **rand** function.
readdir	Identical to the Perl version.
realloc	C-specific.
remove	Identical to the Perl **unlink** function.
rewind	Seeks to the beginning of the specified filehandle.
rewinddir	Identical to the Perl version.
scanf	C-specific. Use the <> operator and regular expressions.

Constant	Description
setbuf	Sets how a filehandle will be buffered.
setgid	Sets the group ID for the process. Equivalent to setting the value of $(.
setjmp	C-specific. Use **eval** instead.
setlocale	Sets the current locale. See the **local_h** import set section below.
setpgid	Sets the process group ID.
setsid	Creates a new session and sets the process group ID of the current process.
setuid	Sets the user ID. Equivalent to setting the value of $<.
setvbuf	Sets and defines how the buffer for a filehandle works.
sigaction	Defines a signal handler. See the **POSIX::SigAction** section below.
siglongjmp	C-specific. Use the **die** function instead.
signal	C-specific. Use the **%SIG** hash instead.
sigpending	Returns information about signals that are blocked and pending. See the **POSIX::SigSet** section following.
sigprocmask	Changes or examines the current process's signal mask. See the **POSIX::SigSet** section following.
sigsetjmp	C-specific. Use **eval** instead.
sigsuspend	Installs a signal mask and suspends the process until a signal arrives. See the **POSIX::SigSet** import set section following.
sin	Returns the sine for a given value.
sinh	Returns the hyperbolic sine for a given value.
sleep	Identical to the Perl function.
sprintf	Identical to the Perl function.
sqrt	Identical to the Perl function.
srand	Identical to the Perl function.
sscanf	C-specific. Use regular expressions.
stat	Identical to the Perl function.
strcat	C-specific. Use .= instead.
strchr	C-specific. Use the built-in **index** function instead.
strcmp	C-specific. Use **eq** instead.
strcoll	Compares two strings using the current locale.

III

Constant	Description
strcpy	C-specific. Use = instead.
strcspn	C-specific. Use regular expressions instead.
strerror	Returns the error string for a specific error number.
strftime	Returns a formatted string based on the supplied date and time information.
strlen	C-specific. Use the built-in **length** function instead.
strncat	C-specific. Use .= or **substr** instead.
strncmp	C-specific. Use **eq** or **substr** instead.
strncpy	C-specific. Use **eq** or **substr** instead.
strpbrk	C-specific.
strrchr	C-specific. Use **eq** or **substr** instead.
strspn	C-specific.
strstr	Identical to the Perl **index** function.
strtod	C-specific.
strtok	C-specific.
strtol	C-specific.
strtoul	C-specific.
strxfrm	Transforms the supplied string.
sysconf	Retrieves values from the system configuration tables.
tan	Returns the tangent of a value.
tanh	Returns the hyperbolic tangent of a value.
tcdrain	See the section on the **POSIX::Termios**.
tcflow	See the section on the **POSIX::Termios**.
tcflush	See the section on the **POSIX::Termios**.
tcgetattr	See the section on the **POSIX::Termios**.
tcgetpgrp	See the section on the **POSIX::Termios**.
tcsendbreak	See the section on the **POSIX::Termios**.
tcsetattr	See the section on the **POSIX::Termios**.
tcsetpgrp	See the section on the **POSIX::Termios**.
time	Identical to the Perl function.

Constant	Description
times	Similar to the Perl function, but returns five values (realtime, user, system, childuser, and childsystem) counted in clock ticks rather than seconds.
tmpfile	Use the **FileHandle::new_tmpfile** method instead.
tmpnam	Returns the name for a temporary file.
tolower	Identical to the Perl **lc** function.
toupper	Identical to the Perl **uc** function.
ttyname	Returns the path to the terminal associated with the supplied filehandle.
tzname	Returns the offset and daylight savings time settings for the current time zone.
tzset	Sets the current time zone using the **$ENV{TZ}** variable.
umask	Identical to the Perl function.
uname	Returns the system name, node name, release, version, and machine for the current operating system.
ungetc	Use the **FileHandle::ungetc** method instead.
unlink	Identical to the Perl function.
utime	Identical to the Perl function.
vfprintf	C-specific.
vprintf	C-specific.
vsprintf	C-specific.
wait	Identical to the Perl function.
waitpid	Identical to the Perl function.
wcstombs	Converts a wide character string to a multibyte character string.
wctomb	Converts a wide character to a multibyte character.
write	Writes to a file descriptor opened with **POSIX::open**.

III

Supported Classes

The **POSIX** module provides three new classes: **POSIX::SigSet**, **POSIX::SigAction**, and **POSIX::Termios**.

POSIX::SigSet

This provides an interface to the **sigset** function for creating signal sets. For installing handlers for these sets use the **SigAction** class. See the **signal_h** import set for information about the available signal constants to use with the methods.

```
$sigset = POSIX::SigSet->new;
```

Creates a new **SigSet** object. Additional methods are described here.

```
addset SIGNAL
```

Adds a **SIGNAL** to an existing set.

```
delset SIGNAL
```

Deletes a **SIGNAL** from a set.

```
emptyset
```

Empties a signal set.

```
fillset
```

Populates a signal set with all the available signals.

```
ismember SIGNAL
```

Returns true if the signal set contains the specified signal.

POSIX::SigAction

This installs a signal handler against a specific **SigSet** object.

```
$sigaction = POSIX::SigAction->new('main::handler',
$sigset, $flags);
```

The first parameter must be the fully qualified name of the signal handler routine. The second argument is the previously created **SigSet** object. The value of *flags* is a list of signal actions.

POSIX::Termios

This supports an interface to the termios interface driving system.

```
$termios = POSIX::Termios->new;
```

Creates a new **Termios** object. The following additional methods are supported.

```
getattr FD
```

Gets the attributes for the file descriptor specified. Uses zero (**STDIN**) by default.

```
getcc EXPR
```

Gets the value from the **c_cc** field. The information is an array, so you must use an index value.

```
getcflag
```

Returns the value of the **c_cflag**.

```
getiflag
```

Returns the value of the **c_iflag**.

```
getispeed
```

Returns the input baud rate.

```
getlflag
```

Returns the value of the **c_lflag**.

```
getoflag
```

Returns the value of the **c_oflag**.

```
getospeed
```

Returns the output baud rate.

```
setattr FD, EXPR
```

Sets the attributes for the file descriptor **FD**.

```
setcc EXPR, INDEX
```

Sets the value of the **c_cc** field. The information is an array, so you must specify an index value.

```
getcflag EXPR
```

Sets the value of the **c_cflag**.

```
getiflag EXPR
```

Sets the value of the **c_iflag**.

```
getispeed EXPR
```

Sets the input baud rate.

```
getlflag EXPR
```

Sets the value of the **c_lflag**.

```
getoflag EXPR
```

Sets the value of the **c_oflag**.

```
getospeed EXPR
```

Sets the output baud rate.

See the **termios_h** import set for the lists of supported constants.

Symbol Sets

For convenience and compatibility, the functions and constants defined within the **POSIX** module are also grouped into symbol sets to import the required elements. The sets are grouped by the name of the header file that would be required if you were programming directly in C. To use, specify the header name, substituting underscores for periods and prefixing the name with a colon. For example, to include the elements of the fcntl.h file:

```
use POSIX qw/:fcntl_h/;
```

For reference, the sets and functions they import, along with the constants they define, are listed below.

assert_h

This symbol set imports the following function: **assert**.

The following constant function is also imported: **NDEBUG**.

ctype_h

This symbol set imports the following functions:

isalnum	Isalpha	iscntrl	isdigit
isgraph	Islower	isprint	ispunct
isspace	Isupper	isxdigit	tolower
toupper			

dirent_h

There are no imported elements for this symbol set, since the functions of dirent.h are supported as built-in functions within Perl.

errno_h

The constants defined within errno.h are those that specify the numerical error number normally contained within $!. The list of imported constants is as follows:

E2BIG	EACCES	EADDRINUSE
EADDRNOTAVAIL	EAFNOSUPPORT	EAGAIN
EALREADY	EBADF	EBUSY
ECHILD	ECONNABORTED	ECONNREFUSED
ECONNRESET	EDEADLK	EDESTADDRREQ
EDOM	EDQUOT	EEXIST
EFAULT	EFBIG	EHOSTDOWN
EHOSTUNREACH	EINPROGRESS	EINTR
EINVAL	EIO	EISCONN
EISDIR	ELOOP	EMFILE
EMLINK	EMSGSIZE	ENAMETOOLONG
ENETDOWN	ENETRESET	ENETUNREACH
ENFILE	ENOBUFS	ENODEV
ENOENT	ENOEXEC	ENOLCK
ENOMEM	ENOPROTOOPT	ENOSPC
ENOSYS	ENOTBLK	ENOTCONN
ENOTDIR	ENOTEMPTY	ENOTSOCK
ENOTTY	ENXIO	EOPNOTSUPP
EPERM	EPFNOSUPPORT	EPIPE
EPROCLIM	EPROTONOSUPPORT	EPROTOTYPE
ERANGE	EREMOTE	ERESTART

EROFS	ESHUTDOWN	ESOCKTNOSUPPORT
ESPIPE	ESRCH	ESTALE
ETIMEDOUT	ETOOMANYREFS	ETXTBSY
EUSERS	EWOULDBLOCK	EXDEV

fcntl_h

This symbol set imports the following function: **creat**.

This symbol set imports the following constants:

FD_CLOEXEC	F_DUPFD	F_GETFD	F_GETFL
F_GETLK	F_RDLCK	F_SETFD	F_SETFL
F_SETLK	F_SETLKW	F_UNLCK	F_WRLCK
O_ACCMODE	O_APPEND	O_CREAT	O_EXCL
O_NOCTTY	O_NONBLOCK	O_RDONLY	O_RDWR
O_TRUNC	O_WRONLY	SEEK_CUR	SEEK_END
SEEK_SET	S_IRGRP	S_IROTH	S_IRUSR
S_IRWXG	S_IRWXO	S_IRWXU	S_ISBLK
S_ISCHR	S_ISDIR	S_ISFIFO	S_ISGID
S_ISREG	S_ISUID	S_IWGRP	S_IWOTH
S_IWUSR			

float_h

This symbol set imports the following constants:

DBL_DIG	DBL_EPSILON	DBL_MANT_DIG
DBL_MAX	DBL_MAX_10_EXP	DBL_MAX_EXP
DBL_MIN	DBL_MIN_10_EXP	DBL_MIN_EXP
FLT_DIG	FLT_EPSILON	FLT_MANT_DIG
FLT_MAX	FLT_MAX_10_EXP	FLT_MAX_EXP
FLT_MIN	FLT_MIN_10_EXP	FLT_MIN_EXP
FLT_RADIX	FLT_ROUNDS	LDBL_DIG
LDBL_EPSILON	LDBL_MANT_DIG	LDBL_MAX
LDBL_MAX_10_EXP	LDBL_MAX_EXP	LDBL_MIN
LDBL_MIN_10_EXP	LDBL_MIN_EXP	

limits_h

This symbol set imports the following constants:

ARG_MAX	CHAR_BIT	CHAR_MAX
CHAR_MIN	CHILD_MAX	INT_MAX
INT_MIN	LINK_MAX	LONG_MAX
LONG_MIN	MAX_CANON	MAX_INPUT
MB_LEN_MAX	NAME_MAX	NGROUPS_MAX
OPEN_MAX	PATH_MAX	PIPE_BUF
SCHAR_MAX	SCHAR_MIN	SHRT_MAX
SHRT_MIN	SSIZE_MAX	STREAM_MAX
TZNAME_MAX	UCHAR_MAX	UINT_MAX
ULONG_MAX	USHRT_MAX	_POSIX_ARG_MAX
_POSIX_CHILD_MAX	_POSIX_LINK_MAX	_POSIX_MAX_CANON
_POSIX_MAX_INPUT	_POSIX_NAME_MAX	_POSIX_NGROUPS_MAX
_POSIX_OPEN_MAX	_POSIX_PATH_MAX	_POSIX_PIPE_BUF
_POSIX_SSIZE_MAX	_POSIX_STREAM_MAX	_POSIX_TZNAME_MAX

locale_h

This symbol set imports the following functions:

localeconv	setlocale

The **localeconv** function returns a reference to a hash with the following, self-explanatory, elements:

currency_symbol	decimal_point	frac_digits
grouping	int_curr_symbol	int_frac_digits
mon_decimal_point	mon_grouping	mon_thousands_sep
n_cs_precedes	n_sep_by_space	n_sign_posn
negative_sign	p_cs_precedes	p_sep_by_space
p_sign_posn	positive_sign	thousands_sep

This symbol set imports the following constants:

LC_ALL	LC_COLLATE	LC_CTYPE
LC_MONETARY	LC_NUMERIC	LC_TIME
NULL		

math_h

This symbol set imports the following functions:

acos	asin	atan	ceil
cosh	fabs	floor	fmod
frexp	ldexp	log10	modf
pow	sinh	tan	tanh

This symbol set imports the following constant: **HUGE_VAL**.

setjmp_h

This symbol set imports the following functions:

longjmp	setjmp	siglongjmp	sigsetjmp

signal_h

This symbol set imports the following functions:

raise	sigaction	signal	sigpending
sigprocmask	sigsuspend		

This symbol set imports the following constants:

SA_NOCLDSTOP	SA_NOCLDWAIT	SA_NODEFER
SA_ONSTACK	SA_RESETHAND	SA_RESTART
SA_SIGINFO	SIGABRT	SIGALRM
SIGCHLD	SIGCONT	SIGFPE
SIGHUP	SIGILL	SIGINT
SIGKILL	SIGPIPE	SIGQUIT
SIGSEGV	SIGSTOP	SIGTERM
SIGTSTP	SIGTTIN	SIGTTOU
SIGUSR1	SIGUSR2	SIG_BLOCK
SIG_DFL	SIG_ERR	SIG_IGN
SIG_SETMASK	SIG_UNBLOCK	

stddef_h

This symbol set imports the following function: **offsetof**.

This symbol set imports the following constant: **NULL**.

stdio_h

This symbol set imports the following functions:

clearerr	fclose	fdopen	feof	ferror
fflush	fgetc	fgetpos	fgets	fopen
fprintf	fputc	fputs	fread	freopen
fscanf	fseek	fsetpos	ftell	fwrite
getchar	gets	perror	putc	putchar
puts	remove	rewind	scanf	setbuf
setvbuf	sscanf	stderr	stdin	stdout
tmpfile	tmpnam	ungetc	vfprintf	vprintf
vsprintf				

This symbol set imports the following constants:

BUFSIZ	EOF	FILENAME_MAX	L_ctermid
L_cuserid	L_tmpname	NULL	SEEK_CUR
SEEK_END	SEEK_SET	STREAM_MAX	TMP_MAX

stdlib_h

This symbol set imports the following functions:

abort	atexit	atof	atoi	atol
bsearch	calloc	div	free	getenv
labs	ldiv	malloc	mblen	mbstowcs
mbtowc	qsort	realloc	strtod	strtol
strtoul	wcstombs	wctomb		

This symbol set imports the following constants:

EXIT_FAILURE EXIT_SUCCESS MB_CUR_MAX NULL
RAND_MAX

string_h

This symbol set imports the following functions:

memchr	memcmp	memcpy	memmove	memset
strcat	strchr	strcmp	strcoll	strcpy

strcspn	strerror	strlen	strncat	strncmp
strncpy	strpbrk	strrchr	strspn	strstr
strtok	strxfrm			

This symbol set imports the following constant: **NULL**.

sys_stat_h
This symbol set imports the following functions:

fstat	mkfifo

This symbol set imports the following constants:

S_IRGRP	S_IROTH	S_IRUSR	S_IRWXG	S_IRWXO
S_IRWXU	S_ISBLK	S_ISCHR	S_ISDIR	S_ISFIFO
S_ISGID	S_ISREG	S_ISUID	S_IWGRP	S_IWOTH
S_IWUSR	S_IXGRP	S_IXOTH	S_IXUSR	

sys_utsname_h
This symbol set imports the following function: **uname**.

sys_wait_h
This symbol set imports the following constants:

WEXITSTATUS	WIFEXITED	WIFSIGNALED	WIFSTOPPED
WNOHANG	WSTOPSIG	WTERMSIG	WUNTRACED

termios_h
This symbol set imports the following functions:

cfgetispeed	cfgetospeed	cfsetispeed	cfsetospeed
tcdrain	tcflow	tcflush	tcgetattr
tcsendbreak	tcsetattr		

This symbol set imports the following constants:

B0	B110	B1200	B134
B150	B1800	B19200	B200
B2400	B300	B38400	B4800

B50	B600	B75	B9600
BRKINT	CLOCAL	CREAD	CS5
CS6	CS7	CS8	CSIZE
CSTOPB	ECHO	ECHOE	ECHOK
ECHONL	HUPCL	ICANON	ICRNL
IEXTEN	IGNBRK	IGNCR	IGNPAR
INLCR	INPCK	ISIG	ISTRIP
IXOFF	IXON	NCCS	NOFLSH
OPOST	PARENB	PARMRK	PARODD
TCIFLUSH	TCIOFF	TCIOFLUSH	TCION
TCOFLUSH	TCOOFF	TCOON	TCSADRAIN
TCSAFLUSH	TCSANOW	TOSTOP	VEOF
VEOL	VERASE	VINTR	VKILL
VMIN	VQUIT	VSTART	VSTOP
VSUSP	VTIME		

time_h

This symbol set imports the following functions:

asctime	clock	ctime	difftime
mktime	strftime	tzset	tzname

This symbol set imports the following constants:

CLK_TCK	CLOCKS_PER_SEC	NULL

unistd_h

This symbol set imports the following functions:

_exit	access	ctermid	cuserid
dup	dup2	execl	execle
execlp	execv	execve	execvp
fpathconf	getcwd	getegid	geteuid
getgid	getgroups	getpid	getuid
isatty	lseek	pathconf	pause
setgid	setpgid	setsid	setuid
sysconf	tcgetpgrp	tcsetpgrp	ttyname

This symbol set imports the following constants:

F_OK	NULL
R_OK	SEEK_CUR
SEEK_END	SEEK_SET
STDIN_FILENO	STDOUT_FILENO
STRERR_FILENO	W_OK
X_OK	_PC_CHOWN_RESTRICTED
_PC_LINK_MAX	_PC_MAX_CANON
_PC_MAX_INPUT	_PC_NAME_MAX
_PC_NO_TRUNC	_PC_PATH_MAX
_PC_PIPE_BUF	_PC_VDISABLE
_POSIX_CHOWN_RESTRICTED	_POSIX_JOB_CONTROL
_POSIX_NO_TRUNC	_POSIX_SAVED_IDS
_POSIX_VDISABLE	_POSIX_VERSION
_SC_ARG_MAX	_SC_CHILD_MAX
_SC_CLK_TCK	_SC_JOB_CONTROL
_SC_NGROUPS_MAX	_SC_OPEN_MAX
_SC_SAVED_IDS	_SC_STREAM_MAX
_SC_TZNAME_MAX	_SC_VERSION

re

The **re** pragma alters regular expression behavior. The pragma has three options: **taint**, **debug**, and **eval**. One additional pragma is really just a modification of an earlier one, called **debugcolor**. The only difference is in the color of the output.

The **taint** option ensures that variables modified with a regular expression are tainted in situations where they would be considered clean:

```
use re 'taint';
```

That is, in situations where matches or substitutions on tainted variables would ordinarily produce an untainted result, the results are in fact marked as tainted.

The **debug** and **debugcolor** options force Perl to produce debugging messages during the execution of a regular expression:

```
use re 'debug';
use re 'debugcolor';
```

This is equivalent to using the **–Dr** switch during execution if the **–DDEBUGGING** option were specified during the build process. The information provided can be very large, even on a relatively small regular expression. The **debugcolor** option prints out a color version if your terminal supports it.

The **eval** option enables regular expressions to contain the **(?{...})** assertions, even if the regular expression contains variable interpolation:

```
use re 'eval';
```

Ordinarily, this is disabled because it's seen as a security risk, and the pragma is ignored if the **use re 'taint'** pragma is in effect.

Safe

This module creates a safe compartment for executing a Perl script.

```
use Safe;

$compartment = new Safe;
```

The created compartment has the following attributes:

- A new name space. The new package has a new root name space, and code within the compartment cannot access the variables outside of this root name space. The parent script can optionally insert new variables into the name space, but the reverse is not true. Only the "underscore" variables (**$_**, **@_**, and **%_**) are shared between the parent and safe compartment.

- An operator mask. This is generated using the opcode names and tags as defined in the **Opcode** module. Executing code within the new compartment that contains a masked operator will cause the compilation of the code to fail. By default, the operator mask uses the **:default** opcode set.

To create a new compartment:

```
$compartment = new Safe;
```

An optional argument specifies the name of the new root name space. The module then supports the following methods.

```
permit(OP, ...)
```

Adds the specified opcodes or sets to the mask when compiling code in the compartment.

```
permit_only(OP, ...)
```

Exclusively sets the specified opcodes or sets in the mask when compiling code in the compartment.

```
deny(OP, ...)
```

Deletes the specified opcodes or sets from the current mask.

```
deny_only(OP, ...)
```

Denies only the listed opcodes or sets.

```
trap(OP, ...)
```

Synonymous with **deny**.

```
untrap(OP, ...)
```

Synonymous with **permit**.

```
share(NAME, ...)
```

Shares the specified variables with the compartment.

```
share_from(PACKAGE, ARRAY)
```

Shares the list of symbols defined in the array of references **ARRAY** from the specified **PACKAGE** with the compartment.

```
varglob(VARNAME)
```

Returns a glob reference for the symbol table entry of **VARNAME** with the package of the compartment.

```
reval(STRING)
```

Evaluates **STRING** within the compartment.

```
rdo(FILENAME)
```

Executes the script **FILENAME** in the compartment.

```
root(NAMESPACE)
```

Returns the name of the package that is the root of the compartment's name space.

```
mask(MASK)
```

When **MASK** is not specified, returns the entire operator mask for the compartment. If **MASK** is specified, then it sets the compartment's operator mask.

References:

See **Opcode, ops**

SDBM_File

```
use SDBM_File;
use Fcntl;

tie(%db, 'SDBM_File', 'db', O_RDWR|O_CREAT, 0640);
untie %db;
```

This is an interface supporting access to the Perl-supplied **SDBM** database using **tie**.

References:

See **AnyDBM_File, DB_File, GDBM_File, NDBM_File, ODBM_File**

Search::Dict

```
use Search::Dict;
look *FILEHANDLE, $key, $dict, $fold;
```

The **look** function sets the current location within the
FILEHANDLE to the first occurrence of **$key**, or the closest match
that is greater than or equal to it. This can be used, as the name
suggests, to locate a word within a dictionary that lists words, one
per line. If **$dict** is true, the search is conducted in strict dictionary
(alphabetical) order, ignoring everything that is not a word
character. The dictionary file should have been sorted with the
Unix **sort** command and the **–d** option. If **$fold** is true, the case is
ignored.

References:

See **Text::Abbrev**, **Text::Soundex**

SelectSaver

This module provides an alternative to the **select** function for
selecting the default output filehandle.

```
use SelectSaver;
```

You use it within a block:

```
use SelectSaver;

#STDOUT is selected
{
    my $saver = new SelectSaver(MYOUT);
    #MYOUT is selected
}
#STDOUT is selected again
```

Once the block exits, the selected filehandle returns to the value
selected before the block.

SelfLoader

This module provides a system similar to **AutoLoader** except that functions are self-loaded from the script rather than from separate files.

```
package MyPackage;
use SelfLoader;
```

Like **AutoLoader**, the module delays the loading of functions until they are called. Unlike **AutoLoader**, the functions themselves are defined after the **__DATA__** token. This token signifies to Perl that the code to be compiled has ended, and the functions defined in **__DATA__** are available via the **MyPackage::DATA** filehandle.

The **__DATA__** definitions for a single package can span multiple files, but the last **__DATA__** token in a given package is the one accessible via the **MyPackage::DATA** filehandle. Reading from the **DATA** filehandle ends when it sees the **__END__** token. But it will restart if the **__END__** token is immediately followed by a **DATA** token (not to be confused with the **__DATA__** token).

The method used by the **SelfLoader** package is to read in the contents of the filehandle to identify the defined functions. When the function is first called, it uses **eval** to parse the requested subroutine. The **SelfLoader** exports an **AUTOLOAD** subroutine to be used for loading the packages from the **DATA** filehandle.

Unlike **AutoLoader**, there is a small overhead for having the definitions parsed once at compile time. Other than that, execution will seem faster because functions are only compiled when used, thus negating the need to compile unused functions. There is no advantage to defining often-used functions with **SelfLoader**.

Note that lexically defined values (via **my**) are visible to functions only up to the **__DATA__** token. Functions that rely on lexicals cannot be autoloaded, either by **AutoLoader** or **SelfLoader**. Remember to use the **vars** pragma if you are also using the **strict** pragma.

References:

See **AutoLoader**, **Devel::SelfStubber**

Shell

This module allows you to use shell commands directly without the need to use backticks or the **system** function.

```
use Shell;
```

If you do not specify explicitly any commands, then all are assumed.

Once loaded, you can use the shell commands just like a normal Perl function:

```
use Shell;

print ps('-ef');
```

If you want to use them without parentheses, either import explicitly or declare the shell command as a function before you use it:

```
use Shell;
sub ps;
print ps -ef;
```

The actual method of supporting this operation is to use the **AUTOLOAD** system to call the supported command.

sigtrap

The **sigtrap** pragma enables simple signal handling without the complexity of the normal signal handling routines.

```
use sigtrap;
```

The pragma supports three handlers: two are supplied by the module itself (one provides a stack trace, and the other just calls **die**), and the third is one that you supply yourself. Each option supplied to the module is processed in order, so the moment a signal name is identified, the signal handler is installed.

Without any options specified, the module defaults to the
stack-trace and **old-interface-signals** options. The individual
options are listed following.

```
use sigtrap qw/stack-trace HUP INT KILL/;
```

Generates a Perl stack trace to **STDERR** when the specified signals
are received by the script. Once the trace has been generated, the
module calls **dump** to dump the core.

```
use sigtrap qw/die HUP INT KILL/;
```

Calls **croak**, reporting the name of the message that was caught.

```
use sigtrap 'handler' => \&my_handler, HUP, INT, KILL;
```

Installs the handler **my_handler** for the specified signals.

The pragma defines some standard signal lists. If your system does
not support one of the specified signals, the signal is ignored rather
than producing an error.

```
normal-signals
```

These are signals that might ordinarily be trapped by any program:
HUP, **INT**, **PIPE**, **TERM**.

```
error-signals
```

These are the signals that indicate a serious error: **ABRT**, **BUS**,
EMT, **FPE**, **ILL**, **QUIT**, **SEGV**, **SYS**, **TRAP**.

```
old-interface-signals
```

The list of signals that were trapped by default by the old **sigtrap**
pragma. This is the list of signals that are used if you do not specify
others and include **ABRT**, **BUS**, **EMT**, **FPE**, **ILL**, **PIPE**, **QUIT**, **SEGV**,
SYS, **TERM**, **TRAP**.

```
untrapped
```

This special option selects from the following signal list or
specification all the signals that are not otherwise trapped
or ignored.

```
any
```

Applies handlers to all subsequently listed signals; this is
the default.

Socket

This module defines the core functions and utility routines for supporting socket-based communication.

```
use Socket;
```

The module defines a core set of functions, as shown in the following table.

Function	Description
inet_aton HOSTNAME	Returns a 4-byte packed IP address for **HOSTNAME**, or **undef** if it cannot be resolved.
inet_ntoa IP_ADDRESS	Returns a string in the form **x.x.x.x** based on the supplied 4-byte packed IP address.
INADDR_ANY	Returns a 4-byte packed string defining the wildcard address for accepting connections.
INADDR_BROADCAST	Returns a 4-byte packed string defining the broadcast address
INADDR_LOOPBACK	Returns a 4-byte packed string defining the loopback address for the current host.
INADDR_NONE	Returns a 4-byte packed string defining the invalid IP address.
sockaddr_in PORT, ADDRESS	Packs **PORT** and **ADDRESS** into a **sockaddr_in** structure.
sockaddr_in SOCKADDR_IN	Unpacks and returns the **SOCKADDR_IN** structure into port and IP address.

Function	Description
pack_sockaddr_in PORT, ADDRESS	Packs **PORT** and **ADDRESS** into a **sockaddr_in** structure.
unpack_sockaddr_in SOCKADDR_IN	Unpacks and returns the **SOCKADDR_IN** structure into port and IP address.
sockaddr_un PATHNAME	Packs **PATHNAME** into a **sockaddr_un** structure.
sockaddr_un SOCKADDR_UN	Unpacks **SOCKADDR_UN** structure into a pathname.
pack_sockaddr_un PATHNAME	Packs **PATHNAME** into a **sockaddr_un** structure.
unpack_sockaddr_un SOCKADDR_UN	Unpacks **SOCKADDR_UN** structure into a pathname.

References:

See **IO::Socket**

strict

The **strict** pragma restricts those constructs and statements that would normally be considered unsafe.

```
use strict;
```

In particular, it reduces the effects of assumptions Perl makes about what you are trying to achieve and, instead, imposes limits on the definition and use of variables, references, and bare words that would otherwise be interpreted as functions. These can be individually turned on or off using **vars**, **refs**, and **subs**.

Although it imposes these limits, the pragma generally encourages (and enforces) good programming practice. However, for casual scripts it imposes more restrictions than are really necessary. In all cases, the pragmas are lexically scoped, which means you must specify **use strict** separately within all the packages, modules, and individual scripts you create.

subs

The **subs** pragma predeclares **func** so that the function can be
called without parentheses even before Perl has seen the full
definition.

```
use subs qw(func);
```

This can also be used to override internal functions by predefining
subroutines:

```
use subs qw(chdir);
chdir $message;
sub chdir
{
...
}
```

Symbol

This module provides a set of functions for manipulating Perl
symbols and their names.

```
use Symbol;

$glob = gensym;
print qualify($symbol, $pkg);
print qualify_to_ref($symbol, $pkg);
```

The **gensym** function returns a reference to an anonymous glob.
The resulting reference is suitable for use as a file or directory
handle. This is useful when you want to use a filehandle but do
not want to name it directly.

The **qualify** function returns a string containing the qualified
variable name for the supplied **$symbol** (which should be a string).
If you supply **$pkg**, it will be used as the default package for
variables not defined within a separate package in place of the

normal **main::**. In all cases, the returned string contains the true qualification, such that function **foo** in package **Bar** will always resolve to **Bar::foo**. The two lines below would print the same value:

```
print qualify('foo','Bar'),"\n";
print qualify('foo','foo'),"\n";
```

References are assumed to be glob references and therefore return their true, qualified name by their very nature.

The **qualify_to_ref** function is identical to **qualify** except that it returns a glob reference rather than a string.

The optional **delete_package** function deletes all of the symbol table entries and therefore the related variables, functions, and other structures:

```
use Symbol qw/delete_package/;

delete_package('Foo');
```

Sys::Hostname

This module provides a semireliable method of determining a host's name by trying every conceivable method until the hostname is found.

```
use Sys::Hostname;
print "Hostname is ", hostname, "\n";
```

It tries **syscall(SYS_gethostname)**, **'hostname'**, **'uname –n'**, and the file /com/host, stripping any white space, line termination, or null characters as necessary. If it is still unable to find the hostname, it calls **croak**.

Note that this method may fail on non-Unix operating systems.

References:

See **Carp**

Sys::Syslog

This module supports an interface to the Unix **syslog** logging system.

```
use Sys::Syslog;
```

There are four main functions imported by default: **openlog**, **syslog**, **setlogmask**, and **closelog**:

```
openlog IDENT, LOGOPT, FACILITY
```

Opens the system log. The string **IDENT** will prepend every message. The **LOGOPT** is a comma-separated list of options that equate to the standard **openlog** constants. See the following table for a list.

String	C Constant	Description
pid	LOG_PID	Logs the process ID with each message.
ndelay	LOG_NDELAY	Opens the connection to the **syslogd** daemon immediately. Normally the interface waits until the first message is posted to open the log.
cons	LOG_CONS	Writes messages to the system console if the **syslogd** daemon cannot be contacted.
nowait	LOG_NOWAIT	Doesn't wait for child processes (from **fork**) to log messages to the console.

The **FACILITY** argument is a string that defines the part of the system for which to record the log entries. Valid values are **user** for user-level entries, **kern** for kernel problems, and **daemon** for system daemons. These equate to the **LOG_USER**, **LOG_KERN**, and **LOG_DAEMON** constants used in the C interface. The exact list of supported values is system dependent.

```
syslog PRIORITY, FORMAT, LIST
```

This records an entry in the system log of the level specified by **PRIORITY**. Note that the priority definition is the same as for the **LOGOPT** parameter to the **openlog** function and should be expressed as a string (see the following table). Individual priorities can be combined using the I symbol. The **FORMAT** and **LIST** are passed to **sprintf** to format and output the supplied arguments in a format. The resulting string is then used as the log entry.

String	C Constant	Description
emerg	**LOG_EMERG**	A panic condition, normally broadcast to all users.
alert	**LOG_ALERT**	An urgent problem that needs immediate attention.
crit	**LOG_CRIT**	Critical error such as a hardware error/failure.
err	**LOG_ERR**	Simple errors.
warning	**LOG_WARNING**	Warning messages.
notice	**LOG_NOTICE**	Notification of particular events. Not considered critical, but may still require immediate attention.
info	**LOG_INFO**	Informational messages.
debug	**LOG_DEBUG**	Debugging information, normally of no use outside a debugging procedure.

The **FORMAT** string supports one additional option not supported by **printf**. The **%m** format inserts the value of the latest error message found in **$!**.

```
setlogmask MASK
```

Sets the mask priority for further **syslog** calls. Returns the old mask value.

```
closelog
```

Closes the connection to the **syslogd** daemon.

You can optionally import the **setlogsock** function, which allows you to change the type of socket used to communicate with the **syslogd** daemon.

```
setlogsock SOCKTYPE
```

Valid values for **SOCKTYPE** are "unix" for Unix domain sockets and "inet" for INET domain sockets. The function returns true on success and **undef** on failure.

Term::Cap

This module provides a simplified interface to the termcap terminal driver system.

```
use Term::Cap;
```

The module supports an object interface to **Tgetent**:

```
Tgetent(TERM)
```

The **Tgetent** function extracts the entry of the specified terminal type **TERM**, returning a reference to a **Term::Cap** object. For example:

```
$terminal = Tgetent Term::Cap { TERM => 'vt220',
                   OSPEED => $ospeed
               };
```

The **OSPEED** is the output bitrate for the terminal, specified either in POSIX format (absolute bitrates such as 9600), or as BSD-style relative values, where 13 equals 9600.

```
$terminal->Trequire(LIST)
```

The **Trequire** method enables you to specify the list of required capabilities for the terminal driver.

```
$terminal->Tgoto(EXPR, COL, ROW, HANDLE)
```

This decodes a cursor addressing string **EXPR**, passing it **COL** and **ROW**. The value of the string is returned, or printed directly to the **HANDLE** if specified.

```
$terminal->Tputs(EXPR, COUNT, HANDLE)
```

Caches the control string **EXPR** for **COUNT** times, returning the string. Alternatively, you can have it sent directly to **HANDLE** if specified.

You can access the extracted termcap entry by accessing the **TERMCAP** hash key element.

Term::Complete

This module provides an interface for completing words on a command line interface, similar to that provided by the Bourne Again SHell (**bash**).

```
use Term::Complete;
```

It supports a single function, **Complete**:

```
Complete(PROMPT, LIST)
```

This provides **PROMPT** to the screen and supports completion on the words in **LIST**. The return value is the completed word:

```
$input = Complete('$ ', qw/echo ls/);
```

You can type any character into the prompt. Pressing TAB completes the word (if possible). The default ^D prints a list of completion words. The ^U combination deletes the current line, and the DEL and BACKSPACE keys work as you would expect. You can modify the keys used for the last four options using the **$Term::Complete::complete, $Term::Complete::kill, $Term::Complete::erase1**, and **$Term::Complete::erase2** variables.

Specification should be done using the normal **stty** values, and the **stty** command is required for the module to function correctly. Note that you can continue to edit the line using the above keyboard sequences. The completion value is not returned until ENTER is pressed.

References:

See **Text::Abbrev**

Term::ReadLine

This module supports an interface to the available readline packages.

```
use Term::ReadLine;
```

Readline is a function library that supports the input of text in a line-by-line editable format. The interface is object based:

```
use Term::ReadLine;

$line = new Term::ReadLine 'Line Interface';
$input = $line->readline('Name? ');

print "Got $input\n";
```

The supported methods are described here.

```
readline(EXPR)
```

Returns the string entered, using the value of **EXPR** as a prompt. The trailing newline character is removed from the returned value.

```
ReadLine
```

Returns the name of the actual package being used to support the readline operation.

```
new
```

Creates a new **Term::ReadLine** object. You can optionally supply two arguments that specify the input and output filehandles to use for the readline operation.

```
addhistory(EXPR)
```

Adds **EXPR** to the history of input lines.

```
IN
OUT
```

Returns the filehandles for input or output.

```
MinLine(EXPR)
```

If specified, defines the minimal size of a line to be included in the history list.

```
findConsole
```

Returns an array of two strings containing the names for files for input and output, specified in the normal **shell** style of **<file** and **>file**.

```
Attribs
```

Returns a hash reference describing the internal configuration parameters of the package.

```
Features
```

Returns a hash reference describing the features of the current readline package being used.

Test

This module provides a simple framework for writing Perl test scripts, using a format similar to Perl's own testing systems.

```
use Test;
```

You use the framework by importing the module and then using a **BEGIN** block to specify the parameters for the tests you are about to conduct. For example:

```
use Test;
BEGIN { plan tests => 2}

ok(1);
ok(0);
```

Each call to **ok** should indicate a successful test or failure. The resulting report and output matches the format used by Perl's own testing system available when Perl has been built from a raw distribution. For example, the above script would output

```
1..2
ok 1
not ok 2
# Failed test 2 in test.pl at line 5
```

Note that each call to **ok** iterates through the available test numbers, and failures are recorded and reported.

You can embed expressions into the **ok** call:

```
ok(mytest());
```

The return value or resolved expression must be expected to return true or false according to the success or otherwise of the test. You can also use a two-argument version that compares the values of the two arguments:

```
ok(mytest(),mytest());
```

If you want to trap additional information with the error, you can append additional arguments to the **ok** function:

```
ok(0,1,'Math Error');
```

The resulting error and mismatch information is reported when the script exits:

```
1..2
ok 1
not ok 2
# Test 2 got: '0' (test.pl at line 5)
#   Expected: '1' (Didn't work)
```

You can mark tests as "to do" tests by specifying which test numbers are to be fixed directly within the test suite. These tests are expected to fail. You specify the information to the **plan** function during the **BEGIN** block:

```
use Test;
BEGIN { plan tests => 2, todo = [2]}

ok(1);
ok(0);
```

The resulting failure message notes the existence of an expected failure:

```
1..2 todo 2;
ok 1
not ok 2 # (failure expected in test.pl at line 5)
```

and also warns you when it sees a success in a test it was expecting to fail:

```
1..2 todo 2;
ok 1
ok 2 # Wow! (test.pl at line 5)
```

You can skip tests based on the availability of platform-specific facilities, using the **skip** function:

```
skip(TEST, LIST)
```

TEST is a test that evaluates to true only if the required feature is *not* available. Subsequent values in **LIST** work identically to the **ok** function.

You can supply a subroutine to handle additional diagnostics after the tests have completed. The function is passed an array reference of hash references that describe each test failure. The keys of each hash are **package**, **repetition**, and **result**. To configure the function, specify its reference in the call to **plan** in the **BEGIN** block:

```
BEGIN { plan tests => 2, onfail => \&errdiags }
```

The resulting function is executed within an **END** block and is therefore subject to the normal limitations of such a block.

Test::Harness

This module processes the output of multiple Perl test scripts and reports the success or failure of the scripts accordingly.

```
use Test::Harness;
runtests(LIST)
```

LIST should be a list of valid test scripts to be executed. It parses the output produced by a typical Perl test script and analyzes the output. The output produced by the **Test** module is suitable for correct parsing.

For example, a nine-test script with three failures would output the following:

```
t.p................# Failed test 2 in t.pl at line 5
# Failed test 5 in t.pl at line 8
# Failed test 9 in t.pl at line 12
FAILED tests 2, 5, 9
        Failed 3/9 tests, 66.67% okay
Failed Test  Status Wstat Total Fail  Failed  List of failed
-------------------------------------------------------------------
t.pl                        9    3  33.33%  2, 5, 9
Failed 1/1 test scripts, 0.00% okay. 3/9 subtests failed, 66.67% okay.
```

References:

See **Test**

Text::Abbrev

Given a list of words, this module generates an abbreviation table in a hash. The generated list accounts for possible duplications of abbreviations within the supplied list.

```
use Text::Abbrev;
%abbrev = ();
abbrev(\%abbrev, LIST);
```

For example, the call

```
abbrev(\%abbrev, 'better');
```

will produce a hash like this:

```
b      => better,
be     => better,
bet    => better,
bett   => better,
bette  => better,
better => better,
```

While the call

```
abbrev(\%abbrev, qw/be bet better/);
```

will populate the **%abbrev** hash with

```
b       => be,
be      => be,
bet     => bet,
bett    => better,
bette   => better,
better  => better,
```

References:

See **Term::Complete**

Text::ParseWords

This module parses an array of lines into a list of words using a specified delimiter. Any words or strings contained within quotes are treated as single words, effectively ignoring the supplied delimiter.

```
use Text::ParseWords;
@words = quotewords($delim, $keep, LIST);
```

The **$delim** element is the delimiter to use. This can be a raw string or a regular expression. The **$keep** element affects the way text within the lines is treated. If set to true, quotes are retained in the list of words returned; otherwise they are removed. Also, if **$keep** is true, then the backslashes are preserved in the returned list. If false, then a double backslash is converted to a single backslash, and a single backslash disappears entirely.

Text::Soundex

The **Text::Soundex** module generates a four-character soundex string using the algorithm designed by Donald Knuth. The algorithm translates individual words into the string, which can then be used for comparison and hashing of the supplied words as they sound when they are spoken, rather than how they are spelled.

```
use Text::Soundex;
```

```
soundex LIST
```

The **soundex** function hashes the words supplied in **LIST**, returning a list of soundex codes. Each code is made up of a single character, matching the first character of the supplied word, and three digits. For example,

```
print join(' ',soundex('Martin', 'Brown'),"\n");
```

prints

```
M635 B650
```

On the other hand,

```
print join(' ',soundex('Martin', 'Martian'),"\n");
```

produces

```
M635 M635
```

Note that the soundex string produced cannot be mapped back to the original string. The above example should demonstrate the fact, since M635 refers both to "Martin" and "Martian." Note, however, that the algorithm is not completely fail-safe:

```
print join(' ',soundex('Wood', 'Would'),"\n");
```

This produces the following, perhaps incorrect, sequence:

```
W300 W430
```

If a suitable soundex string cannot be produced, then the function returns **$soundex_nocode**, which is initially set to the undefined value. You can, however, set the value of this variable for your own purposes.

Text::Tabs

This module expands tabs into spaces and "unexpands" spaces into tabs.

```
use Text::Tabs;

$tabstop = 8;
expand LIST
unexpand LIST
```

The **$tabstops** scalar specifies the number of spaces to replace a single tab with **expand**, or the number of spaces to convert into a single tab with **unexpand**. Both functions accept a list of scalars, and each scalar should contain a string to be expanded or unexpanded as appropriate. Each element of **LIST** should not contain any newlines; they should be **split** first into a suitable list. The return value is a list of converted elements.

For example, here is a script for expanding the tabs of files supplied on the command line into four spaces:

```
#!/usr/local/bin/perl -pi.bak

BEGIN
{
        use Text::Tabs;
        $tabstop = 4;
}

$_ = expand $_;
```

You can now do

```
$ expand file.txt
```

To convert it back, create a new script with **unexpand** instead of **expand**:

```
#!/usr/local/bin/perl -pi.bak

BEGIN
{
```

```
        use Text::Tabs;
        $tabstop = 4;
}

$_ = unexpand $_;
```

Text::Wrap

This module intelligently wraps text into paragraphs.

```
use Text::Wrap;

$Text::Wrap::columns = 70;
wrap PREFIRST, PREOTHER, EXPR
```

The width of the resulting paragraph is specified directly in the **$Text::Wrap::columns** scalar. The **wrap** function then wraps **EXPR** indenting the first line of the paragraph with **PREFIRST** and subsequent lines in the paragraph with **PREOTHER**.

Tie::Array

This module provides some simple base class definitions for tying arrays. You normally use this module to inherit base methods from, for example:

```
package MyArray;
use Tie::Array;
@ISA = qw/Tie::Array/;
```

It provides stub **DELETE** and **EXTEND** methods, and also **PUSH**, **POP**, **SHIFT**, **UNSHIFT**, **SPLICE**, and **CLEAR** in terms of basic **FETCH**, **STORE**, **FETCHSIZE**, **STORESIZE**, in addition to the mandatory **new** method for creating the new object.

When developing your own tied-array classes, you will need to define the following methods:

```
TIEARRAY classname, LIST
STORE this, index, value
FETCH this, index
FETCHSIZE this
```

```
STORESIZE this, count
EXTEND this, count
CLEAR this
DESTROY this
PUSH this, LIST
POP this
SHIFT this
UNSHIFT this, LIST
SPLICE this, offset, length, LIST
```

III

Tie::Handle

This module provides core methods for tying handles.

```
package MyHandle;
use Tie::Handle;
@ISA = qw/Tie::Handle/;
```

It supports the basic **new** method in addition to **TIESCALAR**, **FETCH**, and **STORE**.

For developing your own tied-handle classes, you will need to define the following methods:

```
TIEHANDLE classname, LIST
WRITE this, scalar, length, offset
PRINT this, LIST
PRINTF this, format, LIST
READ this, scalar, length, offset
READLINE this
GETC this
DESTROY this
```

Tie::Hash

This module provides base class definitions for tied hashes. It provides the **new**, **TIEHASH**, **EXISTS**, and **CLEAR** methods.

```
package MyHash;
use Tie::Hash;
@ISA = qw/Tie::Hash/;
```

When developing your own class for tying hashes, you will need to implement the following methods:

```
TIEHASH classname, LIST
STORE this, key, value
FETCH this, key
FIRSTKEY this
NEXTKEY this, lastkey
EXISTS this, key
DELETE this, key
CLEAR this
```

Tie::RefHash

This module supports the facility to use references as hash keys through a tied hash. This is normally not allowed, and if **strict refs** is switched on, Perl will fail on compilation.

```
use Tie::RefHash;
tie %hash, 'Tie::RefHash', LIST;
```

Tie::Scalar

This module provides base class definitions for tying scalars. The basic **Tie::Scalar** package provides the **new**, **TIESCALAR**, **FETCH**, and **STORE** methods.

```
package myScalar;
use Tie::Scalar;
@ISA = qw/Tie::Scalar/;
```

If you are developing your own tied scalars, you will need to define the following methods:

```
TIESCALAR classname, LIST
FETCH this
STORE this, value
DESTROY this
```

Tie::SubstrHash

This module provides a class for supporting a hash with fixed key and value sizes. The resulting hash algorithm is a factor of the key and value sizes specified, and the hash is optimized for the specified size. This improves performance but also limits the size of the hash you create. Any attempt to add keys into the hash beyond the specified size results in a fatal error.

```
require Tie::SubstrHash;
tie %hash, 'Tie::SubstrHash', KEYLEN, VALUELEN,  TABLE_SIZE;
```

The above creates a hash in **%hash**. Each key within the hash will be **KEYLEN** long (in bytes), and values will be **VALUELEN** long. Note that **KEYLEN** and **VALUELEN** are not maximum sizes; they are fixed. Attempts to insert data with a key size greater or less than **KEYLEN** will cause a fatal error, as will storing values that are greater or less than **VALUELEN**. The maximum size for the hash is specified as the number of key/value pairs, as specified in **TABLE_SIZE**.

There are two main benefits to this system: speed and memory. With a fixed-size hash the memory footprint is much smaller, and the resulting internal tables used to look up individual key/value pairs are therefore much smaller, resulting in faster and more efficient searches for information.

Time::Local

This module provides the reverse functionality of the **localtime** and **gmtime** functions; that is, it converts a date and time specified in individual variables into the number of seconds that have elapsed since the epoch:

```
use Time::Local;

$time = timelocal(SEC, MIN, HOURS, MDAY, MON, YEAR);
$time = timegm(SEC, MIN, HOURS, MDAY, MON, YEAR);
```

The functions accept the arguments in the same range as the corresponding **localtime** and **gmtime** function, such that the code

```
use Time::Local;

$time = time;

print "Time!" if ($time = (timelocal((localtime)[0..5])));
```

should always print "Time!"

Both **timelocal** and **timegm** return −1 if the upper limit is reached for the integer that stores the time value. On most systems this will be Jan 1 2038.

Time::gmtime

Overrides the built-in **gmtime** function with one that returns an object based on the **Time::tm** module. The individual methods within the returned object are the individual fields of the new time structure. For example:

```
use Time::gmtime;

$time = gmtime;

print "Date is: ",
      join('/',$time->mday,($time->mon+1),
                    ($time->year+1900)),
                    "\n";
```

The individual methods (fields) match the names of the **struct tm** structure, that is, **sec, min, hour, mday, mon, year, wday, yday,** and **isdst**.

It's also possible to obtain the time from the last **gmtime** call via predefined variables. These variables have the same name as the structure fields and object methods with a **tm_** prefix. For example:

```
use Time::gmtime qw/:FIELDS/;

gmtime;
```

```
print "Date is: ",join('/',$tm_mday,
                       ($tm_mon+1),
                       ($tm_year+1900)),
                       "\n";
```

The time variables will not be updated until **gmtime** is called again.

You can access the original **CORE::gmtime** function in a scalar context using the new **gmctime** function:

```
print gmctime(time);
```

To use the object-oriented interface without overriding the **CORE::localtime** function, import the module with an empty import list, and then call the functions explicitly:

```
use Time::gmtime qw//;

$time = Time::gmtime::gmtime;

print "Date is: ",
      join('/',$time->mday,($time->mon+1),
                       ($time->year+1900)),
                       "\n";
```

References:

See **Time::tm**

Time::localtime

This module overrides the built-in **localtime** function with one that returns an object based on the **Time::tm** module. The individual methods within the returned object are the individual fields of the new time structure. For example:

```
use Time::localtime;

$time = localtime;

print "Time is: ",join(':',$time->hour,
                       $time->min,
                       $time->sec),
                       "\n";
```

The individual methods (fields) match the names of the **struct tm** structure, that is, **sec**, **min**, **hour**, **mday**, **mon**, **year**, **wday**, **yday**, and **isdst**.

It's also possible to obtain the time from the last **localtime** call via predefined variables. These variables have the same name as the structure fields and object methods with a **tm_** prefix. For example:

```
use Time::localtime qw(:FIELDS);

localtime;

print "Time is: ",join(':',$tm_hour,
                        $tm_min,
                        $tm_sec),
                  "\n";
```

The time variables will not be updated until **localtime** is called again.

You can access the original **CORE::localtime** function in a scalar context using the new **ctime** function:

```
print ctime(time);
```

To use the object-oriented interface without overriding the **CORE::localtime** function, import the module with an empty import list, and then call the functions explicitly:

```
use Time::localtime qw//;

$time = Time::localtime::localtime;

print "Time is: ",join(':',$time->hour,
                        $time->min,
                        $time->sec),
                  "\n";
```

References:

See **Time::tm**

Time::tm

This module supports the internal functionality of the **Time::localtime** and **Time::gmtime** modules.

References:

See **Time::localtime**, **Time::gmtime**

UNIVERSAL

The **UNIVERSAL** module provides the base class from which all other classes are based. This module provides the essential grounding for all blessed references within. Because all new objects inherit from the base class, the **UNIVERSAL** module also provides the same base methods that are automatically inherited by all classes and objects. Two of the methods, **can** and **isa**, are supported as both methods and functions:

```
isa(TYPE)
UNIVERSAL::isa(REF, TYPE)
```

Returns true if the object or **REF** is blessed into the package **TYPE** or has inherited from the package **TYPE**.

```
can(METHOD)
UNIVERSAL::can(REF, METHOD)
```

Returns a reference to the subroutine supporting **METHOD** if **METHOD** is supported within the class of the object or **REF**. If the specified method does not exist, then it returns **undef**.

```
VERSION ([REQUIRE])
```

Returns the contents of the **$VERSION** variable within the object's class. If the **REQUIRE** value is specified, the script will die if **REQUIRE** is less than or equal to the **$VERSION** variable.

User::grent

This module supports an object-oriented interface to the built-in **getgr*** functions:

```
use User::grent;
$grent = getgrnam('staff');
```

Individual fields are then available as methods to the **$grent** object.
The supported methods are **name**, **passwd**, **gid**, and **members**.
This last item returns a reference to a list; the first three simply
return scalars.

References:

See **User::pwent**

User::pwent

This module provides an object-based interface to the built-in
getpw* functions.

```
use User::pwent;
$pwent = getpwnam('root');
```

Once retrieved, individual fields of the password entry are
available as methods to the newly created object. For example,

```
print "User ID: ",$pwent->uid,"\n";
```

prints the uid of the **root** user. The list of methods supported is
name, **passwd**, **uid**, **gid**, **quota**, **comment**, **gecos**, **dir**, and **shell**.

References:

See **User::grent**

utf8

The **utf8** pragma tells Perl to use the UTF-8 (Unicode) character set
for internal string representation. The pragma is block scoped. For
most installations, there are no differences between Unicode and
normal ASCII representation, since the first 128 characters of the
ASCII code are stored within a single byte. For patterns that are

greater than this value, or for multibyte characters, the differences are significant.

```
use utf8;
```

Once switched on, you can switch off Unicode operation with **no**:

```
no utf8;
```

The main effects of the module are as follows:

III

- Strings and patterns may contain characters that have an ordinal value greater than 255. You can explicitly specify a Unicode character by specifying the hexadecimal prefix with braces and the Unicode character in a 2-byte hexadecimal string, for example **\x{263A}**.

- Symbol table entries within Perl may be specified in Unicode format.

- Regular expressions match characters (including multibyte characters) instead of individual bytes.

- Character classes in regexps match characters instead of bytes.

- You can match Unicode properties using the **\p{}** (which matches a property) and **\P{}** (which does not match a property).

- The **\X** pattern match matches any extended Unicode string.

- The **tr///** operator translates characters instead of bytes.

- Case translation with the **uc**, **lc**, **ucfirst**, and **lcfirst** functions uses internal Unicode tables for conversion.

- Functions that use or return character positions; returns positions correctly in characters, not bytes.

- The **pack** and **unpack** functions are unaffected (the "c" and "C" letters still pack single-byte characters). The "U" specifier can instead be used to pack Unicode characters.

- The **chr** and **ord** functions work on Unicode characters.

- Use of **reverse** in a scalar context works correctly on characters, not bytes.

References:

See **File::Find**, **File::CheckTree**

vmsish

This module is a pragma for imposing VMS-specific and/or style features. This allows for the differences between the VMS platform and Perl's normal behavior.

```
use vmsish;
```

The options for the **vmsish** pragma are listed in the following table.

Option	Description
status	Implies VMS-style treatment of the values returned by backticks and **system**.
exit	Causes the **SS$NORMAL** variable to contain the correct exit status.
time	Forces time values to be localized rather than referenced to GMT.

vars

The **vars** pragma predeclares the variables specified. This solves problems when the **use strict** is in force and also provides the best mechanism for exporting variables from modules and packages.

```
use vars qw/$foo @bar %poo/;
```

References:

See **subs**

warnings

This module is a pragma that can help to control the level of warnings that are produced. There are three options to the pragma: **all**, **deprecated**, and **unsafe**.

```
use warnings 'all';
```

Switches on all warnings for the script.

```
use warnings 'deprecated';
```

Only lists warnings for features that are deprecated in the current version of Perl.

```
use warnings 'unsafe';
```

Only lists warnings that are considered unsafe.

You can switch off specific sets with **no**:

```
no warnings 'deprecated';
```

Part 4
Sample Scripts

Perl is a very versatile language and can be used for a wide variety of tasks. It is perhaps best known for its use on Web sites for CGI (Common Gateway Interface) programming, although it can be used for a great many other things.

In this section, you'll find some nonCGI related scripts that demonstrate some of the different abilities of Perl. These scripts work straight out of the book, although in some cases you may need to download a module or bundle from CPAN. These requirements are mentioned in the descriptions.

Alternatively, use the **CPAN** module to download the necessary **CPAN** modules and any related modules required by them. See Part 3 for details on using the **CPAN** module to download other modules.

Uudecoding Files

To transfer files over e-mail or Usenet, they have to be converted into a 7-bit format. This is a legacy requirement due to the nature of the old e-mail systems, which only supported the 7-bit character set. This gave rise to all sorts of formats, the most well known being Uuencoding, so named because of the uucp system used to exchange files between machines.

Perl supports a function called **unpack** (see Part 2), which translates a packed binary structure into individual typed elements. This is often used in fixed-width database systems and when accessing information written from a C structure. It also provides the facility for decoding a UU-encoded file, which is what we use in the script following to convert a downloaded file into its original format.

```perl
#!/usr/local/bin/perl

use strict;

my ($file, $valid, $filemode, $outfile,
```

```perl
$decodedline);

unless (@ARGV == 1)
{
    die <<EOF
Usage: $0 $file

Where file is the name of the file you want to decode
EOF
}

open(INFILE,"<" . $ARGV [0])
    || die "Can't open the input file";

$valid=0;

while (<INFILE>)
{
    if (/^begin\s+(\d+)\s+(.*)/)
    {
        $filemode=$1;
        $outfile=$2;
        $valid=1;
        last;
    }
}

$valid ? print "Creating $outfile\n"
       : die "Not a UU file";

open(OUTFILE, ">$outfile")
    || die "Can't open the output\n";

while(<INFILE>)
{
    $decodedline = unpack("u",$_);
    die "Invalid uuencoded line"
        if (!defined($decodedline));
    print OUTFILE $decodedline;
    /^end$/ && last;
}

close (INFILE);
close (OUTFILE);
chmod oct($filemode), $outfile;
```

The script automatically identifies the filename and octal mode, which is stored in a uuencoded file. The process is so easy only because of the built-in ability of Perl's **unpack** function to decode a uuencoded string.

Building a named.boot File

If you manage a number of domains and a number of machines that cache details on secondary domain names, then you will have experienced the problems of resolving and updating the details in the **/etc/named.boot** file that stores the configuration information for the **named** domain name server. The format of the file is simple. Each line specifies a different domain or configuration option in the file. For example:

```
directory /var/named
cache . fake/cache
primary 0.0.127.in-addr.arpa primary/0.0.127.in-addr.arpa
primary 10.112.198.in-addr.arpa primary/10.112.198.in-addr.arpa
primary mchome.com primary/mchome.com
secondary mcwords.com 207.240.118.18 secondary/mcwords.com
```

Each field in each line is separated by a space and, depending on the value of the first field, the format of the line is different. In this sample, you can see four different types. The directory line specifies the base directory for the **named** system. The cache line specifies the root point and path name (within the directory specified above) for the root domain name server file.

The primary entries are those domains that you manage on your local machine; the remainder of the fields are the domain name and the path to the primary domain file. The secondary entries specify the domains that you hold details on but do not manage, either in an official or unofficial capacity. The remainder of the fields specify the domain name, the IP addresses of the official domain name servers for the domain, and the path in which to store the domain file. The named daemon refreshes the contents of these secondary files by contacting, in order, the list of hosts specified by each address.

The first three types—directory, cache, and primary—are easy to manage, since you have all of the information at hand. The secondary entries are more difficult to build, since you need to find out the IP addresses of the servers before you list them in the

IV

named.boot configuration file. Furthermore, if you are officially holding the domains as a secondary domain name server, you need to omit your own IP address from the list. If you have a number of servers holding secondary information on your site, it's also a good idea to list them last in the list of servers from which to obtain the latest copy of the domain file.

The script following makes the process easier by automatically building the **named.boot** file. The script automates the process by interrogating the local domain name server to obtain the list of domain name servers for a specified domain. It then builds the list of IP addresses, taking account of local servers and the current machine in order to produce the final configuration information for the domain and, eventually, the entire file.

This script uses the **Net::DNS** module from Michael Fuhr and the **libnet** module from Graham Barr.

```perl
#!/usr/local/bin/perl5 -w

use strict;

use Net::DNS;
use Net::Domain;

my $hostfqdn = Net::Domain::hostfqdn();
my ($dnsdir,$cache,@secondaries,
    @primaries,%dnshosts);

open(DNSCONF,"<$ARGV[0]")
    or die "Couldn't open $ARGV[0], $!";

while(<DNSCONF>)
{
    chomp;
    s/\s+//g;
    my ($type,$opt) = split(/:/,$_,2);
    if ($type eq 'dir')
    {
        $dnsdir = $opt;
    }
    elsif ($type eq 'cache')
    {
        $cache = $opt;
    }
    elsif ($type eq 'primary')
    {
```

```perl
            push(@primaries,$opt);
        }
        elsif ($type eq 'secondary')
        {
            push(@secondaries,$opt);
        }
}
close(DNSCONF)
    or die "Couldn't close $ARGV[0], $!";

open(NAMED,">$ARGV[0].boot")
    or die "Couldn't open $ARGV[0].boot, $!";

print NAMED "directory $dnsdir\n";
print NAMED "cache . $cache";

for my $primary (sort @primaries)
{
    print NAMED ("primary $primary ",
                "primary/$primary\n");
}

my $res = new Net::DNS::Resolver;
unless ($res)
{
    die "Error creating resolver";
}

for my $domain (sort @secondaries)
{
    my $query = $res->query($domain,"NS");
    unless ($query)
    {
        print("Error processing query for $domain:",
              $res->errorstring,"\n");
        next;
    }
    my (@remote,@local);

    for my $rr ($query->answer)
    {
        next unless($rr->type eq 'NS');
        next if ($rr->nsdname eq $hostfqdn);
        my $islocal = 0;
        for my $dom (@primaries)
        {
```

```
        if ($rr->nsdname =~ /$dom$/)
        {
            $islocal=1;
            last;
        }
    }
    if ($islocal)
    {
        push(@local,$rr->nsdname);
    }
    else
    {
        push(@remote,$rr->nsdname);
    }
    }
    print NAMED "secondary $domain ";
    for my $host (@local,@remote)
    {
        unless(defined($dnshosts{$host}))
        {
        $dnshosts{$host} =
            join('.',
                unpack('C4',
                    gethostbyname($host)));
        }
        print NAMED "$dnshosts{$host} "
            if(defined($dnshosts{$host}));
    }
    print NAMED " secondary/$domain\n";
}

close(NAMED)
    or die "Couldn't close $ARGV[0].boot, $!";
```

If you use the script on a configuration file like this:

```
dir:/var/named
cache:fake/cache
primary:0.0.127.in-addr.arpa
primary:mcslp.com
primary:mcwords.com
primary:10.112.198.in-addr.arpa
secondary:mcgraw-hill.com
secondary:stok.co.uk
```

You will get a resulting **named.boot** file like this:

```
directory /var/named
cache . fake/cacheprimary 0.0.127.in-addr.arpa
    primary/0.0.127.in-addr.arpa
primary 10.112.198.in-addr.arpa
    primary/10.112.198.in-addr.arpa
primary mcslp.com primary/mcslp.com
primary mcwords.com primary/mcwords.com
secondary mcgraw-hill.com 199.221.47.8 207.24.245.179
    207.24.245.178 199.221.47.7
secondary/mcgraw-hill.com
secondary stok.co.uk 194.207.0.129 194.207.13.1
    secondary/stok.co.uk
```

IV

This result can be renamed and copied directly into the **/etc/ named.boot** file. I've used this script for a number of years to manage the 60 secondary domains that we host in collaboration with another site. It has yet to fail on me and, in fact, it normally highlights differences between domains—especially those that no longer exist—long before a notification e-mail arrives.

Checking the Alias Database

Aliases under Unix are mapped using a text file that relates incoming addresses into single people or groups of people to forward the e-mail to. The relation is circular—it's possible to have aliases that contain further aliases to other people, or more aliases. For speed, the file is translated into a DBM file that is then used directly by **sendmail**. The only problem is that debugging the file requires that it be translated, which places a version of a possibly buggy alias file onto a live system.

To get around this problem, you can use the script below to debug the text file used to build the DBM database.

```perl
#!/usr/local/bin/perl5 -w

use strict;
use FileHandle;
use Getopt::Std;
```

```perl
my $usage = "Usage: [-r | [-e|m alias...]]"
            . " [-f aliasfile]";
use vars qw/$opt_e $opt_f $opt_m $opt_r/;
die $usage unless (getopts('merf:'));
$opt_e = 1 unless($opt_r || $opt_m);
$opt_f = '/etc/aliases' unless ($opt_f);
die $usage unless @ARGV or $opt_r;

my %alias = readaliases($opt_f);
expand_aliases(\%alias) if $opt_e;
member_of(\%alias) if $opt_m;
report_bad_aliases(\%alias) if $opt_r;

sub member_of
{
  local *alias = shift;
  my %members = memberalias(\%alias);

  for $_ (@ARGV)
  {
    if ($members{$_})
    {
      print "$_ is member of $members{$_}\n";
    }
    else
    {
      print "$_ is not member of anything\n";
    }
  }
}

sub expand_aliases
{
  local *alias = shift;
  for $_ (@ARGV)
  {
    my @expand=expandalias(\%alias,$_);
    if ($expand[-1])
    {
      print "$_ expands to @expand\n";
    }
    else
    {
```

```
          print "$_ not found in alias DB\n";
      }
   }
}

sub report_bad_aliases
{
   local *alias = shift;
   my %erroralias;
   for my $aliasname (keys %alias)
   {
      my @members = expandalias(\%alias,$aliasname);
      for my $member (@members)
      {
         if ($member)
         {
            unless (($member =~ /.*@.*/) ||
                    ($member =~ /^\/.*/) ||
                    ($member =~ /["!|]/))
            {
               $erroralias{$aliasname} .=
                   "$member "
                   unless getpwnam(lc($member));
            }
         }
      }
   }
   if (keys %erroralias)
   {
      for my $aliasname (keys %erroralias)
      {
         print("Alias $aliasname has ",
               "missing members:",
               $erroralias{$aliasname},"\n");
      }
   }
   else
   {
      print "No problems found";
   }
}
```

```perl
sub readaliases
{
  my $file = shift;
  my (%alias,$aliasname,$members);
  open(D,"<$file")
    || die "Cannot open $file, $!";
  while (<D>)
  {
    next if /^#/;
    chomp;
    ($aliasname,$members) = split /:\s+/;
    $alias{(lc($aliasname))} = lc($members);
  }
  close(D) || return 0;;
  return(%alias);
}

sub expandalias
{
    *alias = shift;
    my $expand = shift;
    my @expanded;
    my @toexpand = split /\s*,\s*/,$expand;

    return(0) unless $alias{$expand};

 OUTEXPAND:
  {
    while ($#toexpand >= 0)
    {
        my $toexpand = pop @toexpand;
      EXPAND:
        {
          if (defined($alias{$toexpand}))
          {
            if (defined($alias{$alias{$toexpand}}))
            {
              $toexpand = $alias{$alias{$toexpand}};
              redo EXPAND;
            }
            $toexpand = $alias{$toexpand};
          }
        }
```

```perl
      if ($toexpand =~ /,/)
      {
        push @toexpand,split(/\s*,\s*/,$toexpand);
        redo OUTEXPAND;
      }
      else
      {
        push @expanded,$toexpand;
      }
    }
  }
  my %dedupe;
  for (@expanded)
  {
    $dedupe{$_} = 1;
  }
  return (keys %dedupe);
}

sub expandaliases
{
  *alias = shift;

  EXPAND:
  {
    for $_ (sort keys %alias)
    {
      if (defined($alias{$alias{$_}}))
      {
        delete $alias{$_};
        redo EXPAND;
      }
    }
  }
}

sub memberalias
{
  *alias = shift;
  my %mteams;

  for my $aliasname (keys %alias)
  {
```

```
    for my $member (split /,/,$alias{$aliasname})
    {
      $mteams{$member} .= "$aliasname ";
    }
  }
  return %mteams;
}
```

The script is quite straightforward—the **read_aliases** function imports the alias file into an internal hash (which is essentially what a DBM file is) and then resolves the addresses when requested.

The report option verifies that an alias resolves fully, either to other aliases, or to log in entries from the **/etc/passwd** file. For example:

```
$ chkalias.pl -r -f alias.txt
```

Or, we can individually expand an alias:

```
$ chkalias.pl -f alias.txt -e postmaster
```

Simple HTTP Server

Here's a script that does the opposite: it provides a Web server that could be used for serving some very simple Web sites. It supports the basic GET method used to transfer information and uses nothing but the standard Perl library, so it can be used on any machine that supports sockets and Perl without you having to worry about installing additional modules.

```
#!/usr/local/bin/perl5

use Socket;
use FileHandle;
use Cwd;
use Getopt::Std;
use strict;

my ($error, $opt_d, $remaddr);

getopts('d');

sub listensocket
{
```

```perl
my ($SOCKETHANDLE, $service_name,
    $protocol_name, $queuelength) = @_;
my ($port_num, $sock_type, $protocol_num,
    $local_socket);

$protocol_num
    = (getprotobyname($protocol_name))[2];
unless ($protocol_num)
{
  $error = "Couldn't find protocol $protocol_name";
  return;
}
$sock_type = $protocol_name eq "tcp"
    ? SOCK_STREAM : SOCK_DGRAM ;

if( $service_name =~ /^\d+$/)
{
  $port_num = $service_name;
}
else
{
  $port_num = (getservbyname($service_name,
                             $protocol_name))[2];
  unless($port_num)
  {
    $error = "Can't find service $service_name";
    return;
  }
}

unless(socket($SOCKETHANDLE, PF_INET,
              $sock_type, $protocol_num))
{
  $error = "Couldn't create a socket: $!";
  return;
}
unless(setsockopt($SOCKETHANDLE,SOL_SOCKET,
                  SO_REUSEADDR,pack("l",1)))
{
  $error = "Couldn't set socket options: $!";
  return;
}
$local_socket = sockaddr_in($port_num, INADDR_ANY);
unless(bind($SOCKETHANDLE, $local_socket))
{
  $error = "Failed to Bind to socket: $!";
  return;
}
unless(listen($SOCKETHANDLE, $queuelength))
{
```

```perl
    $error = "Couldn't listen on socket: $!";
    return;
  }
  return(1);
}

$SIG{'INT'} = $SIG{'QUIT'} = \&exit_request_handler;
$SIG{'CHLD'} = \&child_handler;

my ($res);
my ($SERVERPORT) = 4003;

unless(listensocket(*SERVERSOCKET, $SERVERPORT, 'tcp', 5))
{
    die "$0: ", $error;
}

autoflush SERVERSOCKET 1;

chroot(getcwd());
die "$0: Couldn't change root directory, you root?"
    unless (getcwd() eq "/");

print "Changing root to ", getcwd(), "\n" if $opt_d;

print "Simple HTTP Server Started\n" if $opt_d;

while(1)
{
 ACCEPT_CONNECT:
  {
     ($remaddr = accept(CHILDSOCKET, SERVERSOCKET))
        || redo ACCEPT_CONNECT;
  }
  autoflush CHILDSOCKET 1;
  my $pid = fork();
  die "Cannot fork, $!" unless defined($pid);
  if ($pid == 0)
  {
    my ($remip)
     = inet_ntoa((unpack_sockaddr_in($remaddr))[1]);
    print "Connection accepted from $remip\n"
        if $opt_d;
    $_ = <CHILDSOCKET>;
    print "Got Request $_" if $opt_d;
    chomp;

    unless (m/(\S+)  (\S+)/)
    {
```

```perl
            print "Malformed request string $_\n"
                if $opt_d;
            bad_request(*CHILDSOCKET);
        }
        else
        {
            my ($command) = $1;
            my ($arg) = $2;
            if (uc($command) eq 'GET')
            {
                if (open(FILE, "<$arg"))
                {
                    while(<FILE>)
                    {
                        print CHILDSOCKET $_;
                    }
                    close(FILE);
                }
                else
                {
                    bad_request(*CHILDSOCKET);
                }
            }
        }
        close(CHILDSOCKET);
        exit(0);
    }
    close(CHILDSOCKET);
}

sub bad_request
{
    my ($SOCKET) = shift;

    print $SOCKET <<EOF
<html>
<head>
<title>Bad Request</title>
</head>
<body>
<h1>Bad Request</h1>
The file you requested could not be found
</body>
</html>
EOF
    ;
}

sub child_handler
{
```

```
    wait;
}

sub exit_request_handler
{
    my ($recvsig) = @_;
    $SIG{'INT'} = $SIG{'QUIT'} = 'IGNORE';
    close(SERVERSOCKET);
    close(CHILDSOCKET);
    die "Qutting on signal $recvsig\n";
}
```

The **listensocket** function is a general-purpose function used to initialize a socket handle for listening for connections—you can use this in other scripts if you want to support your own network server. The script also demonstrates the use of **fork** for supporting multiple client connections on a single server. This is a form of multiprocessing within a single script, but it does not quite offer the same advantages of threads.

Mail Filter

In the modern world, it is next to impossible to have an e-mail account without getting some level of junk e-mail. On a Unix system, you can use a mail filter and your **.forward** mail forwarding file to filter your e-mail based on a simple processing language. Many different systems have been produced, but most rely on a simple processing and rules-based language that is somewhat restrictive.

The alternative is to use something like the script below to parse your incoming e-mail messages, and then make use of Perl, a far less restrictive language, to make decisions about what you want to do with your e-mail.

This script requires the **libnet** package by Graham Barr, which is available on your local CPAN archive. You need the **Net::SMTP** module so that you can communicate directly with a mail server for forwarding or replying to e-mail automatically.

```
#!/usr/local/bin/perl5

use Net::SMTP;
use strict;
```

```perl
my (%mailheader,@message,@mailbody,$keyword,
    $value,$field,$error);
my ($filtscript);
my ($user) = $ENV{'USER'} || $ENV{'LOGNAME'} ||
             getlogin || (getpwuid($>))[0];
my ($homedir) = (getpwnam($user))[7];

close(STDERR);
close(STDOUT);
my $state=1;

while(<STDIN>)
{
    chomp;
    push @message,$_;
    if (length($_) eq 0)
    {
        $state=0;
        next;
    }
    if ($state)
    {
        if ( m/^From\s/)
        {
            next;
        }
        elsif ( m/(^[\w\-\.]+):\s*(.*\S)\s*$/)
        {
            $keyword = lc($1);
            $value = $2;
            $mailheader{$keyword} = $value;
        }
        else
        {
            $mailheader{$keyword} .= "\n" . $_;
        }
    }
    else
    {
        push @mailbody,$_;
    }
}
close(STDIN);

$filtscript
    = read_parse_script("$homedir/.mailfilt.cfg");
```

```perl
eval $filtscript;

if ($@)
{
    write_local_mail(join("\n",@message));
    write_local_error($@);
}

sub read_parse_script
{
    my($file) = @_;
    my $permissions = (stat($file))[2];

    unless ($permissions & 00600)
    {
        write_local_error("Bad permissions "
                         . " on config file $file");
        return(undef);
    }
    unless(open(D,"<$file"))
    {
        write_local_error("Can't open "
                         . "config $file, $!");
        return(undef);
    }
    {
        local $/;
        $file=<D>;
    }
    close(D)
        || write_local_error("Can't close "
                             "config $file, $!");
    $file;
}

sub write_local_error
{
    my ($error) = @_;

    my $message = "To: $user\n";
    $message .= "From: Mailfilter "
              . "(local program) <$user>\n";
    $message .= "Subject: Mail Filter Error\n\n";
    $message .= "$error\n";
    write_local_mail($message);
}
```

```perl
sub write_local_mail
{
    my ($message) = @_;
    my ($sec,$min,$hour,$mday,$mon)
        = (localtime(time))[0-4];
    my $tempfile
        = "/tmp/ml.$user.$mday$mon$hour$min$sec.$$";
    open(T,">$tempfile")
        || die "Cant open temp file,$!";
    print T $message,"\n";
    close(T);
    system('/bin/rmail -d $user < $tempfile');
    unlink("/tmp/ml.$$");
}

sub forward_mail
{
    my ($to) = @_;
    $mailheader{to} = $mailheader{'apparently-to'}
                    unless $mailheader{to};
    my $subject = $mailheader{subject} ?
        "FWD: $mailheader{subject}"
        : "FWD: <no subject>";

    unless(mail_a_message($subject,$to,
                    clean_address($mailheader{to}),
                    join("\n",@message)))
    {
        write_local_mail(join("\n",@message));
        write_local_error("Forwarding mail, "
                        . $SMTPwrap::error");
    }
}

sub anonymous_forward
{
    my ($toaddress) = @_;
    my $message;
    my @fields = qw(Date From Reply-To
                    Organization X-Mailer
                    Mime-Version Subject
                    Content-Type
                    Content-Transfer-Encoding);

    foreach $field (@fields)
    {
```

```perl
        $message .= "$field: " . $mailheader{$field}
                . "\n"
            if defined($mailheader{$field});
    }

    $message .= "\n";
    $message .= join("\n",@mailbody);
    $message .= "\n";

    unless(send_smtp($toaddress,
                    $mailheader{from},
                    $message))
    {
        write_local_mail(join("\n",@message));
        write_local_error("Anonymous Forward, "
                        . "$SMTPwrap::error");
    }
}

sub send_smtp
{
    my ($to,$from,$message) = @_;
    my $smtp = Net::SMTP->new('mail');
    unless($smtp)
    {
        $error = "Couldn't connect to mail server";
        return 0;
    }
    unless($smtp->mail($from))
    {
        $error = "Bad 'From' address specified";
        return 0;
    }
    unless($smtp->to($to))
    {
        $error = "Bad 'To' address specified";
        return 0;
    }
    unless($smtp->data())
    {
        $error = "Not ready to accept data";
        return 0;
    }
```

```perl
    $smtp->datasend($message);
    unless($smtp->dataend())
    {
        $error = "Bad response when sending data";
        return 0;
    }
    unless($smtp->quit())
    {
        $error = "Error closing SMTP connection";
        return 0;
    }
    1;
}

sub mail_a_message
{
    my ($subject,$to,$from,$message) = @_;
    my ($newmessage);

    $newmessage .= "To: $to\n";
    $newmessage .= "From: $from\n";
    $newmessage .= "Subject: $subject\n";
    $newmessage .= "\n" . $message;

    send_smtp($to,$from,$newmessage);
}

sub return_address
{
    my ($hash) = shift;

    $$hash{'reply-to'} || $$hash{'from'} ||
        $$hash{'return-path'} ||
        $$hash{'apparently-from'};
}

sub clean_address
{
    local($_) = @_;
    s/\s*\(.*\)\s*//;
    1 while s/.*<(.*)>.*/$1/;
    s/^\s*(.*\S)\s*$/$1/;
    $_;
}
```

IV

The process for the script is to digest an incoming e-mail into the e-mail headers and the message body. The information is placed into variables, which can then be used in combination by an external script (in **.mailfilt.cfg**), which is parsed by the **eval** function to process and forward, format, reject, or file e-mail.

To use the script, you need to write some Perl that identifies the message contents before either writing the message to the local mail file, or forwarding it elsewhere. You also need to specify the script as the mail handler within your **.mailfilt.cfg** file:

```
"|/usr/local/bin/mailfilt.pl"
```

If you specify nothing else, or if you don't want your mail to be filtered, then you must at least specify that a message is written to your mailbox. Otherwise, all incoming will be deleted:

```
write_local_mail(join("\n",@message));
```

If you want to specify an option, you can just use standard Perl. For example, to forward all mail with a subject of "Win," you would put the following line into your mail filter configuration file:

```
forward_mail('mc@foo.bar')
    if ($mailheader{subject} eq 'Win');
```

Of course, because the mail filtering rules are based on Perl, you can put any Perl code into the mail filter configuration. This doesn't restrict you to a list of available options when an e-mail is received. You could use this script to automatically print e-mail when it arrived, or even to automatically forward failure warnings on your network to your home e-mail address when e-mail was received outside of normal working hours. The possibilities are, quite literally, limitless.

Web Site Mirror

If you are a Web developer, you are bound to have come across the situation where you need to download one or more pages from a Web site. There are many tools that can do this for you, but when you have Perl available to you, there seems little reason to look for an alternative solution.

You can use the network tricks seen in earlier examples to
download a single page, but how do you download the pages and
graphics contained within the HTML? The trick is to parse the file
that you download to identify the graphics and links that need to
be downloaded. Furthermore, you need to be able to record which
pages you've downloaded so you don't download the same page
more than once.

The first problem is solved by the excellent **LWP** module bundle by
Gisle Aas. This module, perhaps better known as **libwww-perl**,
provides everything you should need to create and extract
information to and from HTML files. The module bundle also
includes an **LWP::UserAgent** module that provides a much simpler
system for downloading files from the Internet by supplying a
simple URL. Using a combination of the download and parsing
features, you can retrieve a file, extract a list of links, add it to the
list, and then repeat the process on the next entry.

IV

```perl
#!/usr/local/bin/perl

use strict;
use LWP::Simple;
use LWP::UserAgent;
use HTML::LinkExtor;
use URI::URL;
use Getopt::Long;
use File::Basename;

my ($file,$host,$localdir,$curhost);
my ($url, $specdir, $quiet,
    $silent, $inchost, $unrestrict);

usage() unless(GetOptions("d=s" => \$specdir,
                           "s"   => \$silent,
                           "q"   => \$quiet,
                           "h"   => \$inchost,
                           "u"   => \$unrestrict
                          ));

usage() unless($url=shift);
$specdir = '.' unless defined($specdir);
$specdir = "$specdir/" unless ($specdir =~ m#/$#);
$quiet = 1 if ($silent);
```

```perl
my %fullurl;
my @urlstack = ($url);
my @urls = ();
my $p = HTML::LinkExtor->new(\&callback);

my $ua = new LWP::UserAgent;
my $res
    = $ua->request(HTTP::Request->new(GET => $url));
my $base = $res->base;
$curhost = $host = url($url,'')->host;

print "Retrieving from $url to $specdir",
      ($inchost ? "$host\n" : "\n")
          unless ($silent);

while ($url = pop(@urlstack))
{
    $host = url($url,'')->host;
    if ($host ne $curhost)
    {
        my $ua = new LWP::UserAgent;
        my $res
          = $ua->request(HTTP::Request->new(GET=>
                                            $url));
        my $base = $res->base;
        $host = url($url,'')->host;
        $curhost = $host;
        print "Changing host to $host\n"
            unless $quiet;
    }
    $localdir = ($inchost ? "$specdir$host/"
                          : "$specdir/");

    $file = url($url,$base)->full_path;
    $file .='index.html' if ($file =~ m#/$#);
    $file =~ s#^/#$localdir#;

    print "Retrieving: $url to $file\n"
        unless ($quiet);
    my $dir = dirname($file);
    unless (-d $dir)
    {
        mkdirhier($dir);
    }
    getfile($url,$file);
```

```
      if (-e $file)
      {
        $p->parse_file($file);
        @urls = map {$_ = url($_, $base)->abs;} @urls;
        addtostack(@urls);
      }
}

sub addtostack
{
    my (@urllist) = @_;

    for my $url (@urllist)
    {
        next if ($url =~ /#/);
        next unless ($url =~ m#^http#);
        my $urlhost = url($url,$base)->host;
        unless (defined($unrestrict))
            { next unless ($urlhost eq $host); };
        push(@urlstack,$url)
            unless(defined($fullurl{$url}));
        $fullurl{$url} = 1;
    }
}

sub callback
{
    my($tag, %attr) = @_;
    push(@urls, values %attr);
}

sub getfile
{
    my ($url,$file) = @_;
    my $rc = mirror($url, $file);

    if ($rc == 304)
    {
        print "File is up to date\n" unless ($quiet);
    }
    elsif (!is_success($rc))
    {
        warn "sitemirr: $rc ",
            status_message($rc),
            " ($url)\n"
```

```
                      unless ($silent);
              return(0);
      }
}

sub mkdirhier
{
  my ($fullpath) = @_;
  my $path;

  for my $dir (split(m#/#,$fullpath))
  {
    unless (-d "$path$dir")
    {
      mkdir("$path$dir",0777)
        or die "Couldn't make dir $path/$dir: $!";
    }
    $path .= "$dir/";
  }
}

sub usage
{
    die <<EOF;
Usage:
    sitemirr.pl [-d localdir] [-s] [-q] URL

Where:

localdir is the name of the local directory you want
        files copied to (default: .)
h        Include host in local directory path
q        Retrieve quietly (show errors only)
s        Retrieve silently (no output)
u        Unrestrict site match (will download ALL
        URL's, including those from other hosts)
EOF
}
```

You can see the options for using the script in the last part of the example preceding. For example, to download the Osborne/McGraw-Hill site to your local machine, you might use this command line:

```
$ sitemirr.pl -h www.mcgraw-hill.com
```

This would download the entire site to the current directory, within a directory called www.mcgraw-hill.com.

Note that the default option is to restrict the downloaded URLs only to those from the same machine as the original. Using the **–u** option will solve this, since it will allow you to download pages from other machines too—unfortunately, it also has the side effect of potentially downloading the entire Internet!

FTP Synchronization

IV

The typical process for developing and publishing a Web site is to first design the site, then check it, and finally release it. Unless you are hosting your site on one of your own servers, chances are you are using a Web hosting service provided by an Internet Service Provider (ISP). The process for getting your site uploaded to the site usually involves using FTP to transfer the files over to a secure directory on the remote server.

Although there are tools that help in the process of uploading sites, the programs are often limited to copying over the selected set of files in a single directory. Even if they do support the option of uploading an entire directory structure, you have to copy the entire directory structure to the destination. To speed up the process of updating an existing Web site, it makes sense to copy to the server only any items that have changed.

I wrote the script below to download my Web sites from my local machine to my Web hosting service without all the pain and difficulties associated with manually uploading the files. The script uses the **File::Find** module (see Part 3) to process through a local directory and choose which files to upload to the remote host using the **Net::FTP** module, which is part of the **libnet** bundle. The module takes automatic account of the times the files were updated at each end and automatically switches the connection between binary and ASCII modes as it progresses through the local file hierarchy.

```
#!/usr/local/bin/perl5

use Net::FTP;
use Getopt::Long;
```

```perl
use File::Find;
use Cwd;

my $debug       = 1;
my $remserver   = undef;
my $remport     = '21';
my $user        = 'anonymous';
my $password    = 'me@foo.bar';
my $dir         = '.';
my $localdir    = './';
my $curxfermode = 'ASCII';

unless (GetOptions("d" => \$debug,
                   "s=s" => \$remserver,
                   "r=s" => \$dir,
                   "p=i" => \$remport,
                   "u=s" => \$user,
                   "w=s" => \$password,
                   "l=s" => \$localdir
                   ))
{
    usage();
}

usage() unless $remserver;

$localdir = './' unless ($localdir);
my $ftp = Net::FTP->new($remserver,
                        'Port' => $remport);
die "Could not connect to $remserver"
    unless $ftp;
$ftp->login($user, $password)
    or die "Couldn't login to $remserver";
$ftp->cwd($dir)
    or die "Invalid directory ($dir) on FTP Server";
$ftp->ascii()
    or warn "Couldn't change set xfer mode, continuing";

chdir($localdir);
my $currentdir = getcwd();
find(\&sendfile,'.');

$ftp->quit();

sub sendfile
{
  my $file       =  $File::Find::name;
  $file          =~ s#^\./##g;
  my $localfile  =  "$currentdir/$file";
  $localfile     =~ s#//#/#g;
```

```perl
my $remfile   =  $file;

print "Processing $localfile rem($remfile)\n"
    if $debug;

if (-d $localfile)
{
  my $remcurdir = $ftp->pwd();
  unless($ftp->cwd($remfile))
  {
    unless ($localfile eq '..')
    {
      print "Making directory $remfile\n";
      $ftp->mkdir($remfile,1) or
        die "Couldn't make directory $remfile";
    }
  }
  else
  {
    $ftp->cwd($remcurdir) or
        die "Couldn't change to directory $currentdir";
  }
}
else
{
  my ($remtime,$localtime,$upload) = (undef,undef,0);
  unless($remtime = $ftp->mdtm($remfile))
  {
      $remtime = 0;
  }
  $localtime = (stat($file))[9];
  if (defined($localtime) and defined($remtime))
  {
      if ($localtime > $remtime)
      {
          $upload=1;
      }
  }
  else
  {
      $upload=1;
  }
  if ($upload)
  {
    if (-B $localfile)
    {
        if ($curxfermode eq 'ASCII')
        {
          if ($ftp->binary())
          {
```

IV

```perl
          $curxfermode = 'BIN';
          print "Changed mode to BINary\n"
            if $debug;
        }
        else
        {
          warn "Couldn't change transfer mode";
        }
      }
    }
      else
      {
        if ($curxfermode eq 'BIN')
        {
          if ($ftp->ascii())
          {
            $curxfermode = 'ASCII';
            print "Changed mode to ASCII\n"
              if $debug;
          }
          else
          {
            warn "Couldn't change transfer mode";
          }
        }
      }
      print "Uploading $localfile to $remfile\n"
        if $debug;
      $ftp->put($localfile,$remfile)
          or warn "Couldn't upload $remfile";
    }
    else
    {
      print "File $remfile appears up to date\n"
          if $debug;
    }
  }
}

sub usage
{
    print <<EOF;
Usage:

    uplsite.pl [-d] [-r remdir] [-p remport]
               [-u user] [-w password]
               [-l localdir] -s server

Description:
```

```
Uploads directory structure to the server using FTP.

Where:

-d  Switch on debugging output
-r  Remote directory to upload to (defaults to .)
-p  The remote port to use (defaults to 21)
-u  The user name to login as (default anonymous)
-w  The password to use (defaults to me\@foo.bar)
-l  The local directory to upload from (default .)
-s  The remote server address to upload to (reqd.)

EOF
    exit 1;
}
```

For example, if you wanted to upload the directory of your local Web site to one provided by an ISP, you might use this command line:

```
$ uplsite.pl -r public_html -l /usr/local/etc/httpd/htdocs
            -s www.mcwords.com -u user -w password
```

Although I've marketed this as a script for uploading Web sites, it could in fact be used to duplicate any structure on any remote machine acting as an FTP server. I successfully used this script to back up a Unix machine to a MacOS server—it is the Mac that has the backup tape drive attached, and the network backup allows me to avoid detaching and attaching the tape drive between the two machines.

IV

Part 5
Execution Environment

The execution and invocation of Perl can be controlled through a combination of the internal switches and command line switches. Script-based configurations change the execution of the script every time it is executed, but command line switches can be selected and used during individual invocations. Perl also takes some of its configuration information from optional environment variables.

Command Line Options

Perl supports a number of command line options. These can be specified either on the actual command line if you are manually executing Perl, or within the #! line at the start of the script. If you are using the latter method, be aware that some Unix systems place a limit on the size of the line.

In either case, command line options can either be selected individually, as in:

```
$ perl p -i.bak -e "s/foo/bar/g"
```

or combined, as in:

```
$ perl -pi.bak -e "s/foo/bar/g"
```

You can also specifically terminate command-line options by using a double hyphen. Any further arguments will be passed on to the script as the contents of @**ARGV**.

-a

Turns on autosplit mode (implies the **split** function); fields are split into the @**F** array. The use of the **-a** option is equivalent to

```
while (<>)
{
    @F = split(' ');
}
```

This is generally used with the **–n** or **–p** options to automatically split and/or summarize a group of input files.

–c

This checks the syntax of the script without executing it. Only **BEGIN** and **END** blocks and **use** statements are actually executed by this process since they are considered an integral part of the compilation process.

–d(:module)

Without the optional **module**, this invokes the Perl debugger after your script has been compiled and places the program counter within the debugger at the start of your script. If **module** is specified, then the script is compiled and control of the execution is passed to the specified module. For example, **–d:Dprof** invokes the Perl profiling system.

–Dflags

This specifies the debugging options defined by **flags**, as seen in the following table. Note that options can be selected by either their letter combination or by specifying decimal value of the combined options. For example, to switch on taint checks and memory allocation you would use **–Dmu** or **–D2176**.

Number	Letter	Description
1	p	Tokenizing and parsing
2	s	Stack snapshots
4	l	Context (loop) stack processing
8	t	Trace execution
16	o	Method and overloading resolution
32	c	String/numeric conversions
64	P	Print preprocessor command for **–P**
128	m	Memory allocation

Number	Letter	Description
256	f	Format processing
512	r	Regular expression parsing and execution
1024	x	Syntax tree dump
2048	u	Tainting checks
4096	L	Memory leaks (you need to have used the **–DLEAKTEST** directive when compiling Perl)
8192	H	Hash dump
16384	X	Scratchpad allocation
32768	D	Cleaning up
65536	S	Thread synchronization

You will need to have compiled Perl with the **–DDEBUGGING** compiler directive for these debugging flags to work.

-e commandline

The **commandline** will be interpreted as a single line Perl script. For example,

```
$ perl -e 'print 4+5,"\n";'
```

will print 9. You can define multiple lines by placing all of the semicolon-terminated lines within the quotes. This can also be split over multiple lines:

```
$ perl -e '
$result =  4+5;
print "$result\n";
'
9
```

-F regex

This specifies the pattern to use for splitting when the **-a** command line option is in use. By default, the value used is a single space. The **regex** can be specified including any of the normal delimiters allowed by **split**, that is, ", "", and //.

–h

This prints the Perl usage summary but does not execute the Perl interpreter.

–iext

This edits the file "in place," that is, modifications and edits are carried out on the file directly, rather than sending the modifications to the standard output. The optional **ext** defines the extension to append to the old version of the file. What actually happens is that the file is moved to the backup version (with **ext** appended), and then the file and edits are written back into a file with the original name. If **ext** is not specified, then a temporary file is used.

This option is generally used with the **–p** and **–e** options to edit a series of files in loop. For example, the command line,

```
$ perl -pi.bak -e "s/foo/bar/g" *
```

replaces every occurrence of *foo* with *bar* in all the files in the current directory. The contents of the original files are stored in the files with names ending **.bak**.

Note that you must append the extension including a period if desired; Perl does not add any characters to the backup file except those specified.

–Idir

Prepends the directory **dir** to the list used to search for modules (**@INC**) and the directories for the C preprocessor (invoked with **–P**) to look for include files. See also the **use lib** pragma in Section 3 and the **PERLLIB** and **PERL5LIB** environment variables.

–l(char)

This option sets the character **char** that will automatically be appended to all printed output and uses **chomp** to remove the existing line termination character on input. The specification should be via the octal equivalent. By default, no characters are automatically added to printed lines. If **char** is not is not specified, the value of the output record separator (**$**) will equal the value of the input record separator (**$/**).

This can be used to help convert files between formats. For example, to reverse the field order of a colon-delimited database, you might use something like this:

```
$ perl -lpi -e '$_ = join(":",reverse split /:/);'
passwd
```

If you didn't use the –l option, then the new first field of each line would have a trailing new line.

–mmodule

See –Mmodule.

–Mmodule

Includes the module specified by **module** before executing your script and allows you to specify additional options to the **use** statement generated. For example, the command line

```
$ perl -MPOSIX=:fcntl_h,:float_h
```

is equivalent to

```
use POSIX qw/:fcntl_h :float_h/;
```

The **−M** form also allows you to use quotes to specify the options; for example, the above line could be written as:

```
$ perl -M'POSIX qw/:fcntl_h :float_h/'
```

In both cases, a single hyphen as the first character after **−M** or **−m** indicates that **no** should be used in place of **use**.

This option causes Perl to assume the following code around your script for each file specified on the command line:

```
while(<>)
{
# Your script
}
```

Note that the contents of the files are not printed or otherwise output during execution, unless specified within the script itself. Any files in the list of those to be opened that cannot be opened are reported as errors, and execution continues on to the next file in the list.

This option causes Perl to assume the following code around your script for each file specified on the command line:

```
while(<>)
{
# Your script
}
continue
{
    print or die "-p destination: $!\n";
}
```

As you can see, an error during printing/updating is considered fatal. The **–p** option overrides the **–n** option.

Any files in the list of those to be opened that cannot be opened are reported as errors, and execution continues on to the next file in the list.

–P

This invokes the C preprocessor on the script before it is parsed by the Perl interpreter. Care should be taken when using comments in the original C source, since lines starting with a # character and a keyword such as **if**, **else** or **define** will be interpreted as a preprocessor directive.

–s

This enables basic command line switching. Once this option has been set, any command line options specified after the script name are interpreted as the names of variables, with their value being set to true within the script. For example,

```
$ perl -s t.pl -true
```

will create a variable **$true** within the current invocation of t.pl.

A more advanced system is to use the **Getopt::Long** or **Getopt::Std** modules.

–S

This uses the **$PATH** environment variable to find the script. It will also add extensions to the script being searched for if a lookup on the original name fails.

–T

This switches on taint checking. Variables and information that originates or derives from external sources are considered to be unsafe and will cause your script to fail when used in functions such as **system**. This is most often used when a script is executed on behalf of another process such as a Web server. You should specify this option at the start of the command line options to ensure that taint checking is switched on as early as possible.

–u

This causes Perl to dump the program core of the interpreter and script after compilation (and before execution). In theory, this can be used with an **undump** program to produce a standalone executable. The Perl-to-C compiler has superceded this option (refer to the information on the Perl Compiler in Section 7). See also the **dump** function in Section 2.

–U

This allows the Perl script to do unsafe operations. These currently include only the unlinking of directories when you are a superuser. This option will also turn fatal taint checks into warnings, provided the **–w** option is also specified.

–v

This option prints the version and patch level of the Perl interpreter but does not execute the interpreter.

–V(:var)

This option prints the version and configuration information for the Perl interpreter. If the optional **var** is supplied, then it prints out only the configuration information for the specified element as discovered via the **Config** module. Here is the default output from the function:

```
perl -V
Summary of my perl5 (5.0 patchlevel 5 subversion 53) configuration:
  Platform:
    osname=solaris, osvers=2.4, archname=sun4-solaris
    uname='sunos twinspark 5.4 generic_101945-59 sun4c sparc '
    hint=previous, useposix=true, d_sigaction=define
    usethreads=undef useperlio=undef d_sfio=undef
  Compiler:
    cc='gcc -B/usr/ccs/bin/', optimize='-O', gccversion=2.8.1
    cppflags='-I/usr/local/include'
    ccflags ='-I/usr/local/include -DDEBUGGING'
    stdchar='unsigned char', d_stdstdio=define, usevfork=false
    intsize=4, longsize=4, ptrsize=4, doublesize=8
    d_longlong=define, longlongsize=8, d_longdbl=define,
    longdblsize=16, alignbytes=8, usemymalloc=y, prototype=define
  Linker and Libraries:
    ld='gcc -B/usr/ccs/bin/', ldflags =' -L/usr/local/lib'
    libpth=/usr/local/lib /lib /usr/lib /usr/ccs/lib
    libs=-lsocket -lnsl -lgdbm -ldb -ldl -lm -lc -lcrypt
    libc=/lib/libc.so, so=so, useshrplib=false, libperl=libperl.a
  Dynamic Linking:
    dlsrc=dl_dlopen.xs, dlext=so, d_dlsymun=undef, ccdlflags=' '
    cccdlflags='-fPIC', lddlflags='-G -L/usr/local/lib'


Characteristics of this binary (from libperl):
  Compile-time options: DEBUGGING
```

V

```
Built under solaris
Compiled at Mar 18 1999 08:15:07
@INC:
  /usr/local/lib/perl5/5.00553/sun4-solaris
  /usr/local/lib/perl5/5.00553
  /usr/local/lib/perl5/site_perl/5.00553/sun4-solaris
  /usr/local/lib/perl5/site_perl/5.00553
  .
```

−w

This prints out warnings about possible typographical and interpretation errors in the script.

−x(dir)

This option extracts the script from an e-mail message or other piped data stream. Perl will ignore any information up to a line that starts with #! and contains the word **perl**. Any directory name will be used as the directory in which to run the script, and the command line switches contained in the line will be applied as usual. The script must be terminated either by an EOF or an __END__ marker.

This option can be used to execute code stored in e-mail messages without first requiring you to extract the script element.

−0(val)

This option specifies the initial value for the input record separator **$/**.

Perl Environment Variables

The effects of certain elements of Perl and Perl functions can be modified by environment variables. Many of these variables are set automatically by your shell. In the case of MacPerl, these values can be configured within the MacPerl environment.

HOME

This is the home directory for the script. It's used by **chdir** if no argument is specified.

LOGDIR

This option is used by **chdir** if no argument is specified and the **HOME** environment variable is not set.

PATH

This is the list of directories searched when invoking a command via **system**, **exec**, **backticks**, or other external application callers. This is also the directory list searched with the **–S** command line option.

PERLLIB

This is the colon-delimited list of directories used to look for the modules and libraries required for the Perl script. Note that this list overrides the values defined within the interpreter. This variable is ignored if **PERL5LIB** has been set.

PERL5LIB

This is the colon-delimited list of directories used to look for the modules and libraries required for the Perl script. Note that this list overrides the values defined within the interpreter.

The values here can be added to or overridden entirely using the **use lib** pragma (see Part 3, "User Interface") and the –l command line option (see above). Note that only the **use lib** pragma is supported when taint checking is in effect.

PERL5OPT

This option allows you to predefine any of the **DIMUdmw** command line switches for every invocation of the Perl interpreter. The variable is ignored when taint checking is in effect.

PERL5DB

This is the command used to load the debugger code when the –d option is specified on the command line. The default value is

```
BEGIN {require 'perl5db.pl' }
```

You can use this variable to permanently enable profiling or use an alternative debugger (including those with windowed interfaces).

PERL5SHELL

This is specific to the Win32 port of Perl. This specifies the alternative shell that Perl should use internally for executing external commands via **system** or **backticks**. The default under

Windows NT is to use the standard **cmd.exe** with the **/x/c** switches. Under Windows 95, the **command.com /c** command is used instead.

PERL_DEBUG_MSTATS

This option causes the memory statistics for the script to be dumped after execution. It only works if Perl has been compiled with the Perl's own version of the **malloc()** function. You can use

```
$ perl -V:d_mymalloc
```

to determine whether this is the case. A value of **define** indicates that Perl's **malloc()** is being used.

PERL_DESTRUCT_LEVEL

This controls the destruction of global objects and other references, but only if the Perl interpreter has been compiled with the **–DDEBUGGING** compiler directive.

Threads

Threads are an experimental feature of Perl with v5.005, and must be explicitly built into the Perl interpreter. They offer a simpler and more controllable method of performing multiple tasks than the usual **fork** method. The details below may be subject to change in later versions, although the basic principles outlined here should remain constant.

To create a new thread, import the **Thread** module and then create a new **Thread** object.

For example, to create a new thread that uses the subroutine **process_queue**:

```
use Thread;
$thread = new Thread \&process_queue,"/usr/
    local/queue";
```

You can supply arguments to be sent to the function as additional arguments to the new object creation. The **$thread** variable in the above example contains a reference to the newly created thread and will provide a link from the main program to the thread. The thread can obtain a reference to itself with the self method:

```
$me = Thread->self;
```

Each thread is given its own unique thread ID. The main program has a thread ID of 0, and subsequent threads are given a sequential thread number up to a current maximum of $2^{32}-1$. You can discover the thread ID using the **tid** method:

```
$tid = $thread->tid;
```

Or for a thread to find its own ID:

```
$mytid = Thread->self->tid;
```

You can also get a list of all the running and finished threads (providing the thread has not been joined—see the next section) by using the **list** method:

```
@threads = Thread->list;
```

You'll need to process the information yourself, but the list of object references should be enough.

Controlling a Thread

There are three basic methods for controlling a thread once created and one function for controlling the processor cycles available to each thread. The **detach** method explicitly detaches a thread so that it runs independently.

The **join** method waits for a thread to end, returning any values the thread returned during the process of execution:

```
$result = $thread->join;
```

This can be used either to force the thread to block until the specified thread has finished, or to get a return value from the thread at the end of execution. If the specified thread exited as a result of a **die** function, then the error returned during the **die**, as would be trapped by **$@**, is returned instead. Since the join effectively combines the two threads, care will need to be taken if the specified thread dies after the **join** method has been called. If you want to prevent the calling thread from also dieing, then you should enclose the **join** method call in the eval statement.

The **eval** method on a thread automatically wraps an eval function around the **join** method. Return values from the thread are placed into **$@** as usual.

The **yield** function gives up processor cycles for the current function and redistributes them to other threads. This provides a crude method for prioritizing individual threads and assigning them processor time.

Controlling Variables

Sharing variables across threads is as dangerous and prone to error as sharing a database file across many processes. The basis for controlling access to the variables is much the same. You set a "lock" on the variable to indicate its status. Also, like the file locks that are available, the variable locks are advisory. Although you can lock a variable, there is nothing to prevent a thread from accessing or updating it. It is entirely up to the programmer to check the lock status and decide whether the variable should or should not be used. The main function for locking a variable is the **lock** function:

```
lock($var);
```

The lock set on the variable lasts as long as the scope of the current block. If a lock is already set on the variable by another thread, then the **lock** function will block execution of the current thread until the other has finished using it. Note that the lock is on the entity, not the contents, so a call such as

```
lock(@var);
```

only sets the lock on the **@var** variable, not the individual elements of the array.

Therefore, another call to **lock($var[0])** will not block. Also, references are only followed to one level such that a reference to lock **\$var** will work, but **\\$var** will not work. In addition, since subroutines are just other objects, you can also lock them using the lock function. Again, this blocks execution only if another thread tries to lock the subroutine.

Once a variable is locked, you can control the unlocking process with three separate functions: **cond_wait**, **cond_signal**, and **cond_broadcast**. The **cond_wait** function is the main one. It unlocks the variable and blocks until another thread does a **cond_signal** or **cond_broadcast** call for the variable. The function therefore enables you to wait until another process indicates (either through the **cond_signal** or **cond_broadcast** function) that the thread has finished using the variable. Once the **cond_wait** unblocks, the variable is locked again.

The **cond_wait** function takes one argument—a locked variable—and unblocks a random thread that is waiting for the variable via **cond_wait**. It is not possible to specify which thread is unblocked. You can unblock all waiting threads using the **cond_broadcast** function, which also takes a single (locked) variable as an argument.

This is a very complicated description of what is basically a simple process of indicators and signals that allow you to control access to a variable. Consider that you have two threads, A and B, and they both want to update a variable **$var**. Thread A locks the variable with lock and then starts its update. Meanwhile, thread B decides that it needs to update the variable, so it calls **cond_wait($var)**, effectively halting the B thread until A has finished.

Once A has completed the update, it calls **cond_signal($var)**, indicating to thread B that it has finished with the variable. The **cond_wait** function called from thread B then locks the variables for its own use and continues execution. This process of waiting and signaling the status of locked variables allows you to control access to them and prevent the corruption that could occur if two threads were to update the variable at the same time.

Fortunately, in the example, there are only two threads, and so the locking method is relatively straightforward. In a multithreaded process, controlling access to a single variable may be more difficult. You may want to try using either the queuing or semaphore method for divining information about the variables that you want to share among processes.

Queues

Although you can use ordinary variables for exchanging information between running threads, it often requires careful use of the **lock** function to ensure you are using the right value at the right time. If all you want to do is exchange simple information between threads, a better method is to use a simple stack. However, you can't use a simple scalar array, since that will exhibit the same (if not more complex) problems that you already know about regarding the **lock** and other functions.

Instead, the Perl thread system supports a message queue object. This is basically a standard array, except that it is thread compatible and handles additions and removals from the list safely without the normal risk of corruption to the variables.

To create a new queue:

```
use Thread::Queue;
my $queue = new Thread::Queue;
```

The list operates strictly on a LILO (last in, last out) format, so new entries are added to the end of the list, and entries are removed and returned from the start of list. The **enqueue** method adds a list of values to the end of the queue:

```
$thread->enqueue('Martin', 'Brown');
```

The **dequeue** function returns and removes a single scalar from the beginning of the queue:

```
$value = $thread->dequeue;
```

If the queue is empty, the thread blocks until there is an entry in the queue. To immediately return from a **dequeue** operation, you use the **dequeue_nb**, which does not block; it simply returns **undef** if the list is empty.

Finally, you can use the **pending** method to find out how many items are left on the queue. Note that this information is correct at the time the method was called, but this does not guarantee this is the actual value if multiple threads are accessing and using the queue simultaneously. To get around this, you can use the **lock** function seen earlier to lock the object so that its state is consistent between the pending method and when you use it.

Semaphores

A *semaphore* is defined in the dictionary as a system of signaling. In the realm of threads a semaphore can be used to indicate a particular occurrence to a thread. The information is provided in the form of a number, and this number can be increased or decreased accordingly. The method for employing the semaphore is to use the **Thread::Semaphore** module and create a new object:

```
$sema = new Thread::Semaphore;
```

The default value is one, or you can specify the initial value:

```
$sema = new Thread::Semaphore(256);
```

Two methods, **up** and **down**, then increase or decrease the value, either by the default value of one, or by the amount specified. For example, the code

```
$sema->up;
$sema->down(256);
```

will set the value of the **$sema** semaphore back to one.

How you use the semaphore value is entirely up to you. The usual method is to create a semaphore that relates to the available quantity of a specific resource.

Signals

Because signals could interrupt the normal execution process of the script, and even more so when working with threads, it can be a good idea to create a separate thread just for handling signals. This is practical not only for multithreaded applications, but also for applications that make use of pipes, non-blocking I/O, and even networking. Of course, by creating a new thread for signals, your script is now multithreaded, but it doesn't mean you have to create additional threads.

To create a new signal-handling thread, all you do is import the **Thread::Signal** module:

```
use Thread::Signal;
```

This automatically generates a new thread and causes all signals to the program to be handled within this thread. There is no difference in the way you set up signal handlers.

They can be assigned to existing functions or handled by anonymous subroutines, as usual. The difference is that the signal handlers execute within the realm of a new thread. This allows execution of the current process to continue when a signal is received.

There are some traps in this. Using **die** within a signal handler executed in the signal thread will cause the thread to exit, but won't necessarily cause the main thread to quit. This also means you will have problems when using exit within an extension, since this too will affect the signal handler thread and not the main program.

V

Part 6
Compiler and Debugger

Perl Compiler

The Perl compiler is available in Perl 5.005 and provides a method for converting Perl scripts into standalone executables. Note that the C code provided here is not a C version of the script, but a C-based representation of the internal Opcode structure used to execute all Perl scripts. In all cases, the compiler is considered experimental.

Perl Interface

You can use the **B** and **O** modules to convert a Perl script into a number of different formats. The method of operation is to use the following command line:

```
$ perl -MO=Backend[,OPTIONS] foo.pl
```

The supported Backends are summarized in the following table.

Backend	Description
C	Produces C code based on the state of the Perl script just before execution begins.
CC	Produces C code based on the state of the Perl script just before execution begins, with optimizations for the C-based environment.
Bytecode	Produces a platform-independent binary representation of the script in its compiled form.
Terse	Produces an Opcode tree in the script's compiled format.
Debug	Generates a more in-depth Opcode tree analysis of the execution process.
Xref	Generates a list of cross references for the functions and variables used within a script, specifying enclosing package or function names and line numbers.
Lint	Performs additional code-check tests beyond those normally produced with the **-w** command line option.

Backend	Description
Deparse	Produces an optimized version of the original Perl script by running the original through Perl's built-in compiler and optimizer.
ShowLex	Lists the lexical variables (as defined by **my** or **local**) used by a subroutine or file.

perlcc Interface

If what you want to achieve is a precompiled binary of your Perl script, then you can use the quicker **perlcc** Perl script that generates the C source and then compiles and links it for you automatically. The command

```
$ perlcc foo.pl
```

will compile **foo.pl** into the executable **foo**. If you specify a module, for example, **foo.pm**, then it will be compiled into a loadable shared object library **foo.so**. The various command line options available are listed next.

```
-L DIRS
```

adds the directories specified in **DIRS** to the C/C++ compiler. A colon should separate directories.

```
-I DIRS
```

adds the directories specified in **DIRS** to the C/C++ compiler. A colon should separate directories.

```
-C FILENAME
```

gives the generated C code the filename specified by **FILENAME**. This is only applicable when compiling a single-source script.

```
-o FILENAME
```

gives the generated executable the filename specified by **FILENAME**. This is only applicable when compiling a single-source script.

```
-e LINE
```

is identical to the Perl **–e** option and compiles **LINE** as a single-line Perl script. The default operation is to compile and then execute the one-line script. If you want to save the executable generated, use the **–o** flag.

```
-regex NAME
```

NAME should specify a regular expression to be used when compiling multiple-source files into multiple executables. For example, the command

```
$ perlcc -regex 's/\.pl/\.bin/' foo.pl bar.pl
```

would create two executables, **foo.bin** and **bar.bin**.

```
-verbose LEVEL
```

sets the verbosity of the compilation process to the level specified by **LEVEL**. This should be either in the form of a number or a string of letters. Except where specified via the **–log** option, the information is sent to **STDERR**. The available levels are given in this table:

Numeric	Letter	Description
1	g	Code Generation Errors to STDERR
2	a	Compilation Errors to STDERR
4	t	Descriptive text to STDERR
8	f	Code Generation Errors to file (**–log** flag needed)
16	c	Compilation Errors to file (**–log** flag needed)
32	d	Descriptive text to file (**–log** flag needed)

For example, to set the maximum verbosity level you might use the following:

```
$ perlcc -v 63 -log foo.out foo.pl
```

Note that some options require that the name of a suitable file be given via the **–log** option. See below for more details. If the **–log** tag has been given and no specific verbosity level has been specified, then the script assumes a verbosity level of 63, which sends all of the output to the screen and a log file. If no verbosity or log file is specified, then a level of 7 is implied, sending all the output to **STDERR**.

```
-log NAME
```

logs the progress of the compilation to the file **NAME**. Note that the information is appended to the file; the contents are not truncated before more information is added. The effect of this option is to make the entire process of compilation silent—all output is redirected to the specified file.

```
-argv ARGS
```

must be used with the **–run** or **–e** options. It permanently populates the **@ARGV** array with the contents of **ARGS**. If you want to specify more than one argument, use single quotes and separate each argument with a space.

```
-sav
```

The intermediate C source code that is generated during the compilation is saved in a file with the same name as the source with *.c* appended.

```
-gen
```

tells **perlcc** to only generate the C source code—the file will not be compiled into an executable.

```
-run
```

immediately runs the executable that was generated. Any remaining arguments to **perlcc** will be supplied to the executable as command line arguments.

```
-prog
```

specifies that all files supplied are programs. This causes Perl to ignore the normal interpretation that **.pm** files are actually modules, not scripts.

```
-mod
```

specifies that the files should be compiled as modules, not scripts. This overrides the normal interpretation that files ending in **.p**, **.pl**, and **.bat** are Perl scripts.

Perl Debugger

To start the debugger, you need to specify the **–d** option on the command line to the Perl interpreter:

```
perl -d t.pl
```

Alternatively, it can be used with a dummy **–e** statement to drop you straight into a dummy debugger environment:

```
perl -de 1
```

Once invoked, you are placed into the debugger at the first executable statement within the defined script.

h

```
h COMMAND
h
```

prints out help information for **COMMAND** or general help, if **COMMAND** is not specified. If you use the special **h h** command, then a condensed version of the general help is printed—it should fit onto a standard screen without scrolling. You can use the pipe symbol to parse the output through a pager. See the **O** command later in this chapter for details on how to change the default paging program.

p

```
p expr
```

prints the evaluated value of **expr** using the standard print built-in function. The value of **expr** can include variables and functions defined within the current script being debugged.

The usual rules to the print function apply—nested structures and objects will not be printed correctly. See the **x** command below for a more useful version of this.

x

```
x expr
```

evaluates its expression in list context and dumps out the result in a pretty-printed fashion. Nested data structures are printed out recursively, unlike the `print` function. See the Option column in Table 6-1 later in this chapter.

```
V PACKAGE VARS
V PACKAGE
V
```

displays the list of variables specified in **VARS** within the package **PACKAGE** if both are specified. If **VARS** is omitted, then all variables for **PACKAGE** are printed. If no arguments are specified, then it prints out all the variables for the **main** package. Information is intelligently printed with the values of arrays and hashes and nested structures being formatted before output. Control characters are also converted into a printable format.

If you specify the variables, then you should omit the variable type character (**$**, **@**, or **%**). You can also specify a pattern to match or a pattern not to match using ~**PATTERN** and !**PATTERN** arguments.

```
X VARS
X
```

Same as **V VARS** for the current package.

```
T
```

prints out a stack backtrace, as determined by the **caller** function and the value of the current stack frame array.

s

```
s EXPR
s
```

executes only the next statement (single step), following
subroutine calls, if necessary. If **EXPR** is supplied, then it executes
EXPR once, descending into subroutine calls as necessary. This
can be used to drop directly into a subroutine outside of the normal
execution process.

n

```
n EXPR
n
```

single-steps the next statement but steps over the subroutines
instead of stepping into them. If **EXPR** is specified, then any
subroutines are stepped into.

Carriage Return

This repeats the last **n** or **s** command.

c

```
c LINE
c SUB
c
```

continues execution (all statements) until the next configured
breakpoint of the end of the script. If **LINE** or **SUB** is specified, then

a breakpoint, active for one break only, is inserted before **LINE** or the subroutine **SUB**.

```
l
```

lists the next page of lines for the current script from the current line.

```
l MIN+INCR
```

lists **INCR+1** lines from the line specified by **MIN**.

```
l MIN-MAX
```

lists the lines from line **MIN** to **MAX**.

```
l LINE
```

lists the line **LINE**.

```
l SUB
```

lists the first page of lines for the subroutine **SUB**.

This lists the previous page of lines.

```
w LINE
w
```

lists a page of lines surrounding the current line, or **LINE** if specified.

This returns the line pointer to the last line executed and prints it out.

f

```
f FILENAME
```

changes the file currently being viewed to **FILENAME**. The value of **FILENAME** should match either the main script, or the name of a file identifiable within the **%INC** variable. If still not found, then it is interpreted as a regular expression that should resolve to a file name.

/PATTERN/

This searches forward within the current file for the regular expression **PATTERN**.

?PATTERN?

This searches backward within the current file for the regular expression **PATTERN**.

L

This lists all the currently set breakpoints and actions.

```
S
```

```
S  PATTERN
S  !PATTERN
S
```

lists all subroutines matching the regular expression **PATTERN**. If
PATTERN is preceded by an exclamation mark, then it lists those
not matching the regular expression **PATTERN**.

```
t
```

```
t  EXPR
t
```

toggles trace mode. Trace mode enables the printing of each
statement as it is executed. If **EXPR** is specified, it traces the
execution of **EXPR**. See also the **AutoTrace** option listed in
Table 6-1. For example, the script,

```
sub one { 1 };
sub two { 2 };
print one()*two();
```

only prints out the final value of two—with trace mode switched
on, it also prints the statements:

```
DB<1> t
trace = on
DB<1> r
main::one(t2.pl:2):    sub one { 1 };
main::two(t2.pl:3):    sub two { 2 };
2
```

b

```
b LINE CONDITION
b LINE
b CONDITION
b
```

sets a breakpoint on the current line when no arguments are specified. If **LINE** is specified, then the breakpoint is set on the specified line. If **CONDITION** is specified, then each time the breakpoint is reached it only breaks execution if the condition resolves to true. The **CONDITION** does not use an **if** statement—it is purely the test. If you use **/PATTERN/**, then the breakpoint only breaks if the statement matches the regular expression **PATTERN**.

```
b SUB CONDITION
b SUB
```

sets a breakpoint on the first line of the subroutine **SUB**, using **CONDITION** if specified.

```
b postpone SUB CONDITION
b postpone SUB
```

sets a breakpoint on the first line of the subroutine **SUB** only after it has been compiled.

```
b compile SUB
```

sets a breakpoint on the first executable statement of the subroutine **SUB** after it has been compiled.

```
b load FILENAME
```

sets a breakpoint at the first executed line of **FILENAME**. **FILENAME** should be the full name, as defined within the **%INC** hash.

VI

```
d LINE
d
```

deletes the breakpoint specified on **LINE** or the breakpoint on the line that is about to be executed.

This deletes all the currently set breakpoints.

```
a LINE COMMAND
a COMMAND
```

sets the action specified by **COMMAND** to be executed before the current line, or the line specified by **LINE** is executed. For example, this can be used to print out the value of a variable before it is used in a calculation.

This deletes all currently installed actions.

```
W EXPR
W
```

sets a watch on the variable specified by **EXPR**. A change to the specified variable will be printed before the next line to be executed is printed. If **EXPR** is not specified, then all watch points are deleted.

```
O OPT?
O OPT=VALUE
O
```

The first form, **O OPT?**, prints the value of the option named **OPT**. The second format specifies the value for **OPT**; if no value is specified, then it defaults to one. If no arguments are given, then the value of all the current options are printed. The option name can be abbreviated to the minimum identifiable name, for example, the **pager** option can be reduced to **p**.

VI

The most used options are shown in Table 6-1. For others, refer to the **perldebug** man page.

Option	Description
recallCommand	The character(s) used to recall a command.
ShellBang	The character(s) used to spawn a shell. The shell executed.
pager	The program to use for paging the output using the l command within the debugger. The value of the **PAGER** environment variable will be used by default.
tkRunning	Run **Tk** when prompting.
signalLevel	The level of verbosity applied to signals. Default operation is to print a message when an uncaught signal is received. Set to zero to switch this off.
warnLevel	The level of verbosity applied to warnings. Default operation is to print a backtrace when a warning is printed out. Set to zero to switch this off.

Table 6-1. Internal Options for the Debugger

Option	Description
dieLevel	The level of verbosity applied to warnings. Default operation is to print a backtrace when a warning is printed out. Set this option to a value of two to enable messages to be printed by surrounding **eval** statements. Set to zero to switch this off.
AutoTrace	Trace mode, identical to the **t** option on the command line. Set to zero to disable tracing.
LineInfo	The file or pipe to print line number information to. This is used by debugger interfaces with a pipe to enable them to obtain the information.
inhibit_exit	When set to zero, allows you to step to a point beyond the normal end of the script.
PrintRet	When set to zero, does not print the return value resolved when the **r** command is used. When set to one (the default), the return value is printed.
frame	Controls how messages are printed during the entry and exit process from subroutines. The value is numeric, based against a bit set. If the value is zero, then messages are printed only on entry to a new subroutine. If bit 1 (value of 2) is set, then both entry and exit to the subroutine is printed. If bit 2 (2) is set, then the arguments to the subroutine are printed as well as the context and caller info, and bit 4 (8) prints the values parsed to **tied** functions and methods. Bit 5 (16) also causes the return value from the subroutine to be printed. Thus, a value of 18 prints the entry and exit to a subroutine with the returned value.
maxTraceLen	The maximum number of arguments printed when bit 4 of the **frame** option is set.
arrayDepth	The maximum number of elements printed from an array. An empty string prints all elements.

Table 6-1.   Internal Options for the Debugger *(continued)*

Option	Description
hashDepth	The maximum number of keys and values printed from a hash. An empty string prints all keys.
compactDump	Sets the style of the array or hash dump. Short arrays may be printed on a single line.
veryCompact	Sets the style of the array or hash dump to be very compact.
globPrint	Sets whether the resolved filename globs are printed.
TTY	The TTY device to use for debugging I/O.
noTTY	If set, goes into a nonstop debugging mode, as if there is no controlling terminal.
ReadLine	When set to zero, disables readline support within the debugger so that scripts that use ReadLine can be debugged.
NonStop	Automatically set by **noTTY**, sets the debugger into noninteractive mode.

Table 6-1. Internal Options for the Debugger *(continued)*

< EXPR
<

sets a Perl command, specified in **EXPR**, to be executed before each debugger prompt. If **EXPR** is omitted, the list of statements is reset. You can enter multiple lines by backslashing the newline character.

<< EXPR

sets a Perl command, specified in **EXPR**, to be executed before each debugger prompt. You can enter multiple lines by backslashing the newline character.

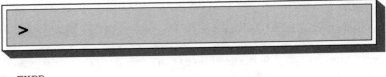

```
> EXPR
>
```

sets the Perl command **EXPR** to be executed after each debugger prompt and after any command on the prompt has been executed. If **EXPR** is not specified, then the list of commands is reset.

```
>> EXPR
```

sets the Perl command **EXPR** to be executed after each debugger prompt and after any command on the prompt has been executed.

```
{ EXPR
{
```

sets a debugger command, specified in **EXPR**, to be executed before each debugger prompt. If **EXPR** is omitted, the list of statements is reset.

```
{{ EXPR
```

sets a debugger command, specified in **EXPR**, to be executed before each debugger prompt.

!

```
! EXPR
!
```

redoes the previous command specified by the number **EXPR** (as shown in the debugger prompt) or the previous command, if **EXPR** is not specified.

```
! -EXPR
```

redoes the command referred to by **EXPR**, starting from the end of the list.

```
! PATTERN
```

redoes the last command starting with **PATTERN**.

VI

!!

```
!! EXPR
```

runs **EXPR** in a subprocess.

H

```
H -EXPR
```

displays the last **EXPR** commands. If **EXPR** is omitted, then it lists them all.

q or ^D

This quits from the debugger.

r

This returns immediately from the current subroutine. The remainder of the statements are ignored.

R

This restarts the debugger. Some options and history may be lost during the process, although the current specification allows for histories, breakpoints, actions, and debugger options to be retained. Also, the command line options specified by **-w**, **-I**, and **-e** are preserved.

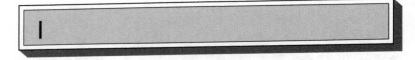

|

| EXPR

runs the command **EXPR** through the default pager.

| |

| | EXPR

runs the command **EXPR** through the default pager, ensuring that the filehandle **DB::OUT** is temporarily selected.

=

= ALIAS EXPR
ALIAS

assigns the value of **EXPR** to **ALIAS**, effectively defining a new command called **ALIAS**. If no arguments are specified, then the list of current aliases is listed. Note that the aliases do not accept arguments, but you can simulate the effects of arguments by defining **EXPR** as a regular expression:

```
$DB::alias{'strlen'} = 's/strlen(.*)/p length($1)/';
```

This effectively re-executes the original **strlen** command as **print length($1)**, where **$1** is the value of the first matching parentheses.

m

m EXPR

evaluates expression and lists the currently valid methods that could be applied to it.

m PACKAGE

lists the available methods defined in **PACKAGE**.

VI

Appendix
Resource Reference

Perl has, for obvious reasons, gained a huge following, both in printed form and online on Web sites, discussion groups, and mailing lists. You will find a selection of the most popular books, magazines, and online resources in this appendix.

Printed Material

While it's impossible to list all the books, journals, and other publications that promote Perl as a programming language, there are some standard books that all Perl programmers should probably keep on their bookshelf.

Books

Asbury, S., M. Glover, A. Humphreys, E. Weiss, J. Matthews, and S. Sol. 1997. *Perl 5 How-To*. 2d ed. Corte Madera, CA: Waite Group

In a question-and-answer style, this book covers nearly the entire range of Perl's abilities. By solving specific problems and giving step-by-step examples of the solutions, the book manages to explain even the most complex areas of Perl development.

Brown, M. C. 1999. *Perl: The Complete Reference*. Berkeley, CA: Osborne McGraw-Hill

As the title suggests, this is a complete reference to the Perl language. It covers all of the different aspects of Perl programming, both those supported in the standard distribution and those available via external modules. It also covers in detail the processes behind developing Perl extensions.

Brown, M. C. 1999. *Perl Annotated Archives*. Berkeley, CA: Osborne McGraw-Hill

This is a library of scripts and modules that are annotated, line by line, in order to demonstrate both the abilities of Perl and the logic behind the scripts' execution. The book should help both beginners and advanced users, and it is an excellent companion to *Perl: The Complete Reference*.

Brown, V., and C. Nandor. 1998. *MacPerl: Power and Ease.* **Sunnyvale, CA: Prime Time Freeware**

This book is a perfect guide to programming Mac-specific Perl scripts, as well as a general guide to Perl programming and making the best of the MacPerl development environment.

Johnson, E. F. 1996. *Cross-Platform Perl.* **Foster City, CA: IDG Press**

This book concentrates on creating code that can be easily transported between Unix and NT hosts. Special attention is given to scripts that deal with systems administration and Web sites, although the book covers a wide range of other topics.

Orwant, J. 1997. *Perl 5 Interactive Course: Certified Edition.* **Corte Madera, CA: Waite Group**

This book is a thorough guide to Perl 5 programming, taking the reader through a series of different tasks and topics that range from building basic scripts to the proper use of variables, functions, and Perl-style regular expressions.

Srinivasan, S. 1997. *Advanced Perl Programming.* **Sebastopol, CA: O'Reilly**

This book is an excellent guide to data modeling, networking, and the Tk widget interface. It also covers the internal workings of Perl, which will help the advanced programmer write more efficient and smaller code, while providing all the information necessary for extending Perl with external C code.

Wall, L., T. Christiansen, and R. L. Schwartz. 1996. *Programming Perl.* **2d ed. Sebastopol, CA: O'Reilly**

Written by the three modern Perl architects, this is the definitive guide to Perl programming. This is what most people refer to as the "Camel" book, since there is a picture of one on the cover.

Wall, L., T. Christiansen, and N. Torkington. 1998. *Perl Cookbook.* **Sebastopol, CA: O'Reilly**

This cookbook of recipes for programming in the Perl language is written by the same team as the classic Camel book and is based on two chapters from the original first edition.

Journals

The Perl Journal

A periodical devoted entirely to Perl, *The Perl Journal* covers a wide range of topics from basic principles for beginners to the advanced topics of Perl internals.

SunExpert Magazine

A magazine targeted at Sun and Unix users, *SunExpert* also covers the use of Perl in systems administration and Web serving roles.

SunWorld Online (www.sunworldonline.com)

SunWorld Online is a monthly Web magazine that covers a number of topics, including using Perl to help manage and monitor Sun workstations.

Web Resources

A

Although Perl's history is rooted in a simple reporting language, it became rapidly apparent that it could be used as a suitable language for CGI programming, and there are therefore a vast number of Web sites dedicated to Perl. The main site is the Perl Institute at www.perl.org. This is the home of Perl and is a good place to start looking for more information.

If you don't find what you are looking for under one of the sites below, try visiting Yahoo (www.yahoo.com) or AltaVista (www.altavista.digital.com). The former lists hundreds of sites within its directory.

www.perl.org

The Perl Institute—the "official" home of Perl. You'll find general information on Perl, links to sources, ports, and a vast amount of background and support information on the Perl world.

www.perl.com

Tom Christiansen's Perl Web site. Christiansen is one of the major contributors to the modern Perl effort and Perl itself and is author of a number of books on the topic (see "Books," preceding). His site is primarily geared to providing general information, sample scripts, and modules.

www.cpan.org

The Comprehensive Perl Archive Network (CPAN) is an online library of scripts, modules, and extensions to Perl. Originally produced with script-specific archives in mind, CPAN now concentrates on supporting and supplying perl5 modules. You should use CPAN as the second port of call (after the CD-ROM) for the modules I've used throughout this book.

www.iis.ee.ethz.ch/~neeri/macintosh/perl.html

The MacPerl homepage contains links and information on using Perl on the Mac.

www.ActiveWare.com

ActiveWare offers a port of perl5 that is usable with Windows NT Web servers (such as Microsoft's Internet Information Server [IIS]). If you want a more general version of Perl for NT, you need the "core" port available on CPAN.

www.roth.net/perl

This site is maintained by Dave Roth, the author of the Win32::AdminMisc Perl module for Windows 95 and NT. There is also some general information and example scripts.

www.virtualschool.edu/mon/Perl/index.html

You'll find a wealth of information on both Mac- and Unix-based Perl scripts and modules here.

www.metronet.com/perlinfo/perl5.html

This brilliant independent source for perl5 scripts, modules, and examples is an excellent starting point for Perl programmers, beginner or advanced, to further their knowledge.

FTP Sites

If you are looking for a specific module, script, or idea, then it's best to visit the CPAN archives (see preceding), since the CPAN system will automatically take you to a local FTP site. However, if all you want to do is browse around the available files or download the entire contents, then try some of the sites in the following table.

Server name	Directory
coombs.anu.edu.au	/pub/perl/CPAN/src/5.0
ftp.cis.ufl.edu	/pub/perl/CPAN/src/5.0
ftp.cs.ruu.nl	/pub/PERL/perl5.0/src
ftp.funet.fi	/pub/languages/perl/CPAN/src/5.0
ftp.metronet.com	/pub/perl/source
ftp.netlabs.com	/pub/outgoing/perl5.0
sinsite.doc.ic.ac.uk	/pub/computing/programming/languages/perl/perl.5.0
sungear.mame.mu.oz.au	/pub/perl/src/5.0

A

Mailing Lists

Mailing lists fall into two distinct categories: announcements or discussions. If the list is for announcements, you are not allowed to post to the group. These tend to be low volume and are useful for keeping in touch with the direction of Perl. If it's a discussion list, you can post and reply to messages just as you would in a Usenet newsgroup. These are higher volume lists, and the number of messages can become unmanageable very quickly.

That said, a discussion list is likely to have the experts and users in it that will be able to answer your questions and queries with authority.

General Mailing Lists

Perl Institute Announce

This list carries announcements from the Perl Institute on general Perl issues. To subscribe, send e-mail to majordomo@perl.org with "subscribe tpi-announce" in the body of the message.

Perl-Unicode (from the Perl Institute)

This list is concerned with issues surrounding Unicode and Perl at both porting and using levels. To subscribe, send e-mail to majordomo@perl.org with "subscribe perl-unicode" in the body of the message.

Perl5-Porters

If you are porting Perl or Perl modules or want to help in the development of the Perl language in general, you should be a member of this discussion list. Don't join if you are just interested. This is a high-volume, highly technical mailing list.

To subscribe, send e-mail to majordomo@perl.org with "subscribe perl5-porters" in the body of the message.

Platform-Specific Mailing Lists

MacOS

This is a general discussion list about using Perl on the Mac. To subscribe, send e-mail to mac-perl-request@iis.ee.ethz.ch with "subscribe" in the body of the message.

Windows Users

The Perl-Win32-Users mailing list is targeted for Perl installation and programming questions. There are two versions: standard and digest. To subscribe to the standard version, send e-mail to ListManager@ActiveState.com with "SUBSCRIBE Perl-Win32-Users" in the body of the message. To subscribe to the digest version, send e-mail to ListManager@ActiveState.com with "DIGEST Perl-Win32-Users" in the body of the message.

Windows Announce

This mailing list is for announcements of new builds, bugs, security problems, and other information. To subscribe to the standard version, send e-mail to ListManager@ActiveState.com with "SUBSCRIBE Perl-Win32-Announce" in the body of the message. To subscribe to the digest version, send e-mail to ListManager@ActiveState.com with "DIGEST Perl-Win32-Announce" in the body of the message.

Windows Web Programming

This mailing list focuses on using Perl as a CGI programming alternative on Windows NT servers. To subscribe to the standard version, send e-mail to ListManager@ActiveState.com with "SUBSCRIBE Perl-Win32-Web" in the body of the message. To subscribe to the digest version, send e-mail to ListManager@ ActiveState.com with "DIGEST Perl-Win32-Web" in the body of the message.

Windows Admin

Here you will find information and discussion about using Perl for administering and managing Windows 95 and NT machines. To subscribe to the standard version, send e-mail to ListManager@ ActiveState.com with "SUBSCRIBE Perl-Win32-Admin" in the body of the message. To subscribe to the digest version, send e-mail to ListManager@ActiveState.com with "DIGEST Perl-Win32-Admin" in the body of the message.

A

Newsgroups

To reach a more general Perl audience, you might want to post a question or announcement to one of the many Perl newsgroups. These are available on ISP's Usenet news servers, and many will be happy to add you to their list if you ask nicely.

comp.infosystems.www.authoring.cgi

Deals with using Perl as a tool for writing CGI programs. This is a general CGI discussion group; it is not specifically targeted at Perl users. However, it does provide a lot of useful information on extracting, receiving, and returning information from Web servers and clients.

comp.lang.perl.announce

For announcing news from the Perl world. This includes new book releases, new version releases, and occasionally major Perl module releases.

comp.lang.perl.misc

A general discussion forum for Perl. Everything from queries about how best to tackle a problem to the inside machinations of Perl is discussed here. Some of the discussion can get quite technical and be more biased to someone interested in the internal Perl workings, but it is still the best port of call if you are having trouble with a Perl script.

comp.lang.perl.modules

This was set up to specifically discuss the use and creation of Perl modules. Unlike comp.lang.perl.misc, you should only find problems related to modules in this group. If you are having trouble with something downloaded from CPAN, this is the best place to start asking questions.

comp.lang.perl.tk

Tk is a toolkit that provides a set of functions to support a graphical user interface (GUI) within Perl. Tk was originally developed in combination with Tcl (Tool command language) but has been massaged to work with other scripting systems, including Perl. Tk's strength, like Perl's, is that it is available for a number of platforms; therefore, building a GUI-style interface within X Windows (under Unix), Microsoft Windows (on the PC), and MacOS, among others, becomes very much easier.

You may also want to refer to "Joseph's Top Ten Tips for Answering Questions Posted to comp.lang.perl.misc," available at http://www.5sigma.com/perl/topten.html. This will provide you with some hints and tips on how best to make use of the question-and-answer nature of many of these groups.